FRACASSA

The Man, the Times and the Teams

FRACASSA
The Man, the Times and the Teams

By Bud Krause and Tom Martin
with Michael Coughlin and Jerome J. Malczewski

PUBLISHING TEAM

Authors Bud Krause and Tom Martin
with Michael Coughlin and Jerome J. Malczewski
Copy Editor Anne Berry Daugherty
Cover and Inside Illustrations Garth Glazier
Designer Ken Cendrowski

ISBN: 9798857633823

"Success is no accident. It is hard work, perseverance, learning, studying, sacrifice, and most of all, love of what you are doing or learning to do."

— *Edson Arantes do Nascimento (Pelé)*

"A coach will impact more people in one year than the average person will in an entire lifetime."

— *Billy Graham*

"A good coach can change a game. A great coach can change a LIFE."

— *John Wooden*

Special thanks to Phyllis and the entire Fracassa family: Rick, David, Kathy, and Susie, for sharing your dad so generously with all of us at Royal Oak Shrine and Birmingham Brother Rice. Coach Fracassa has been a role model and inspiration to thousands. It has been our privilege to be coached, mentored, and loved by him.

Contents

Foreward

In October 1983, I was named president and general manager of the Michigan Panthers of the United States Football League. I moved my family from New York to the northwest suburbs of Detroit, where my sons Vince and John enrolled at Brother Rice High School.

The Brother Rice football team, coached by Al Fracassa, was in the middle of another championship season that year. It wouldn't be an understatement to say that the exploits of Coach Fracassa and his football players were generating more buzz than the Tigers, Lions, and Pistons. That year, the Warriors won their fourth state title, and the team and its legendary coach would go on to win six more state titles before Al Fracassa's retirement in 2013.

My son John was able to play for Coach Fracassa for two seasons, and during that time I came to know that Al was a great admirer of my father — which is to be expected of football coaches who began their careers in the 1960s and '70s. I also learned that Al shared many of the same qualities and attributes that made my father successful.

First, both my father and Al were men of faith. My father attended Mass almost daily. Coach Fracassa and his football players went to Mass every Wednesday and Saturday morning during the football season, and Al and I would, on occasion, have the opportunity to interact just before or after the service. Those talks in the narthex of St. Regis church allowed me to learn much about Al and why he was such a successful football coach.

Secondly, Al understood how to inspire young men. Not just his football players, but also his students and the athletes from other sports who participated in the football team's winter agility drills. Al had a talent for taking a group of individuals and channeling them toward a common purpose. My father's Green Bay teams won five championships in nine seasons because every Packers player was dedicated to a common goal.

My father once said, "It is essential to understand that battles are primarily won in the hearts of men." Al Fracassa understood this. Both he and my father were skilled readers of men who knew that different methods of coaching were required for different players.

Al's career as a head football coach spanned 54 seasons: 1960 to 2013. Human nature has many constants, but a 16-year-old in 1960 had different challenges and different motivations than one in 2013. Al's ability to be successful as the culture and the players changed around him was remarkable. Some players need a kick in the pants and some need a pat on the back. Often, those techniques are needed with the same player in the course of a single drill or practice.

Al Fracassa, like my father, knew how to get the most out of each of his players.

Al's career and lengthy list of accomplishments are not only a study in how to attain a goal, but a study in how to maintain a goal. I suggest to you that those are two very different things. If you've been around a while and experienced some success, then you know what I'm talking about. It's tougher to stay on top than it is to get to the top. The truth of the matter is that Al Fracassa's suc-

Vince Lombardi

cess was due to his remarkable ability to both attain and maintain his goals over a 54-year coaching career.

I've had the opportunity to write numerous books on leadership and give talks on leadership to many organizations. I often get asked why Vince Lombardi's achievements and impact as a professional football coach still resonate today. The reasons why this is so are the same reasons Coach Fracassa has had such a memorable career.

First, both men were leaders who set high standards and achieved those standards while maintaining a high level of integrity and character. Sadly, we live in an era where there is a severe dearth of true leaders.

Vince Lombardi, coaching in a small town in Wisconsin, had a clear sense of who he was and what he believed. He was steadfast and unwavering in those beliefs. He set expectations for his players and held them accountable. The same is true of Al Fracassa.

Secondly, Vince Lombardi was a winner. He got results. He took a loose collection of players who were 1-10-1 the season before he became coach of the Packers and forged them into a team that consistently won.

The Packers were a team of diverse players who experienced turnover, injuries, and adversity. My father instilled in his players the mental toughness to overcome those injuries and adversities, enabling them to win ... and win ... and win. Coach Fracassa's players may not have been the most athletically talented, but they possessed unmatched mental toughness, enabling them to win ... and win ... and win.

Coaching at Brother Rice High School has its own challenges compared to coaching the Green Bay Packers, but the situations are more alike than they are different. Al Fracassa and Vince Lombardi coached at different places and made different choices along the way, but their accomplishments are equally admirable and noteworthy.

—*Vince Lombardi Jr.*

Author's Note

Writing about Al Fracassa has been a privilege. Here are a few special things that happened along the way.

I was interviewing Mike Knuff (Brother Rice '70) over the phone and it didn't take long before he was overwhelmed with emotion. Mike was describing the night in 2014 at Coach Fracassa's retirement party when he reunited with Coach in a small reception room before the event. As he approached his former coach, Mike pulled out of his wallet a 3x5 card on which Fracassa had written out life principles for success back in the fall of 1969, when Mike was struggling. Mike had carried that card in his wallet for 45 years! Through college and football at Cornell. Through marriage and raising a family. Through a successful business career. When Fracassa spoke that night, he held up the card, worn and crinkled, and called up Mike and his twin brother, Pat, to share the moment. My phone interview with Mike, and the raw emotion of his memories of Coach Fracassa, confirmed my conviction that writing this book was a calling.

I met Karen Rottenberk, marketing and communications director for Brother Rice, at Coach Fracassa's 90th birthday party. She was helping me secure photos for the book, and one day she told me: "When I first met my husband Mark (Brother Rice '85), I was just out of college and I couldn't understand the depth of his devotion to his high school football coach." Eventually, of course, Karen met Coach and she remembers: "I understood Mark's devotion to Coach Fracassa right away."

I ran into Pat Simmons (Brother Rice '73) who I knew from our days in the advertising business. He and his four brothers (Bob '70, Terry '76, Tim '77, and Mike '81) had all played for Coach Fracassa. Pat told me a story from the 1971 season, when Rice won an emotional victory over Shrine after losing to them in the 1970 Catholic League Championship Game. Pat was a backup running back, a scout team player who played the role of Shrine's star running back, Tom O'Branovic, in practice as they prepared for the game, and Pat took a bruising from all the tackling in the process. Celebrating the victory, the Rice players wanted to carry Coach Fracassa off the field, but the always humble Fracassa said, "No, carry Simmons off the field!" And the team did — they carried Pat off the field, all the way to the bus. Coach Fracassa loved his scout team players.

Beginning with his 1974 Brother Rice team, Fracassa started the tradition of giving each year's squad its own motto. In 1974, it was "Greatness cannot be achieved without discipline." You'll see these mottos at the beginning of each Rice season.

Coach lent me several of his Black Book Journals, 5x7 hardcover notebooks with the year and the Warrior logo on the front cover. He kept one for each season. Fracassa is a meticulous planner, and these pages contain handwritten details regarding his preparation for practices, plays, and formations. But the Fracassa Black Books are also personal diaries, where he writes about his inner thoughts and feelings. These journals are an insight into Fracassa's unwavering belief in the principles that he taught to everyone who played for him. There's never a year where he doesn't write about his deep love and appreciation for his wife, Phyllis. He humbly prays for the strength and wisdom to be the "best coach I can be." He prays that he can inspire his assistant coaches and players to "strive to do their very best, to do things right EVERY time, not SOME of the time."
He lauds the courage and gallantry of his players in both victory and defeat. One November, at the end of a season, he writes: "Our players fought hard. If you size this team up — pound for pound — we did a lot for what we had. The reason for such a successful season was because of the tremendous attitude and character of our team. They believed that they could — and they did. The leadership of the seniors was extraordinary. They lived right, practiced hard, and were a credit to their school and their families."

— *Bud Krause*

Introduction

On May 10, 2014, an event was held at a conference center in suburban Detroit. A high school football coach was retiring. Such events occur every year in the United States, as friends and family gather at a restaurant or a school gym.

But this particular retirement sendoff was one for the ages. The hall was large and filled with more than 700 of Coach Albert Fracassa's former football players. There were written testimonials from the mayor's office in Detroit, the Michigan governor's office, the U.S. House of Representatives, and the U.S. Senate. There were verbal testimonials from players, coaches, friends, and family. A Friends of Fracassa Committee put together a tribute book for the event: "Coach Al Fracassa, Honoring our Legendary Coach." All of the attendees expressed admiration for a man who had trained them, taught them, shaped them, praised them, and cajoled them. To the players, he was the man who made them what they are. Ron Ranieri, a former player and an assistant coach under Fracassa, put in words what everyone was thinking when he said "I am proud that I was coached by him."

Recently, a group that includes a former Shrine High School team captain, a former Shrine High quarterback, a longtime Brother Rice statistician, and a Brother Rice football historian decided to investigate this coaching phenomenon. Who was he before becoming a high school football coach? What was he like during his early years at Royal Oak Shrine? What characteristics and values launched him on his magnificent career at Birmingham's Brother Rice High School?

COACH, LEADER, LEGEND

Coach Albert Fracassa is a legend. He coached at Royal Oak Shrine High from 1960 to 1968, and finished with a record of 44-19-5. He then moved to Brother Rice High School, located in Bloomfield Hills, where he coached from 1969 to 2013 and posted a record of 386-98-2. At the time of his retirement in 2014, his team's record over 54 years was 430-117-7, making him No. 1 in wins for a Michigan high school football coach and No. 7 in the nation.

His awards include National Football League National High School Coach of the Year; multiple National High School Coach of the Year awards; multiple Michigan High School Coach of the Year awards; and election to the Shrine High School, Brother Rice High School, Catholic League, and Michigan Sports halls of fame. He was the Detroit News Coach of the Year on multiple occasions, the *USA Today*/American Family Insurance All-USA Coach of the Year, and he was even named *The Detroit News'* Michiganian of the Year in 2009. Career awards included the Michigan High School Football Coaches Association Jim Crowley Award and the Michigan State University Duffy Daugherty Memorial Award for Lifetime Achievement in Amateur Sports.

Before he was "Coach Fracassa," he was just Al Fracassa, a three-sport athlete and senior class president at Northeastern High School in Detroit. He was All-State in football and All-City in baseball, and was named the Detroit Public High Schools' Athlete of the Decade for the 1950s. He was awarded a football scholarship to Michigan State University and was a member of the team for four years. As a senior, he was presented with the Fred Danzinger Award, which recognized Fracassa as the most valuable Spartans football player from the Detroit metro area. In other words, he was a true superstar.

Fracassa's accomplishments, as fantastic as they are, fail to tell the entire story. Who was the man behind those numbers and accolades?

FROM SUPINO, ITALY, TO DETROIT, MICHIGAN

Supino, a small village of about 4,500 people, is located approximately 42 miles southeast of Rome. It's at the foot of the Lepini Mountains, near the Sacco River in the Valle Latina; the river and valley support an agricultural community. The northern Italian people labeled the inhabitants of southern Italy "terroni," which is Italian for hick or hayseed, with some racial overtones. Rainfall was erratic, famine was a possibility, public services were limited, local government was questionable, and taxes were high. Bread

From left: Felice Fracassa, Albert Fracassa, Amelia Fracassa.

riots and a cholera outbreak triggered southern Italian immigration to the United States. Supino is also the ancestral home of the Fracassa family.

Between 1880 and 1921, more than 4 million Italians immigrated to the United States. Naples, the port of departure, is located about 100 miles from Supino. In 1928, Felice and Amelia Fracassa, along with their sons Romeo and Guido, made the journey. They cleared the hurdles of health and literacy screening, national and religious prejudice, and employment and housing challenges, and eventually arrived in Detroit, where the population of Italians had increased from 900 in 1904 to 42,000 in 1925. There was a concentration of Italians along Gratiot Avenue, and that's where the Fracassas found a home. Before long they were blessed with a third son, Angelo, followed by Albert in 1932.

THE FRACASSA FAMILY

The story of Coach Albert Fracassa is an immigrant story, and not unusual for the Detroit Catholic High School Football League or the city of Detroit. His parents and two older brothers brought the language, food, and culture of Supino, Italy, to Detroit. His family lived in a mostly Italian neighborhood in the Gratiot-Mount Elliott area and attended Mass at the Assumption of the Blessed Virgin Mary (Assumption Grotto) Church, which is now on the National Register of Historic Places.

Fracsassa Family (from left): Albert, Angelo, Romeo, Guido, Amelia, Felice.

God and country, faith, family, friends, and football were important to the Fracassa family. Felice was a quiet, humble man who attended Mass daily, made his own wine, and enjoyed cigars. The household was a traditional southern Italian one: The father was the patriarch, the sole breadwinner, and the unquestioned authority; and the mother's place was in the home, marketplace, and church. Although Amelia could speak English, she preferred Italian. Fracassa recalls that she made fresh bread every morning and doled out discipline to her sons. The boys were given Saturday chores, and Albert's job was to hunt for wood and coal to heat the family home during the Depression. The Fracassa boys were told to respect others — and not to walk on their neighbors' lawns.

Albert's older brothers looked after him and did their best to keep him out of trouble. Fracassa remembers that he and his brothers would share comic books, pepperoni, cheese, and apples in the evening. His older brothers also

Romeo Fracassa (left) and Albert, brothers and chefs.

enjoyed working on cars but didn't let Albert join them; he showed promise as an athlete, and they felt his time would be better spent on practicing sports. His brothers even covered his job as a paper boy when he was in high school, so he could concentrate on sports.

Loyalty and service to family and country characterized Albert's brothers, who all served in World War II. Guido, his oldest brother, was a sergeant in the European Theater. He spent time in a prisoner-of-war camp but was able to talk a Catholic Czechoslovakian guard into dropping his weapon and escaping with him. Guido's persuasive skills eventually led to a successful insurance sales career.

Romeo was also a sergeant, but he served in the Pacific Theater in World War II. He was in Okinawa preparing to invade Japan when the atomic bombs were dropped. He returned to a career as a mechanic and enjoyed working on electrical systems the most. Angelo, three years older than Albert, served with United States Army counterintelligence in Italy. When he returned home, he earned degrees in accounting and business administration, and worked for the Internal Revenue Service for 60 years.

Years later, when Albert was a high school coach, he was happy and proud that his brothers often came to see his games.

HIGH SCHOOL

At Northeastern High School, Albert played baseball, basketball, and football. The school was integrated, and Fracassa reports that the Black and White players all got along. Among his memorable teammates was Bill Conrad, the great starting tackle on the Northeastern High School Falcons football team.

Despite being 5'8", Fracassa was a playmaking guard on his school's basketball team. His basketball coach, Arthur Thomas "Art" Carty, told him to just "get the ball to Ernie." Ernie was Ernest Wagner Jr., who led Coach Carty's team to the Public High School League Championship. Wagner was awarded a scholarship to Wayne State University, where he played from 1951 to 1953; later, he was a member of the Harlem Globetrotters for 11 years, including one year with Wilt Chamberlain.

High school pitching ace
Al Fracassa (right).

When it came to baseball, Fracassa was a pitcher and an All-City player. He once succeeded in striking out 17 batters in one game, pitched a two-hit ballgame against Cass Tech High School on May 5, 1950, and won a three-hit game over Denby High School on May 20 that same year. But in spite of his successes in baseball, football was his greatest sports love.

From his first football coach, Fracassa learned an important motto that he later used in his coaching career: Do it better than it has ever been done before. He wore the number 22, in honor of legendary quarterback Bobby Layne, and dreamt of a career in the National Football League.

Fracassa was the starting quarterback his senior year in high school and played in a "mafia backfield" with Joe Ignello, Falco Campana, and Romo "Choo-Choo" Renzi. Fracassa called out plays in Italian, which gave him a definite competitive advantage. Renzi claims he never scored a touchdown, and suspected that his quarterback didn't know how to say "fullback" in Italian. Their team was undefeated for the first seven games of the season but lost to Detroit Redford High School and just missed a shot at the Detroit Public School Championship. Northeastern High School's Falcons beat John Matsock's Pershing High team that year. Once they got to college, Matsock and Fracassa became good friends.

Fracassa's ability was praised by sportswriters in Detroit. On Nov. 6, 1950, George DuFour wrote in the *Detroit Free Press* that "Fracassa ... is ... a brainy quarterback with unusual winning incentive. His passing would put many college tossers to shame, but he showed he could run against Pershing last Friday when the chips were piled the highest."

Fracassa was named to the All-State football team in 1950 for his senior year performance and was awarded a football scholarship to Michigan State University.

Albert and Phyllis at Detroit Northeastern High School.

While Fracassa excelled at sports, he also enjoyed other aspects of his high school years. He never missed a day at school, was elected class president in his senior year, and graduated cum laude. He went to Northeastern High School's senior prom with Phyllis Secontine, who eventually became his wife. Although the prom was their first date, Phyllis and Albert were voted "best couple" by their classmates.

MICHIGAN STATE UNIVERSITY

Michigan State University (it was actually known as Michigan Agricultural College at the time and was renamed Michigan State University in 1964) joined the Big 10 conference in 1950 after the University of Chicago chose to drop big-time football to concentrate on academics. Fracassa joined the

At Michigan State, No. 22, Al Fracassa.

team in the fall of 1950, and was known for being the first player on the field for practice. He never missed a day of practice, and dutifully attended all of the team's meetings. His friend, John Matsock, the Spartans' quarterback in the 1954 season, confirms that Fracassa "worked harder than everybody else — sprints, scouting team, spring ball, everything." As a quarterback, though, he had the misfortune of playing behind great quarterbacks — including Earl Morrall, who later played for the NFL's Detroit Lions and went on to win Super Bowls with the Baltimore Colts and the Miami Dolphins.

Fracassa participated in typical college activities, too, such as joining a fraternity on campus in his freshman year. Matsock, his teammate as well as his best friend, says girls were attracted to Fracassa's chiseled Italian good looks and his quiet, unassuming style. A physical education major, Fracassa received his bachelor's degree in 1955.

During his college career, the Michigan State Spartans won the national championship in 1952, and went to the 1954 New Year's Day Rose Bowl game after the 1953 season under Coach Biggie Munn. Fracassa became the quarterback of the scout team, which would help prepare the MSU defense each week by running the plays of the opposing team. He decided he was going to do that job better than it had ever been done before. Matsock says the Spartans "played such good defense because our scout team quarterback was better than most of the opposing quarterbacks."

Coach Fracassa, who stands at 5'8", said in a 2005 interview that the other players "were bigger than me, faster than me, and stronger than me," and he was proud to play on a "really good team."

Believing that it was "an honor to be a Spartan," Fracassa would set out his uniform the night before a game and put it on in front of the mirror. When asked if he were a player today, would he take advantage of the transfer portal that allows players to try for a chance at another school, his answer was that, as a player, he couldn't understand the concept of leaving a beloved coach and teammates. As a coach, he said that if a player left one of his teams, it would "break his heart."

Fracassa's commitment to practice didn't go unnoticed. In the spring of 1954, following the Rose Bowl victory, George S. Alderton of the *Lansing State Journal* was strolling by Jenison Fieldhouse on the MSU campus and stopped to talk with Hank Bullough, a key contributor on the two winning squads. As they were watching Fracassa, an exasperated Bullough said, "That Fracassa." Alderton asked, "What about Fracassa?" Bullough replied, "Look at him sprinting over there! He runs as though he was doing it for money or trying to beat somebody — but that's Al for you."

Bullough went on to point out that even though Fracassa rarely traveled with the team, "He's just as excited back here on campus. He gets nervous, can't eat, and pulls his hair out while listening to the radio." An assistant coach once said, "Nobody out here tries to give more of himself to this football squad than Fracassa."

Fracassa did get his moments to play for the Spartans. On the undefeated, consensus No. 1 team of 1952, he completed 1 of 3 passes for 12 yards. During Duffy Daugherty's first season at Michigan State, in 1954, the team posted three wins and six losses — so Fracassa's playing time was limited. But in a 54-6 victory over Washington State University, he was given a chance to play. According to Robert E. Voges, of the *Benton Harbor News Palladium*, the "workhorse of the squad on the practice field" completed two passes for 34 yards and made one touchdown. As the game was coming to an end, the Spartans were near the goal line again. Fracassa called two or three plays, but the halfbacks refused the play call because they wanted Fracassa to run the ball himself. So, he ran it — and scored a touchdown. "The MSU bench, players and coaches alike cheered with wild enthusiasm," according to Voges. "He stuck at it to take the punishment through the love of football. So, when he made good during his first chance in a game this season, you can understand why his teammates were cheering."

For his efforts, Fracassa was awarded the Fred Danzinger Award, which was given to the Spartan from the Detroit metro area who made the most outstanding contribution to the team. Bullough, his fellow Spartan, gets the prize for the most accurate prophetic statement ever. He said: "Al's going to make somebody a wonderful coach." Amen.

PHYLLIS

Fracassa met Phyllis Secontine in the seventh grade. They were friends but didn't date until years later, when he asked her to the high school senior prom (she accepted). Phyllis also attended Michigan State, and by the time she and Al were sophomores, they were dating regularly.

Phyllis laughs as she remembers Fracassa's trip to the Rose Bowl with the

Spartans wasn't uneventful; although he was the scout team quarterback, he managed to show up in every photograph that appeared in the Detroit newspapers. He was seen on the Groucho Marx television show, on a float in the Rose Bowl Parade, and next to the actress Virginia Mayo. Phyllis confirms that Fracassa didn't date Debbie Reynolds, as rumors at the time had it; she says that was actually his teammate, Billy Wells, a Spartan running back.

Just married! Aug. 4, 1956.

Upon returning to Detroit after their graduation from MSU in 1955, Fracassa and Phyllis became closer than ever. Fracassa took his first coaching job in the fall of 1955 at Flint Mandeville High, which would win one, tie one, and lose seven games during his tenure. That year, the young couple also became engaged.

On Aug. 4, 1956, Albert and Phyllis were married and their journey of life together officially began. Phyllis was aware of the complications of getting involved with a football-obsessed man. Her brother, Vince, played for the University of Michigan Wolverines in the 1940s. Vince coached football at Birmingham High School before establishing the Varsity Shop, which has been a landmark sports destination in Birmingham for decades.

After a short honeymoon trip to northern Michigan, Fracassa, who had already enlisted in the U.S. Army, left for Germany. Phyllis joined him a month later, and they spent two years overseas that both remember fondly. "We were newly married and our life in Germany was wonderful," Phyllis recalls. The newlyweds lived off the Army base in the upstairs flat of a home where the owners, a German couple named Giesla and Manfred, lived downstairs with their three children. Fracassa played on the Army football team and trained the boxing team, learning to jump rope as comfortably as a middleweight champion. Phyllis worked as a substitute teacher at the school for servicemen's children on the Army base. On furlough, they were joined by Phyllis's parents on a trip to Italy, where they visited their family hometowns: Supino (Fracassa) and Costigliole d'Asti (Phyllis).

Just as their two years in Germany were almost complete, their first child — a son, Rick — was born. On the family's return to the U.S. in 1958, Fracassa accepted an assistant football coaching position at Rochester High in Rochester, Mich. The Falcons were a Class B public school and posted a three-win, five-loss record in 1958. The team moved to Class A in 1959 and dramatically improved to seven wins and only two losses. When Fracassa took the head coaching job at Shrine in the fall of 1960, he brought along Tom Urban from Rochester High to serve as his assistant coach.

DAVID FRACASSA

Al and Phyllis Fracassa's second child, David, recalls that "You know you're from a football family when your first solo experience driving a car is picking up a scouting film from another high school coach and bringing it home for (your) dad to study."

He says his father's dedication to football wasn't just something that happened every autumn; it was a year-round thing. Fracassa was sought out as a motivational speaker and was on the circuit for summer football camps. The whole family traveled to these events by car, and David has fond memories of stops along the road at attractions such as national parks.

David says he never felt pressured to be an athlete, but he did enjoy sports and, like his brother Rick, played high school football at Madison Heights Bishop Foley. He was a sophomore running back in 1974, when Bishop Foley played Brother Rice in the Catholic League Championship Game.

"I had a great childhood," David says. "My dad would come home from work to a prepared meal and a quiet evening. My mom ran the household and was always totally supportive of my dad's coaching career. When I was in high school, I would watch game films with my dad, and discuss plays and players. That's a very fond memory of great times with my dad."

A graduate of Michigan State University, David has been very successful in business. "One nice thing for our family has been that with my dad's retirement, he's had time to attend my kids' sporting events as they were growing up. That's been great."

KATHY FRACASSA

Like her brother David, Kathy Fracassa says she had a great childhood. Kathy, the third of Al and Phyllis Fracassa's four children, says: "Our summer vacations involved going to football camps where my dad would speak and coach. I remember a drive to California in a station wagon with a luggage rack on top of the car. The stops along the way were football camps, and I loved staying in the school dormitories — and it was a thrill to meet Terry Bradshaw! We would also stop at sites like the Grand Canyon or Yellowstone National Park. On one trip we went to the Orange Bowl — I think my dad got tickets from one of his former players. We did a side trip to Disney World."

Kathy jokes about her "failure to inherit the family's athletic gene," but she did play volleyball at Madison Heights Bishop Foley. She graduated from Central Michigan University with a Bachelor of Science in elementary education, and later moved into medical and pharmaceutical marketing. Her work took her to Nebraska, where she met her husband. Ironically, her brother-in-law, Terry Connealy, was co-captain of the University of Nebraska Cornhuskers in 1994, when they were co-National Champions with the University of Michigan Wolverines. Kathy's daughter is a high school basketball player of note, and played in the Nebraska State Finals in 2022 — so apparently, she inherited her grandfather's athletic gene.

"My dad is the most successful man I've ever met," Kathy says. "He has touched so many. His life is rich with wonderful stories."

SUSIE FRACASSA

Susie Fracassa, the youngest of the Fracassas' four children, today lives in Berlin, Germany, where she runs a successful catering business. The MSU graduate credits her father with providing the inspiration she needs to face the challenges of running a small business.

The Fracassa family (from left): Rick, Susie, Phyllis, Albert, Kathy, David.

"I (once) had a Zen moment, reflecting on one of my dad's mottos: Do it right every time," she recalls. "It inspired me to approach my business that way. Don't cut corners, and serve your best dish each time, every time."

As a child, Susie was often her father's sidekick. Players and coaches alike remember seeing her on the sidelines of games and even on the team bus. At Fracassa's very successful quarterback camps, she handled concessions and learned the basics of business.

Susie says her mother was "a huge support" to her dad — she was always there for him, always supportive, never complaining. "One thing I'd like to say about my dad is that he's a human being, just like the rest of us." And, she adds: "I love him so much."

FAITH AND FRACASSA

Fracassa is a man of faith. He has faith in his God, his country, his church, and his family. He has faith in himself, and he had faith in all the teams he coached and all the players on those teams. This faith was his hallmark and carried him through his remarkable career. Fracassa kept annual journals through the years, and he diligently recorded his thoughts on his football players and upcoming games. But the diaries also contained his concerns, his worries, and his thoughts on his role as a teacher and mentor.

Once, when asked about his spiritual life by Don Horkey of *The Michigan Catholic*, Fracassa pulled a rosary from his pocket. "When I'm on the football field, it's in my pocket. I hold it in my hand," he said. "I don't pray for victory. I pray the good Lord to take care of me on the sidelines and for the kids to play to their best ability. I don't ask the Lord to take sides."

At the Shrine of the Little Flower Basilica in Royal Oak, there's a statue of St. Sebastian, known as the patron saint of soldiers and athletes. Fracassa liked to sit close to the statue when he was in the church, because he regarded the saint as his personal favorite. He and his players often invoked the martyr's aid: "St. Sebastian, pray for us."

Coach Fracassa would lead his teams to Mass at 6 a.m. during the week, and they recited the rosary before every game. Fracassa didn't just talk the talk; he walked the walk. And his teams walked right alongside him. The coach's faith was ingrained in him — it was part of all he did. It wasn't loud and it wasn't prideful; rather, it was quiet and humble. It was a strength he passed on to his players. In fact, Fracassa's former players say the coach's faith in his teams led them to achieve more than they thought possible, both on and off the field.

Mike Randall, the captain of the 1961 Royal Oak Shrine High School Knights, is one of those players. He and his wife, Joey, wrote a tribute to Coach Fracassa for his 1999 Michigan Sports Hall of Fame induction:

Strength anchored
Between intense eyes
Chiseled features speak
Of a heritage well worn
Words from his past
Still echo truth
This man
Whose steady hand
Gently forms character
Out of a vulnerable soul
And through God's help
Molds a fragile boy
Into a man.

The 1960s

The Times

The early 1960s were a time of calm before the storm that was to come. America was on a roll. President Dwight D. Eisenhower's two-term presidency was ending. He was proud of the fact that no soldier had died in combat on his watch, the economy was robust, traditional families were thriving, and the suburbs were growing to meet the needs of these families; there were now more suburban families than urban ones. There was a tsunami of children in America, the tail end of the baby boom generation.

In 1946, the demand for marriage licenses had increased by 40 percent from 1945. During the Depression and World War II, there were 2.2 to 2.8 million births per year. That number jumped to 3.5 million births in 1945 and 3.9 million births in 1946, and stayed above 3.5 million in the following years. At least 1 million American boys would reach high school age — and that meant they were eligible to play high school football — in 1960.

With the end of the Korean conflict in 1953, the Cold War became the focus of the world. The Union of Soviet Socialist Republics had dropped the iron curtain and the People's Republic of China loomed large in Asia. Fear of the spread of communism led to President Harry Truman's promise that America would stop the dominoes from falling, Sen. Joseph McCarthy's attempt to uproot any domestic conspiracy, and President Eisenhower's military-industrial complex. Nuclear weapons testing and the fear of nuclear war dominated the 1950s. Those who were students during that era remember the air-raid drills in grade school, requiring them to get under their desks and cover their heads.

The Cold War changed the cities in America. The Interstate Highway System was designed with the country's defense in mind; it meant that soldiers and equipment could be moved more easily from place to place. In addition, defense industries could be decentralized, decreasing the risk of loss due to bombing or missiles. It made the growth and expansion of the suburbs practical, as many people were able to live outside of a city yet work in the city.

In 1960, the city of Detroit was thriving. The city had become known as the "Arsenal of Democracy" in the 1940s and was home to the highest-paid blue-collar workers in America. Detroit experienced economic growth and unprecedented prosperity. The automobile and related industries accounted for one-sixth of the American economy in 1950.

The population of the city increased from 466,000 in 1910 to 1.57 million in 1930. It was the fourth-largest city in America, with a peak population of 1.85 million in 1950. Early and mid-19th century immigration from northern Europe (Ireland and England, for example) was followed in the latter part of the century by Eastern and Southern European immigrants from Germany, Poland, and Italy. Many of these immigrants were Roman Catholic. In 1950, the city of Detroit was about 80 percent White, and 80 percent of those White Detroiters were Catholic. On the heavily Catholic east side of Detroit, families, parishes, and neighborhoods were all tightly intertwined.

Detroit was founded in 1701 by Antoine de la Mothe Cadillac as a fur trading center. In June 1805, what was known as the "Great Fire" leveled the city. In the efforts to rebuild after the fire, Augustus Brevoort Woodward created a grand design with Campus Martius, close to the Detroit River, forming a central point. Woodward Avenue ran northwest, perpendicular to the river. Jefferson Avenue ran parallel to the river. By 1960, these roads were associated with gradients of race, employment, income, and socioeconomic status starting in central Detroit and heading out to the distant suburbs. The parochial high schools of the Detroit Catholic League were located near the borders of the city and enrolled the children of blue-collar and modest white-collar families, who were recent arrivals and nearly all White.

The Roman Catholic Church had a loyal following and in 1955, 75 percent of Catholics reported that they attended weekly Mass. The services were in

Latin, although in 1964, the Second Vatican Council began introducing "the New Mass," or Mass in English, in U.S. parishes. Catholic schools of the time were known for their discipline, exercised by both male and female clergy.

Catholic politicians were enjoying greater acceptance in America and in Detroit. In November of 1960, John F. Kennedy, a Catholic, was elected president. He brought youth and energy to the job. Jerome Cavanaugh, the first Catholic mayor of Detroit, was elected in 1961 and brought the same attributes to the city's government. There was a buzz in the air. Catholics felt pride and responsibility in representing church and school.

Detroit has always been a sports town, but the Detroit Tigers American League baseball team of the era seemed to always struggle under the weight of the mighty New York Yankees. They were fun to watch, though, with players like Al Kaline, Harvey Kuenn, and Jim Bunning. In 1961, the team won an outstanding 101 games, but they still finished in second place in the American League, eight games behind the Yankees.

The Detroit Red Wings National Hockey League team won championships in 1950, 1952, 1954, and 1955. The "Production Line" of Gordie Howe, Ted Lindsay, and Sid Abel (followed by Alex Delvecchio) led the way. The Detroit Pistons basketball team, meanwhile, which arrived from Fort Wayne, Ind., in 1957 and was new to the National Basketball League, was struggling. Things got a little better when Dave DeBusschere, a Detroit Catholic High School League star, played for the team in the '60s when he wasn't pitching for the Chicago White Sox.

The Detroit Lions NFL team was doing very well. They had signed one of their first Black players, the University of Michigan standout Bob Mann, in 1948. He led the league in receiving yards in 1949 but held out after a pay cut and was traded to New York for Bobby Layne in 1950. Quarterback Layne led the Detroit Lions to three championships in 1952, 1953, and 1957. When he was traded to the Pittsburgh Steelers in 1958, he predicted that the Lions would "not win for 50 years," a curse that seems to still hold — and then some.

Professional football was on the crest of a rise in popularity. The 1958 NFL Championship game between the Baltimore Colts and the New York Giants is considered one of the best. Just as television was becoming a fixture in American homes, a new show was coming to town. Pete Rozelle, the 33-year-old general manager of the Los Angeles Rams, brought media savvy to the NFL when became commissioner in 1960.

Vince Lombardi arrived in Green Bay, Wis., in 1959. Coach Lombardi was a working-class son of a close Italian immigrant family. He attended Catholic schools and believed in hard work. He began his career as a high school football coach. His approach to his football team was "drill, baby, drill." The discipline and repetition of practice would be rewarded on game day. He became a model for coaches throughout the game. Coach Lombardi reflected Coach Fracassa's own origin, heritage, and values, and became an inspiration. Professional football would prosper in the 1960s, and the American Football League (AFL) would be established in 1960. The promotion of individual stars; a wide-open, high-risk style of game; and the acceptance of relaxed dress, long hair, and facial hair challenged the standards of 1960.

This was the world awaiting Al Fracassa as he began his football coaching career.

THE DETROIT CATHOLIC HIGH SCHOOL LEAGUE

The Detroit Catholic High School League was a juggernaut in the 1950s and '60s. It was an athletic conference composed of parochial (or parish) high schools and regional non-parish (or more centralized) Catholic high schools. The centralized high schools (such as the University of Detroit Jesuit, Detroit Catholic Central, and Detroit — later Warren — De La Salle) were larger, all-boys schools. The faculty consisted of male clergy (Jesuit priests or Christian Brothers, for example), and these schools were mostly college preparatory institutions. Although the tuition was significant, the schools attracted Catholic boys from across the Detroit metropolitan area.

Parochial, or parish high schools, were most often associated with a single church. These schools tended to be smaller and coeducational. Girls often made up more of the enrollment than boys, possibly due to central boys' schools. The majority of the faculty was female, often consisting of nuns from a variety of orders (Sisters of Charity or Sisters, Servants of the Immaculate Heart of Mary, for example). The tuition was low, and the clientele often reflected the immigrant makeup of the local community. College was a possibility, but not a given.

In Michigan, there were no regional or state playoffs for high school football in the 1950s and '60s. The Detroit City Championship, which pitted the Catholic League champion against the Public League champion, was called the Goodfellows Game, and it was a special event for the Goodfellows Fund, one of the city's favorite charities. The contest was established in 1938 and was played at Briggs Stadium, where the Tigers and Lions played their games, and it wasn't uncommon for as many as 40,000 people to attend.

The Detroit Catholic High School League also had a championship game, with the larger high schools most often playing the smaller parish high schools. This was called the Soup Bowl, as it was sponsored by the Capuchin Soup Kitchen, a charity established by the Capuchin Franciscan friars during the Great Depression that provided food and clothing to the needy. The Soup Bowl winner would go on to play the Detroit Public School League champion in the Goodfellows Game.

In the 1950s and '60s, the Soup Bowl became a showplace for parochial high schools.

St. Anthony, established in 1918, was the first parish high school to dominate the local scene. The team, known as the Teutons, played in two Goodfellows Games in the 1940s and three Soup Bowls in the '50s. St. Anthony was in decline by 1960, and Coach Fracassa's Shrine Knights played the Teutons in his first three years. A drop in enrollment and a required shift to lower divisions led to league realignment on more than one occasion. St. Anthony High School eventually closed in 1969.

The team that dominated the Catholic League in the 1950s was the St. Mary of Redford Rustics. From 1951 to 1958, they were in six Goodfellows Games, and won three of them. St. Mary of Redford, established in 1843, opened its high school in 1922. The school grew like crazy with the expansion of the automobile industry in Detroit. After World War II, the parish became the largest in Michigan, with 4,455 families.

Following his service with the U.S. Marine Corps in Okinawa (where he was awarded a Purple Heart), Dan Boisture coached the Rustics from 1954 to 1958. In 1959, he became an assistant coach at Michigan State University under Duffy Daugherty. At the time, the Catholic League had a revolving door to and from East Lansing. Boisture eventually left MSU and became the head coach at Eastern Michigan University in Ypsilanti. One of the Rustics' stars was Norman Masters, who would eventually become a teammate of Al Fracassa's at Michigan State University. Masters went on to play for the NFL champion Green Bay Packers teams coached by Vince Lombardi.

Norm Masters

The league saw a new powerhouse emerge in 1959. With its first Goodfellows Game victory, Grosse Pointe's St. Ambrose High, coached by Tom Boisture, Dan's younger brother, began to dominate. In 1960, Coach Fracassa, a Michigan State University Spartan alumnus, took the job as the coach at Royal Oak Shrine, and he sent shock waves through the ultra-competitive Catholic League in his very first year.

FR. CHARLES COUGHLIN AND THE SHRINE OF THE LITTLE FLOWER

Albert Fracassa isn't the only superstar to have begun his career at Shrine of the Little Flower, which was established in 1926 when Bishop Michael J.

Gallagher appointed Fr. Charles E. Coughlin as the first parish priest.

Fr. Coughlin built a simple church for 600 parishioners at the corner of Woodward Avenue and 12 Mile Road. Two weeks after its completion, the local Ku Klux Klan burned a wooden cross on the grounds. Fr. Coughlin put out the flames and promised to construct: "... a cross so high ... that neither man nor beast could burn it down." He set about to fulfill this promise. Of course, that meant that he needed to raise money.

Church fundraisers were inadequate for financing such large dreams. Fr. Coughlin approached radio station WJR in Detroit with a proposal for a weekly broadcast. He began by giving a regular Sunday sermon in the early 1930s. His broadcasts turned out to be profitable, and the 28-foot Charity Crucifixion Tower at Woodward Avenue and 12 Mile Road was built in 1931. The tower housed Fr. Coughlin's office, and he prepared his sermons there. The church itself was completed in 1936.

Shrine coaches in 1960, from left: Martin Foley, Al Fracassa, Tom Urban.

Fr. Coughlin's Basilian order was interested in the Catholic "social justice" movement. During the Great Depression, there was a concern that unemployed and disadvantaged factory and farm workers would turn to communist solutions, and that led Fr. Coughlin to become more political in his preaching. He called for monetary reforms, the nationalization of major industries, and the protection of the rights of labor. His audience grew to 30 or 40 million listeners, and he was invited to visit President Franklin D. Roosevelt at the White House. Fr. Coughlin established the National Union for Justice, a political party of sorts.

President Roosevelt eventually had a falling out with Fr. Coughlin over his isolationism, his support of fascist policies, and his anti-Semitism. In 1939, the Roosevelt administration forced the cancellation of his radio program and forbade the dissemination of his newspaper, Social Justice. Fr. Coughlin retreated to the Shrine of the Little Flower, where he remained pastor until 1965.

Fr. Coughlin hired Ted Widgren to be athletic director at Shrine High School in 1959. Martin Foley and Al Fracassa both were looking for a football head coaching job, but Fracassa won a coin toss and began his career the following year (Foley became the basketball and track coach).

ROYAL OAK SHRINE HIGH SCHOOL

After establishing the Shrine of the Little Flower parish, named in honor of the recently canonized St. Therese of Lisieux, Fr. Coughlin decided to open an all-girls high school, Little Flower High School, in the 1930s. An all-boys high school, Shrine High School, soon followed. The two schools merged in 1941, becoming Shrine of the Little Flower High School. In the 1960s, it became Shrine High School. About 700 students were enrolled in the high school, and roughly 60 percent were girls. The Sisters of Charity made up most of the faculty at both the grade school and the high school.

The grade school was located at Woodward Avenue and 12 Mile Road, while the high school was a little farther north, at the corner of Woodward Avenue and 13 Mile Road. Most pupils grew up within one or two miles of Woodward Avenue and met each other in first grade when they were 6 years old.

Like the other parish high schools, the Shrine High School football team benefited from a "farm system." The parochial grade schools had a competitive football league that began in the seventh grade. This system contributed to the quality and enthusiasm of the high school teams in the Detroit Catholic High School Football League. The Shrine seventh- and eighth-grade teams had outstanding coaches in Mike Brown, Tim Sauter, and Bob Peltier.

Shrine High School began to play Catholic League football in 1950. The team struggled, posting a 21-30-3 record in its early years. In 1958, the team found a quarterback named Ron Bishop and they were 6-1, with one loss to St. Mary of Redford just keeping them out of the Soup Bowl. In 1959, they were 5-0-2 under Coach Ron Horvath, and that year they made it to the Soup Bowl. Bishop and his teammate receiver, John Seymour, made a proficient offensive duo. Prior to league restructuring, Shrine beat an excellent Detroit De La Salle team before meeting St. Ambrose in the Soup Bowl. The St. Ambrose Cavaliers blitzed early and often and won with a score of 14-6. Bishop went on to be named the All-City team quarterback and was awarded a scholarship to the University of Detroit.

In 1960, Coach Al Fracassa arrived at Shrine High School and began his long, legendary high school coaching career.

1960

Coach Fracassa took over a Shrine High School Knights team with talent. The 1959 team had made it to the Soup Bowl thanks to Ron Bishop's passing and John Seymour's receiving, but they lost to a great Grosse Pointe St. Ambrose High School Cavaliers team, 14-6, on a sloppy field against a blitz package. St. Ambrose, a small Class C parish high school, went on to beat the powerful, No. 1 Class A Detroit Cooley High, 13-6, for the Detroit City Championship in the

Goodfellows Game at Briggs Stadium, which would be renamed Tiger Stadium in 1961. That year, Bishop was named to the All-League, All-Catholic, and All-State football teams. He was also All-League and All-Catholic in both basketball and baseball and went on to play four years of varsity college football at the University of Detroit and three years of semiprofessional football with the Michigan Arrows of the Continental Football League.

Coach Fracassa inherited several excellent players. One was John Seymour — the first of several Seymour boys to play and star at Shrine. John was a multi-position player for the 1959 team, but Fracassa thought he

Detroit Free Press, Tuesday, Oct. 6, 1960

would excel as a running back. He approached Seymour with the question: "Did you ever think about being a running back?" That change turned out to be a key to Seymour's later college success.

The 1960 season started with shutout wins over both St. Patrick and St. Mary of Redford by matching scores of 13-0. The next opponent was St. Ambrose, coming off its excellent 1959 season. Fracassa's Knights pulled off a "surprising" 33-19 upset win, although St. Ambrose's head coach, Tom Boisture, felt he had his best talent that year. According to Joe Dowdall of the *Detroit Free Press*, "Not only did the Shrine players outplay the city champions on the field, but their young coach outsmarted three of the best high school

John Everly, Jerry McCulloch

coaches in the Detroit area." That trio included Boisture, along with assistant coaches Roger Parmentier (formerly of Cooley High) and Ed Rutherford (formerly of Denby High). Seymour produced touchdowns rushing, receiving, and throwing for the Knights in that game.

The Knights lost to Servite High the following weekend but won the next three games to make it to the Soup Bowl Catholic Championship Game. There, they lost 20-7 to Class A Catholic Central. It was the first of many games Coach Fracassa would play against the Shamrocks in his record-setting, 54-year career.

In addition to Seymour, Coach Fracassa had other talented players on his roster. Most were multis-port athletes. John Everly,

1960 upset kids, offensive line, from left: Pete Saputo, Herb Seymour, Joe Woodall, Mike Nidifer, Pat Carroll, John Everly, Paul Kraemer.

a team captain (along with Jerry McCulloch), was named to the All-Catholic football team and received an honorable mention for the All-State Class B team in 1960. He was a two-year varsity letter-winner in basketball and track. Everly went on to play college football for the University of Detroit Titans and was named a co-captain of their 1964 squad. Mike Nidiffer, who was the senior class president at Shrine, just like Fracassa had been at Northeastern High School, was named to the All-City and All-State Class B teams.

JOHN SEYMOUR

Before the 1964 Army-Navy football game, the United States Naval Academy teams had won five of the service academy matchups in a row. But in 1964, the United States Army's academy, West Point, had a player named John Sey-

mour — the same John Seymour who had played on Fracassa's Shrine team of 1960. He had been on the All-Catholic team for three years in football and was All-Catholic for two years in track, in addition to playing high school basketball and baseball. Seymour was a great all-around athlete, but his passion was football. Following his high school graduation in 1961, Seymour accepted an appointment to West Point and, once there, he excelled academically and was awarded a Superintendent's Trophy as an Outstanding Freshman Cadet.

John Seymour

In 1964, the Naval Academy Midshipmen had a star quarterback named Roger Staubach, who would go on to win the Heisman Trophy and later play for the Dallas Cowboys in the NFL.

The Army-Navy game was always the highlight of the year for the service academy squads. Seymour gained 103 yards on the ground — more than any runner had gained that year against Navy. Army prevailed, claiming an 11-8 victory.

After his education at West Point, John Seymour did his Airborne/Ranger training and later served in Viet Nam. He says the inspiration Coach Fracassa provided to his players extended far beyond the high school walls.

GROSSE POINTE ST. AMBROSE HIGH SCHOOL

To be great at a given sport, you need an outstanding opponent. Coach Fracassa found a spectacular opponent in the St. Ambrose Cavaliers. In his nine-year career at Shrine High School, Fracassa's teams went to the Soup Bowl on two occasions, but mighty St. Ambrose played in five Soup Bowl games in the 1960s. The Cavaliers won the City Championship Goodfellows Game in 1961,

Goodfellows: The Champions of St. Ambrose.

1962, 1964, and 1966. There were no state play-offs in Michigan in those years, so St. Ambrose was often the de facto state champion.

St. Ambrose High School had less than 400 students, making it a class C school by the state of Michigan's classification, but that didn't prevent the school from emerging as a football powerhouse in 1959. Under Coach Tom Boisture, the Cavaliers — after beating the Shrine Knights — played a much larger Class A Detroit City League (later the Detroit Public School League) football champion, Detroit Cooley, in the Goodfellows Game. St. Ambrose stunned Cooley, 13-6. From 1957 to 1967, 12 young men from St. Ambrose High were named to the Michigan All-State team, and two players went on to play in the NFL.

The coaching staff was outstanding during those years, too. Boisture had been a star at Holy Redeemer High in Detroit, played college football at Mississippi State University, and returned to Detroit to coach at Austin Catholic Preparatory School. He took over as head coach at St. Ambrose in 1955, and his teams won both the Soup Bowl games and Goodfellows games in 1959 and 1961. After his career at St. Ambrose, he served as an assistant coach at the University of Houston (1962-1965). He was the head coach at the College of the Holy Cross from 1967 to 1968, before becoming a scout for the New England Patriots of the NFL. Later, he worked as the director of player personnel for the NFL's New York Giants, where he won two Super Bowl rings.

George Perles took over in the 1962 season. He came to St. Ambrose after a college career at Michigan State University and a year at St. Rita High in Chicago. The Cavaliers won Soup Bowl games and Goodfellows games in 1962 and 1964 under Perles, who then returned to Michigan State as the defensive line coach. He caught the eye of Chuck Noll, head coach of the NFL's Pittsburgh Steelers, and was given a position as their defensive line coach. During Perles' 10-year stay with the Steelers, the team won four Super Bowls. In 1983, Perles returned to his alma mater as the Spartans' head coach and stayed there until 1994.

St. Ambrose Church, Grosse Pointe, 1960.

Joe Carruthers took over at St. Ambrose in 1965. He had been a friend of Perles at Michigan State, was the best man at his wedding in 1958, and was godfather to one of his children. The Cavaliers won both the Soup Bowl and the Goodfellows games in 1966. Afterward, Carruthers had a brief stint as head coach at Grosse Pointe North High School, before becoming MSU's offensive line coach in 1968.

What other factors led to a tiny parochial high school in Detroit becoming a football powerhouse for so many years? "Extensive grade school, even freshman and reserve [football] programs, give the Catholic League a decided superiority that City League can't match," was one reason cited by Dr. Robert Luby, health and physical education supervisor of the Detroit Public Schools. All the parochial high schools had this advantage, but Coach Boisture and the St. Ambrose Cavaliers developed a program that took things a step further.

The program was described in Rick Gosselin's book "Goodfellows: The Champions of St. Ambrose" as resembling a college program. The St. Ambrose parish grade-school boys all went on to play for the high school, but Coach Boisture said: "I didn't have enough [football talent] at the grade school to carry me. I knew I had to bring in another 16-17 kids." His solution was to assign a Catholic Youth Organization (CYO) basketball coach to scout grade school athletic talent outside of the parish. The boys who were scouted were brought to St. Ambrose High School and given what was known as the "recruiting pitch." Boisture later said, "I guess it was legal, or the league would have said something to us."

There were other factors, too. The St. Ambrose Dad's Club was "flush with cash" in 1958, so the high school tuition for non-parish families (about $50 at the time) was covered for the football recruits. Some parish boys had their $20 tuition covered, as well.

The Dad's Club also paid for equipment. Ray Macoun, a St. Ambrose High School football player who went on to play at the University of Detroit and Drake University, said: "The equipment we had at St. Ambrose was head and shoulders above anything I had in college." Riddell helmets, fiberglass shoulder pads, lightweight mesh uniforms, and kangaroo leather shoes were among the items provided in 1958. The school's locker room was updated with a whirlpool, and the Dad's Club contracted a chiropractor and provided an ultrasound machine for the team. None of the steps taken to improve the St. Ambrose High School football were illegal; a lot of Catholic High School League teams probably hadn't considered them. And the Cavaliers still had to play the game on the field.

1961

Sometimes a losing season isn't really a losing season. In 1961, Fracassa's Shrine Knights experienced a losing campaign, finishing with 3 wins, 4 losses, and 1 tie. It was to be his only losing season at Shrine, and one of two losing seasons in his 54-year career. The team was recovering from the graduation of a lot of football talent from the 1959 and 1960 Soup Bowl squads.

There was one fine player, though, and his name was Mike Randall. As ear-

ly as elementary school, people recognized that Randall had talent. One special night in 1961, Randall, an eighth-grader, was being honored in the Shrine auditorium as an outstanding athlete. His dad was ill, and Randall recalls he went to the event not knowing whether his father would be able to make it. When Randall looked up from

From left: Mike Randall, Coach Fracassa, Jason Randall, Jon Randall.

where he sat, he saw his father — he appeared weak and unwell, but he was there, proud of his son.

Randall's father died when Mike was a freshman at Shrine. Coach Fracassa arranged a scholarship for Mike and spoke with him frequently, aware that he was struggling with the loss. But Randall's struggles also caused him to be a little "smart-mouthed" with the coach, and one exchange in particular led to Mike challenging the "elderly" 29-year-old coach to a boxing match. Mike had boxed in the Catholic Youth Organization program in grade school, but he wasn't aware of his coach's Army experience. The match was a public affair in the high school gym. Before anyone had time to settle into their seats, the match was over, and Mike was on the floor.

Coach Fracassa and Mike Randall bonded that day after their unusual ritual. Randall was the captain of that losing team in 1961, but he was named to the All-League and the All-Catholic football teams and was second-team All-State. He earned two varsity letters in basketball, three in baseball, and two in track. He played college football at the University of Detroit, where he earned two more varsity letters.

Fracassa had helped a boy who was "at risk" get on the right road to becoming a man, and for that reason, 1961 could hardly be labeled a losing season. Randall later had two sons go on to play for Coach Fracassa at Brother Rice: Jason Randall captained the 1990 State Championship team and Jon Randall captained the 2000 State Championship team.

1962

In 1961, Ted Widgren, Shrine High School's athletic director, and Bart Seymour, along with a group of other Shrine dads, assembled the resources — including blood, sweat, and tears — to build a football and track facility for the Shrine sports teams. An improvement in team performance followed.

Fracassa found a new quarterback in Chuck Lowther, who served as the captain of the team that year. He was an All-League, All-City, and All-State football team honoree, and was named the Most Valuable Player in Oakland County by the *Pontiac Press*. He attended Michigan State on a scholarship, where he was a member of the 1965 Big Ten Championship Team that played in the Rose Bowl, as well as the 1966 National Championship Team.

One of Lowther's Shrine teammates was the first player on a Fracassa team to play in the NFL. Mike Haggerty was a three-year varsity letter winner in basketball and baseball, and an All-League football player who later was a member of the University of Miami Hurricanes. Haggerty was drafted by the Pittsburgh Steelers in the sixth round and played four years there. He also played one year with the Boston Patriots (now the New England Patriots) and one year with the Detroit Lions. After the NFL, he played two years for Jacksonville in the World Football League.

Shrine started the season with four wins, including three shutouts. The fifth game was against the St. Ambrose Cavaliers, who were also undefeated — but their record featured four straight shutouts.

Coach Fracassa had installed a single-wing offense for the game, a new formation for the Knights. The team scored the first touchdown of the game, but St. Ambrose countered with Tom Beer. The trouble with the Catholic League of the time was that the other team always had a guy who was destined to be named to the All-State team, play in college, and play in the National Football League. After high school, Beer played for the University of Houston Cougars and was then drafted by the Denver Broncos.

The Cavaliers were ready for the single wing and won, 25-6. Gosselin, in his book, quotes Beer as saying: "There was a lay teacher at St. Ambrose who knew someone who taught at Shrine. The players were excited that week because Al Fracassa put in a single wing to beat us. The teacher told [George] Perles and we shut them down. That was supposed to be their big surprise. ...We put in some basic stuff to defend the single wing, and the rest is history." The Shrine Knights finished that season with a 6-1-1 record, and the St. Ambrose game kept them out of the Soup Bowl.

This type of subterfuge characterized the football-obsessed Catholic League in the 1960s. For years, Coach Fracassa would watch for people or cars parked around the practice field. While this degree of care occasionally appeared to be excessive, Fracassa insisted it's not paranoia if they're really out to get you (or your game plan).

JOHN GODDARD

Coach Fracassa was a man who inspired others to follow him in the profession. John Goddard was a member of the 1962 Shrine football squad and became a high school football coach himself. He was an assistant coach at Shrine in the 1969-70 season, after Fracassa left to coach Brother Rice. Af-

ter that, Goddard coached at St. Agatha, in Redford, for 17 years, and at Hamtramck Immaculate Conception for one year. He was named the Catholic League's C Division Coach of the Year seven times for his outstanding work. He was also a *Detroit Free Press* Coach of the Year and the Michigan High School Football Coaches Association

Coach John Goddard, left, and Channel 7 Sports Reporter Brad Galli, a Brother Rice grad.

(MHSFCA) Coach of the Year in 1991. He was elected to the Catholic League Coaches Hall of Fame and the Michigan High School Football Coaches Hall of Fame in 1993.

Goddard was able to return to his alma mater in 1993. He remained there for 25 years, until 2017, and led Shrine to three Catholic League championships, 12 Michigan State playoffs, and two district championships. He was Catholic League Coach of the Year and a nine-time MHSFCA Regional Coach of the Year.

One of Goddard's coaching colleagues described him as "a man filled with courage, honesty, integrity, and compassion." One of Fracassa's Shrine football stars, Ron Ranieri, said: "It seems like yesterday when John and I were playing for Coach Fracassa at Shrine." Coach Fracassa's legacy of coaching excellence lives on in the character and memories of the boys and men who followed him into the coaching ranks.

PAT CARROLL

Another football player of note on the league championship teams of 1959 and 1960 was Patrick H. (Pat) Carroll. Carroll was a three-year football letterman named to the All-Catholic and All-County teams following his season with Coach Fracassa.

Carroll was a multisport athlete, a varsity player for three years in baseball and two years in basketball. He attended the Air Force Academy and graduated from the University of Colorado, then joined the U.S. Air Force and, as a first lieutenant, was assigned to the 355th Tactical Fighter Squadron, 31st Tactical Fighter Wing, stationed at the Pho Cat and Tuy Hoa air bases in South Vietnam.

As the Vietnam War increased in intensity, a major supply line for North Vietnam was via the Ho Chi Minh Trail, which ran through the mountains between Laos and Vietnam. In 1967, a group of combat-experienced fighter pilots was gathered to form a top-secret squadron. Its call sign was MISTY, after the commander's favorite song. All of the pilots had volunteered to serve as forward air controllers, flying fast (350 to 550 mph) and very low (to "identify trucks, bridges, bulldozers, whatever"), continually changing direction over enemy territory. They directed Air Force and Navy strikes on identified targets.

On Nov. 2, 1969, Lt. Col. Lawrence W. Whitford Jr., MISTY 136, and 1st Lt. Patrick H. Carroll, MISTY 127, departed Tuy Hoa air base on a mission over the Ho Chi Mihn Trail. Lt. Col. Whitford reported low fuel status over Laos, but the men's two-seat Super Sabre F-100F didn't show up for the scheduled refueling. At the time, there was no evidence of an aircraft crash and no sign of the crew. Several months later the damaged plane was found, but there was nothing indicating that the crew was dead, and no bodies were found. Whitford and Carroll were declared missing in action. Carroll

U.S. Air Force Major Pat Carroll

was awarded the Vietnamese Cross of Gallantry, the Silver Star, and the Purple Heart, and was promoted to the rank of major.

Nearly 600 Americans disappeared in Laos, controlled by the communist Pathet Lao, in the war. No service members were released in the 30 years after the war, nor were reports provided. From 1967 to 1970, when the MISTY program was active, 28 percent of these heroic volunteer pilots were shot down. In 2005, Carroll's daughters, Darleen and Susie, attended a MISTY families reunion and said, "Our family still holds out some hope that we may one day be able to bring our father home."

In this book, football players are considered heroes, but it should be acknowledged that there are other, real heroes. These real heroes remind us that sports are only games.

1963
Catholic League Champions

This was the year of "The Firsts": The first Catholic League Championship for Coach Fracassa and his first Catholic League Coach of the Year award. The 1963 Shrine Knights opened the season with three victories, in which it allowed a total of only six points. These games preceded the season's only loss, a 19-7 rout, to the Dearborn Divine Child Falcons. The Falcons were newcomers to the league but played well under their young coach, Tony Versaci.

The single blemish on Fracassa's regular-season slate was followed by three victories, including a 20-7 win over St. Ambrose, the prior year's Goodfellows Game city champions. In 1963, the AA Division Shrine Knights made a return to the Catholic Football League Championship Soup Bowl game. The Knights had a senior, Ron Ranieri, anchoring their line. Ranieri had been on the All-State team in 1962 and was heading for a repeat of that honor in 1963. The team's other star was junior Jim Seymour, John's brother, an All-State track star in 1963 who would join Ranieri on the All-State team after this season.

The Knights' Central Division opponent in the game was Harper Woods Notre Dame High School, coached by Walt "Bazy" Bazylewicz. Harper Woods Notre Dame was a Catholic, all-boys, college-preparatory high school founded by the Marist Fathers and Brothers in 1956.

The Fighting Irish had finished at 6 and 1; their only loss was handed down by Detroit Cathedral on the second-to-last game of the regular season. Notre Dame had a star of their own. Joe Przybycki was a lineman who would be named to the High School All-America team by *Parade* magazine, play for Michigan State University, and then be drafted by the Philadelphia Eagles of the NFL.

The last game of the season, the Soup Bowl, was played before a crowd of 17,500 fans at the University of Detroit's stadium. The teams battled to a scoreless tie; as a result, both squads would be Catholic League Co-Champions. However, to send a team to the Goodfellows Game, a league rules tiebreaker would apply: The team with the greater total yards gained in the Soup Bowl would represent the Catholic League. Notre Dame advanced to the Goodfellows Game because they had gained four more yards than the Shrine Knights.

Don Horkey from the *Michigan Catholic* reported that, years later, Coach Fracassa was asked if either team came close to scoring. His reply was: "Well, we had one touchdown called back because of a penalty." Coach Bazylewicz was given the game ball.

On Friday, Nov. 22, 1963, John F. Kennedy was assassinated by Lee Harvey Oswald in Dallas, Texas. For a long time, the question was: "Where were you when you heard of the assassination?" If you were a football player with a late-season game or a Thanksgiving Day game, you probably heard the news on the practice field.

In Detroit, the Goodfellows City Championship game was scheduled to take place on Nov. 22, 1963. Ron Pesch, a Michigan high school sports historian, reported that Goodfellows officials decided that "Because the purpose of the game is to provide help to needy children ... canceling it would have deprived thousands of these children." Attendance at Tiger Stadium suffered, as only 23,500 fans were in the stands. The Denby High School Tars won the game, 7-0, "Beneath a cloud of sorrow as a light rain fell," Pesch reported.

RON RANIERI

Ron Ranieri wrote to Coach Fracassa, at the time of his retirement: "Congratulations Coach Fracassa from your first Catholic League Championship team. You never forget the first time, and neither will we. Thanks for being a part of our lives forever."

A four-year varsity letter-winner, Ranieri was a player on the 1960 Soup Bowl squad as well as on the 1963 Catholic League Co-Championship team. He was named to the Detroit All-City Football team in 1961, 1962, and 1963, and was on the Michigan All-State Football teams in 1962 and 1963. He also received two varsity letters in basketball.

Ranieri attended Michigan State University on a football scholarship and was a two-year letter-winner there for Duffy Daugherty, as well as a member of the Big Ten Championship teams of 1965 and

Ron Ranieri

1966. These two teams were both chosen as consensus National College Athletic Association Champion. Ranieri was named second-team All-Big Ten for his play in 1967. Like Fracassa had done before him, he won the Fred Danzinger Award at MSU in 1967, and was honored as the Spartan from the metro Detroit area "who made the most outstanding contribution to the team."

Ranieri was one of the players who would return to coach football teams alongside his former coach. He helped with the Shrine teams informally, and then joined Fracassa on the staff at Brother Rice. In a recent interview, Ranieri said that he believed Coach Fracassa was "a combination of everything that can be right about a football coach ... humor, discipline, honesty. ... Coach had a sense of humor that could make you laugh so hard it could bring you to tears. Of course, he could yell at you and bring you to tears that way."

Ranieri's daughter met Coach Fracassa once and remarked that when Coach talks to you, you feel "like the only person in the room."

1964

In 1964, Shrine had a down year. Maybe it was a letdown, like losing NFL Super Bowl teams occasionally experience. Ron Ranieri had graduated, but Jim Seymour was still on the team. The year started with three wins, followed by a scoreless tie with Detroit Holy Redeemer. The Knights were beaten the next week by Divine Child, 21-14. After a win over Redford, Shrine traveled to Mack Park to play St. Ambrose, a school that had developed a crushing running game under Coach George Perles. St. Ambrose won, 40-19.

St. Ambrose went on to beat Detroit Cathedral, 21-13, in the Soup Bowl and played the first televised Goodfellows Game against the Detroit Southeastern High School Jungaleers in a blizzard. Only 15,000 fans attended on a blustery Thursday night at Tiger Stadium. The St. Ambrose team won, 20-0, and finished 9-0 for the season.

Greg Hacias, a junior quarterback that year for St. Ambrose, was named to the All-State team in 1965 and eventually played for the University of Nebraska Cornhuskers. Shrine High star Seymour was named to his second All-State team and was a consensus High School All-American player. He went on to earn college All-American honors at Notre Dame and played for the Chicago Bears.

JIM SEYMOUR

One day, an assistant football coach at Shrine, Bob McMackin, talked Coach Fracassa into going to a track meet in downtown Detroit. They were there to see an All-State 180-yard low hurdles champion. This athlete was also participating in the 440-yard relay race. There were no meters back then. The race began with a fast start by the public school teams. The lead was extended at each leg of the race. Shrine High's sprinter took the baton 10 yards behind, then made up that deficit and more. The coaches looked at one another, flabbergasted. Although Jim Seymour was an All-State track team star in 1963 and 1964, his best sport was football.

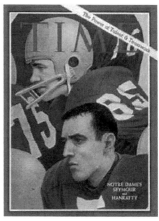

Jim Seymour and Terry Hanratty, Oct. 28, 1966.

Seymour was a 6'4", 210-pound, sure-handed football player who ran a sub-10-second 100-yard dash, set a Catholic High School League record in the 180-yard low hurdles (19.6 seconds), and was named to the All-State teams in basketball, track, and football in 1964. In football, he was named to the All-League and All-Catholic teams for three years, the All-State team for two years, and the All-America team for one year.

In 1965, Coach Ara Parseghian and the University of Notre Dame's Fighting Irish were looking for a replacement for their Heisman Trophy-winning quarterback, John Huarte, and his favorite passing target, Jack Snow, who had finished their careers in 1964. Seymour and Terry Hanratty sat out their freshman year in 1965 (per NCAA rules), and began their college careers in 1966. The first opponent that year was the Purdue University Boilermakers, quarterbacked by Bob Griese. Before the game, Coach Parseghian said, "I would love to see them try to cover Seymour one-on-one."

Seymour presented a "prototype for a new breed of a wide receiver," according to Lou Somogyi of *247Sports*, a website devoted to college sports and recruiting news. Bruce Weber of *The New York Times* reported that he was "bigger and faster than virtually any other college receiver at the time."

In the second series of the game, Seymour's first catch was for 42 yards. He add-

Low Hurdles Champion Jim Seymour.

ed 84-yard, 39-yard, and 7-yard touchdown receptions, finishing with 276 receiving yards on 13 catches. The Irish won 26-14. Throughout college football, the passing game was becoming all the rage. On Oct. 28, 1966, *Time* magazine had a cover graphic that featured Seymour and Hanratty to accompany its football coverage on the inside pages.

Seymour made college All-America teams all three years he played at Notre Dame. When he graduated in 1969, he was the career receiving leader for the Irish, with 138 catches for 2,113 yards (more than 15 yards per catch) and 16 touchdowns. He was drafted No. 10 by the NFL Los Angeles Rams in 1969 and was traded to the Chicago Bears on Sept. 1, 1970. He played three seasons for the Bears and finished his professional career by spending one year with the Chicago Fire of the World Football League.

An injured hamstring muscle from the Hula Bowl, which Seymour aggravated in the Senior Bowl, limited his effectiveness in the professional leagues. "I could still catch the ball, but they wanted speed and it wasn't there anymore," he said. "I was just glad I played as long as I did." Anyone who had the pleasure of seeing him play would agree.

Coach Fracassa has said that Jim Seymour was one of the best — maybe the best — player he ever coached. Of course, that's a question that may remain open for debate.

1965

Shrine's 1965 football season began slowly, with losses to St. Ambrose and Detroit Servite, but team captain Dick Landry rallied the Knights and they went 4-0-1 in their last five games to finish in second place in the tough Double-A division. Fracassa had developed a strong interior line led by Landry, along with Larry Liposky and Roger Schlum. Dave Allen and Ed Busch were the key running backs. Shrine defeated Bishop Gallagher, Holy Redeemer, Divine Child, and Redford St. Mary, and played Benedictine to a tie. St. Ambrose finished the regular season at 7-0, but lost to

Shrine coaches and the team captain in 1965 (from left): Assistant Coach Bob McMackin, Captain Dick Landry, Coach Fracassa.

Notre Dame in the Soup Bowl, 27-21. The Goodfellows Game ended in a 14-14 tie between Notre Dame and Denby at Tiger Stadium, in front of 25,000 fans.

Coach Fracassa didn't take losing lightly. At Shrine, the players experienced a sense of dread after a loss. First, the film of the game was presented for instructional purposes. Fracassa, always thorough and meticulous, would have already reviewed every player's performance on every play. In a team setting, he admonished his players — and not always quietly. Fracassa reminded his team of their errors in judgment, memory lapses concerning the game plan, and possible execution flaws during the game. After reviewing the film, the team would return to the practice field to integrate what they'd learned.

A story appeared on Facebook on June 18, 2018, posted by Mark Schmeling of St. Mary of Redford concerning Coach Bazylewicz possibly "grabbing Buster's [Eugene 'Buster' Parerni] face mask with one of his meaty hands, and ratcheting his head back and forth to 'correct' a mistake he had made on the old gridiron." This technique had been deemed acceptable for treating football-related attention deficit disorder. It had possibly been employed by Coach Fracassa, but no definite confirmation is available from his former players, who say only "ah, no comment."

Coach Fracassa also believed the losses may have been his fault, and he would double the pressure on himself to get his team ready for the next game. Eventually, the mood at practice improved and returned to one of instruction and preparation for the upcoming game.

COACH FRACASSA AND HIS OTHER JOBS

Football wasn't the only sport that attracted Coach Fracassa's attention. In his first year at Shrine, 1960-61, he also coached junior varsity basketball. But his true second coaching joy was baseball. He coached varsity baseball at Shrine from 1961 to 1969 and was the coach at Brother Rice from 1970 to 1982.

During his baseball coaching career, Fracassa guided the Knights to sectional victories in 1966, 1967, and 1968. His teams played in Detroit Catholic League finals in 1968 and 1969 at Tiger Stadium but were knocked out of the finals those years by the Hamtramck St. Ladislaus Greyhounds. The Greyhounds played for a small, Class C school, but were a perennial Detroit baseball power. St. Ladislaus won the first Michigan High School Athletic Association baseball Championship in 1971.

Coach Fracassa took Brother Rice's Warrior squad to Tiger Stadium in 1975, where they defeated Bishop Gallagher High School, 2-1, to win their first Catholic High School League Championship. The Warriors lost in the final in 1976, but returned to win Catholic League High School Championships in both 1978 and 1979. In 1981, Fracassa left his baseball coaching career to devote his attention full time to football. The record for his baseball team during his tenure was 187-121 (0.607), with three Catholic League Championships and one runner-up season. In 1982, his assistant football coach, Ron Kalczynski, took over the reins of the baseball team.

In the Catholic high school setting, additional uses are often found for a football or baseball coach's talents. Because of his background in physical education, the expectation was that Fracassa would teach PE as well as history at Shrine, including segments on health and hygiene. At Brother Rice, he taught history and physical education from 1969 to 1998. He brought the high expectations he had for his athletes to his academic classrooms.

Coaches in the Detroit Catholic high school system provided another function, as well. The parochial schools were often founded and staffed by clergywomen; at Shrine High School, for example, most of the teaching was done by the Sisters of Charity. Although the sisters were tough themselves, adolescent young men — typically an unruly lot — sometimes required additional intervention. The football coach at a Catholic high school often served as a father figure, role model, and disciplinarian who roamed the corridors and smoothed out any behaviors the sisters couldn't handle. Brother Rice was staffed by an order of clerics called the Congregation of Christian Brothers, a tough lot, but the gravitas that Fracassa brought to his role at both high schools was impressive.

1966

The great professional golfer Jack Nicklaus won 18 major golf tournaments in his career, but incredibly, he finished second in 19 majors. A lot of times in a career, a player, a coach, or a team will miss the playoffs, the finals, or the championship by a single game. This was one of those years for Coach Fracassa and his Shrine High School Knights.

The team had a seasoned senior quarterback in Dave Yeager, a three-sport athlete who would eventually become an assistant coach for four years with Fracassa at Brother Rice. Gary Hambell was one of the team's most prominent players that year and went on to play defensive tackle for the University of Dayton Flyers. After college, he was drafted by the Baltimore Colts (before that team moved to Indianapolis). Tom Torongo was outstanding on both the offensive and defensive lines.

Dave Yeager, Brother Rice assistant coach, pictured with Albert Fracassa and fellow assistants Mike Popson and John Walker.

St. Ambrose, under Coach Joe Carruthers, maintained its dominance in both the Catholic League and the city of Detroit. Greg Hacias was still the team's quarterback, and Tom Bialk was an All-State, all-purpose back who ran, passed, and kicked for the Cavaliers in 1966. They had a junior at tight end, Gary Nowak, who would receive a scholarship to Michigan State University and be drafted as an offensive tackle by the NFL's San Diego Chargers in 1971. The game between Shrine and St. Ambrose was the second game of the season. The Cavaliers dominated and won by a score of 19-0.

Shrine allowed an average of 14 points in their first four games and shut out their opponents in the last three games. As demonstrated in this season, one of the characteristics of a Coach Fracassa team was improvement as the season progressed.

St. Ambrose was once again undefeated in the regular season. They went on to beat Notre Dame in the Soup Bowl, 6-0. They also triumphed over Denby in the Goodfellows Game, 33-19. But the impressive run of the Cavaliers would soon come to an end.

DEARBORN DIVINE CHILD HIGH SCHOOL

Divine Child won the Catholic League Second Division Championship in 1961 and 1962, and moved up to the AA first division in 1963. They beat St. Ambrose, 27-19, in their first meeting — an auspicious beginning for Coach Tony Versaci and his high-flying Falcons.

Divine Child, a co-ed parish school, was a recent arrival in the Detroit Diocese. The church was founded in 1950 and the elementary school opened in 1953. Monsignor Herbert Weier founded Divine Child in 1958 with 84 freshmen, a faculty that consisted of two Bernadine Sisters of St. Francis, and one athletic coach, Tony Versaci. Coach Versaci had been a walk-on football player at the University of Detroit and graduated in 1959. He went straight to the coaching job at Divine Child and led the Falcons in their first football game that same year.

The early Falcon teams were considered Class C, playing in the division below the AA Catholic League. In 1960, 1961, and 1962 they were undefeated, winning impressively. Even the national sports press juggernaut, *Sports Illustrated*, in a brief report from Oct. 16, 1961, noted that the "Divine Steamroller" was winning by huge scores. After a 67-0 defeat of Our Lady of Sorrows, the magazine noted that "The coach has been accused of rolling up the score." In their nine-game season in 1961, Divine Child outscored their opponents 460-45, with an average per-game score of 51-5. In 1962, the Falcons scored 332 points and the opposition scored 52 points, an average per-game score of 42-7.

Divine Child continued to grow, along with the suburban city of Dearborn. Before long it became a Class B school and was promoted to the Detroit Catholic League AA Division in 1963. Coach Versaci was named Michigan High School Coach of the Year in 1966.

Fracassa was emotional about the coaching competition with Versaci. Per-

Gary Danielson

haps it was Coach Versaci's early career success. Perhaps it was the scoring differentials. Perhaps it was that early Coach of the Year award. Perhaps it was their shared Italian American heritage. In any case, the enthusiasm of the coaching staff increased before games where Divine Child was the opponent.

In 1966, Coach Versaci moved a sophomore wide receiver to the quarterback position. That player was Gary Danielson, who would play in two Catholic League Championship Soup Bowl games, in one City Championship Goodfellows Game, for four years at Purdue University in the Big Ten, and for 11 years with the Detroit Lions and Cleveland Browns. Danielson was one of the best players to emerge from the Detroit Catholic Football League.

Versaci joined the coaching staff at Michigan State University for one year in 1970 and joined the St. Louis Cardinals' coaching staff for one year in 1971. He was a member of the Michigan Chapter of the National Football Foundation, which supports amateur sports and athletes, for 24 years and was its president for 17 years. When Coach Versaci was honored by the NFF, he said "Having been a high school coach was my fondest memory. Having success on the field was great, but watching the lessons that football taught the young men I coached, which has been converted into their lives, was definitely a marvelous experience." That's something Coach Fracassa and Coach Versaci could agree on.

1967

The 1967 season proved to be outstanding in the Detroit Catholic High School AA League. It was a memorable year for Fracassa's team, too, as four of his players went on to Division I football programs on scholarships. But the team also lost three games.

The first game of the 1967 season was against Divine Child. Their quarterback was Gary Danielson, who dominated the league in his junior and senior years. He attended Purdue University on scholarship following his graduation, and played for World Football League teams in New York, Charlotte, and Chicago in 1974 and 1975. Later, he joined his hometown NFL Detroit Lions, for whom he would play from 1976 to 1984. He closed out his professional career playing with the Cleveland Browns from 1985 to 1988. But in 1967, Danielson and the Falcons beat the Shrine Knights, 20-0.

After a win over St. Mary of Redford in their second game, Shrine played St. Ambrose. St. Ambrose had won both the Soup Bowl and Goodfellows Game in 1966, and was the reigning City Champion. Greg Hacias, their quarterback, went to the University of Nebraska on a scholarship, and Gary Nowak was off to Michigan State University. Although Coach Joe Carruthers had lost two of his best players — Hacias and Nowak — to graduation, he and his best running back, Tom Bialk, were still there, and St. Ambrose prevailed over Shrine, 21-18.

The next week brought a showdown with Servite. The Panthers also had a great quarterback in Frank Kolch. One opponent described Kolch as "The greatest high school athlete I've ever seen." Following his high school graduation, he attended Michigan State University and later transferred to Eastern Michigan University. He was drafted by the Pittsburgh Steelers following his college career. In this game, the Servite Panthers defeated the Shrine Knights, 28-26.

Although Shrine won the rest of their games, Divine Child, St. Ambrose, and Servite tied for the league championship. The league rules gave Divine Child a trip to the Soup Bowl — which they won, 21-6, over Brother Rice. In the Goodfellows Game, Gary Danielson and Divine Child won the City Championship, 14-7, over Denby.

Shrine had a constellation of stars that year. Paul Seymour received a football scholarship to the University of Michigan and was drafted by the NFL's Buffalo Bills. Rick Zimmerman was a kicker and wide receiver and attended the University of Wyoming on scholarship. Ken Caratelli was a multisport athlete with varsity letters in

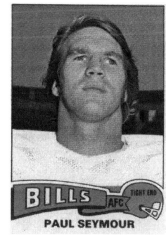

Paul Seymour

basketball, track, and football. In track, he was an All-League and All-Area sprinter in 1967 and 1968. On the football field, he was on the All-Area and All-Catholic teams as a linebacker in 1967. He was awarded an athletic scholarship and lettered at Iowa State University for three years, and was named to the Big 8 All-Conference team. Mick Brzezinski was a multisport athlete who was named to the All-County football team and played quarterback for the Central Michigan University Chippewas. Jim Belleau played football at Ferris State University.

MICK BRZEZINSKI

Mick Brzezinski was the type of player Coach Fracassa loved on his teams. He was an undersized football player with a combination of athletic skills, on-field intelligence, and intestinal fortitude. This type of young man probably reminded Fracassa of his own early sports career.

Brzezinski was an exceptional athlete, and made his first splash for Shrine as a starting guard for the basketball team. He played all four years and was co-captain of the team his senior year. He was named to the All-Area, All-Catholic, and All-State basketball teams after the 1967-1968 season. He

also played baseball for four years, played on sectional champions for three years, and played in the finals at the Catholic League Baseball Championship at Tiger Stadium. His senior year, he was a co-captain of the baseball team. Brzezinski also managed one year of track and lettered in that sport, as well.

While he enjoyed all sports, Brzezinski loved football. He was on the varsity team for four years, lettering three times. He was the captain of the team in his senior year, was named to the All-County football team, and earned an athletic scholarship to Central Michigan University.

Mick Brzezinski gets instructions from Coach Fracassa.

Football was Brzezinski's chosen college sport. He became the starting quarterback for the Central Michigan University Chippewas; in 1970, he was the starting quarterback on a team that went 7-3. There was also a great runner on CMU's run-first team, Jesse Lakes, who ran for 1,296 yards that season while Brzezinski threw for 775 passing yards. The following year, the team was 5-5, with Lakes running for 1,143 yards and Brzezinski throwing for 426 yards. Brzezinski also played basketball at Central Michigan University for one year.

Mick Brzezinski was a version of the young Al Fracassa. He was a four-sport high school phenomenon, was captain of the team in three sports, earned 12 varsity letters, and was named to All-Star teams in two of his sports and All-State in one.

PAUL SEYMOUR

Orenthal James (O.J.) Simpson was a very special athlete who attended the University of Southern California. He was 6'1", 215 pounds, and ran 100 yards in 9.5 seconds. He was the 1968 Heisman Trophy winner and was drafted No. 1 by the NFL Buffalo Bills. Simpson was the first player to rush for more than 2,000 yards in a season, and still leads the yards-per-game and career games rankings with 200 yards rushing for the NFL. The tight end on his offensive line was a Shrine High Knight who had been coached by Al Fracassa.

As the younger brother of John Seymour and Jim Seymour, Paul had big shoes to fill. But he was undaunted. He was too big to participate in grade school football, which had a weight limit that he exceeded by about 40 or 50 pounds when he was 13 years old. He played four years of football for Coach Fracassa's teams, in addition to playing basketball and participating in track and field. After his senior year of football, Paul Seymour was named to the All-League, All-Catholic, and All-State teams. He was awarded a football scholarship to the University of Michigan.

Seymour played two seasons as a tight end for the Wolverines under Bo Schembechler. He caught 19 passes for 257 yards in those two years. In his senior year, he was moved to offensive tackle and was a consensus collegiate All-American player. In the NFL draft, he was the seventh pick in the first round, chosen by the NFL Buffalo Bills. He returned to his tight end position and played for five seasons as the starting tight end. Mostly he blocked for O.J. Simpson as part of the "Electric Company" — but he did manage to catch 62 passes for 818 yards in his career. In 1973, the Bills' offensive line as a group was named Offensive Lineman of the Year.

Many of Coach Fracassa's players have a love of the game that persists after their playing days are over. Seymour says: "I get down to Ann Arbor for games. I'm a big Michigan fan." His only regret is having played in the era that he did; he relates that "Nowadays, you play five years in the NFL and you get to retire for life."

THE SEYMOUR FAMILY

Shrine High School was blessed to have the support of the Seymour family during the time Coach Fracassa was there. Bart and Jane Seymour joined the National Shrine of the Little Flower Parish in November of 1948. Duke, Bart's brother, and his wife, Cis, joined them the following year. The first of their collective 14 children began attending the Shrine schools in 1949.

The Seymours were early supporters of Coach Fracassa when he began his career. Bart told Fracassa that anything the team needed, the Seymours would get it for him. Bart Seymour used to attend football practice and watch from the parking lot. Rick, Bart's son, remembers a day when his father called the coach over to his car to offer some advice. Rick remembers Coach Fracassa gently telling Bart, "You keep selling oil, and I'll coach football." The pair started a habit of meeting for dinner once a week to discuss how things were going.

On Coach Fracassa's retirement, the Seymour family offered him a personal message. To the man who helped shape their children and continued to support them as adults, they wrote: "Proud to have been there at the start and honored to be here at the end of a fabulous and noteworthy career. Thank you for all you have done and continue to do for so many to whom you are truly a mentor and an inspiration. Enjoy your well-earned retirement."

There's a Shrine High School Sports Hall of Fame award that's called the Bart Seymour Service Award. It's given to people who support high school athletics, allowing the coaches to do their jobs. One of the honorees is Rick Seymour, who attended Shrine High School and played on Fracassa's early teams along with his brother, John, and his cousins Herb and Ed. Together with Ted Widgren and his father, Rick helped install the football field at Shrine High School. He was a member of the High School Dads' Club, served as chairman of the school board, and was assistant coach of the grade school football team. Rick is currently a member of the Shrine High School Sports Hall of Fame Committee.

Another Bart Seymour Award honoree was Widgren, the athletic director at Shrine High School during Coach Fracassa's early years. He, along with the Seymour family, led the Dads' Club and was quick to offer support as needed, ranging from providing uniforms and equipment to organizing transportation and all the other little things that make a program possible. Another Bart Seymour Award-winner was Bob Martin, who drove the team bus to home and away games and acted as team photographer on game days. Tom Kirkwood, Shrine High School's onetime principal, also drove the bus when needed and led the cheering section.

Coach Fracassa instilled the concepts of commitment, loyalty, and service in his players — values that would last a lifetime. Martin "Bubba" Glynn, a player on Coach Fracassa's last team at Shrine High School, was given the Bart Seymour Award for his lifetime service. Bubba's two boys played at Shrine High School and later coached the grade school team, following in their father's footsteps of loyalty and service.

THE TIMES

America seemed to be coming apart at the seams in 1968. The Vietnam War was the crucial factor separating people in the country. Four days after Gen. William Westmoreland's statement that the enemy had "experienced only failure" on Jan. 27, 1968, the 70,000 Viet Cong and North Vietnamese Army regulars launched the Tet Offensive, attacking all South Vietnamese government-controlled cities. For eight hours, they controlled the courtyard of the United States Embassy. The Tet Offensive was a military failure but had a demoralizing effect on America's commitment to continuing the war. The gradual erosion of support led to President Lyndon Johnson's decision not to run for re-election and the emergence of the moderate Vice President Hubert Humphrey as the early Democratic Party nominee for president in

1968. Due primarily to opposition to the war, Eugene McCarthy — and, later, Robert Kennedy — became the focus of the party's nomination.

After the "Summer of Love" in 1967, college students in the fall of that year began to adopt a sex, drug, and rock and roll attitude, and their pleas for peace often led to campus unrest. In the summer of 1968, both the demonstrations and the reactions to the student protests had become more violent. More than 100 colleges and universities experienced classroom strikes and campus demonstrations. After Robert Kennedy's victory in the California primary, he was shockingly assassinated. Later that summer, at the Democratic Party's convention in Chicago, frustrations reached a peak, with liberal, anti-establishment protesters fighting the conservative, organized police under Mayor Richard Daley.

Meanwhile, the Roman Catholic Church was going through its own changes. The Second Vatican Council finished its work in 1965 and, in addition to Mass being said in the local vernacular rather than Latin, greater lay participation was encouraged. Ecumenical approaches to Eastern Orthodox and Protestant Christians were begun, as was reconciliation among all faiths with the Jewish community. The right to religious freedom was declared. In 1967, clerical celibacy was affirmed and, in 1968, artificial birth control was forbidden by the Catholic Church. Some said the changes were too liberal, while others believed they were too conservative. From 1955 to 1975, Mass attendance fell from 75 percent to 55 percent for all, and from 73 percent to 36 percent for those 21 to 29 years old. Parishes and parish schools were closing and consolidating.

Sports weren't spared the controversies of the time. Cassius Clay, an Olympic and professional champion boxer, changed his name to Muhammad Ali and joined the Nation of Islam in 1964. In 1967, he refused induction into the United States Armed Services. At the 1968 Olympics in Mexico City, track and field stars John Carlos and Tommie Smith raised gloved fists in a sign of protest during the national anthem.

The world of professional football settled its own war. The NFL and AFL agreed to a merger in 1966. The two leagues kept teams in place, held a common draft, and began interleague play in 1967, with a single league schedule in 1970. But before that, there would be an event called the Super Bowl, named by Lamar Hunt, owner of the Kansas City Chiefs. The first two games weren't called Super Bowls, but the "AFL-NFL World Championship Game." The Green Bay Packers, under Vince Lombardi, convincingly won the first two championships in 1967 and 1968. The 1968 season concluded with what became known as Super Bowl III, played in January 1969. The Baltimore Colts seemed unbeatable under Coach Don Shula and quarterback Johnny Unitas. Coach Weeb Ewbank of the New York Jets countered with Joe

Namath, who predicted a victory. With a concentration on a deep passing game, including pass protection and a quick ball release, the Jets prevailed 16-7. Namath became the new face of professional football.

College football was seen as a "bulwark against radicalism," but around the end of the 1960s, players began to assert their autonomy. Protests involving both Black and White players led Melvin Durslag, of the *Los Angeles Examiner*, to write that a "sharp readjustment" in coaching style would be needed. "The first thing a coach will relinquish is the iron-handed discipline he used to wield. Why should he continue to have this privilege with kids when the rest of us don't? The whole concept of iron-handed discipline is dead anyway. It is dead in our courts, it is dead in our government, it is dead in our homes. Whether this is good or bad is irrelevant. The point is, a coach will have to tailor his methods of handling those in his care." Coach Art Carty, Fracassa's high school football coach, was forced out of his job as principal at Detroit Northern High School in a student-led protest in 1966 because of his "old school authoritarian ways," along with other issues. But the old guard wasn't dead; Woody Hayes and the Ohio State Buckeyes won the NCAA college football championship in 1968.

The decline in Detroit's population, the White flight after the 1967 riots, the change in church participation among younger Catholic families, and the drop in income available to pay for tuition at Catholic schools led to a gradual erosion of leagues and teams in the Detroit Catholic High School Football League. St. Catherine High School closed in 1967, followed by Wyandotte St. Patrick High School and St. Anthony High School in 1969. The Archdiocese of Detroit was forced to close Cathedral High School, Salesian High School, St. Martin of Tours High School, and St. Philip High School in 1970. The last Soup Bowl championship game and the last Goodfellows Game were played in 1967. The Catholic League Championship Game was renamed the Charity Bowl from 1968 to 1970, and then was called the Prep Bowl beginning in 1971.

1968

Shrine graduated 22 varsity lettermen after the 1967 season, including five who would go on to play college football in the fall of 1968. Despite those departures, Coach Fracassa felt that "If we don't have any injuries, we'll be as good as the other teams." Dayton Perrin, the sports editor at the *Royal Oak Daily Tribune*, reported that "The Big Four in AA division contention were Servite, Divine Child, St Mary and St. Ambrose in Fracassa's rating poll." Fracassa added: "Then, hopefully, us." It would be Coach Fracassa's last year at Shrine.

The scrimmage games before the start of the season included a round-robin with three other teams, one of which was Center Line St. Clement, a Catholic League Second Division team that went undefeated in 1967 and 1968 (8-0-1), winning the Second Division Championship Game by a score of 26-7 over Sacred Heart. They had a running back named Joe DeLamielleure. Even so, on this day before the start of the 1968 season, Shrine was able to stop the Center Line rushing game.

Joe DeLamielleure

DeLamielleure, meanwhile, left his running back career behind when he was awarded a scholarship to Michigan State University, where he played offensive guard and earned college All-America honors as a senior. He was drafted by the NFL Buffalo Bills in the first round and blocked for O.J. Simpson as a key member of the "Electric Company." He was All-Pro eight times and was named to the NFL Hall of Fame.

The Shrine Knights opened their regular season with a win over Detroit Holy Redeemer, 27-7. Their next contest was against the reigning Detroit City Champions, Divine Child. Gary Danielson, the eventual Big Ten Purdue Boilermaker and Detroit Lion quarterback, was a senior. The game was close, with a goal-line stand at the end of the first half and a blocked punt in the second half. In the end the Knights won, 14-7. The upset victory was due to great pass defense led by Tom Szostkowski and Bill Simpson, a junior defensive back who later played for Michigan State University and was Coach Fracassa's last Shrine player to be drafted into the NFL.

Next up for Shrine was St. Mary of Redford, which was coached by Walt Bazylewicz. St. Mary prevailed, beating high-flying Shrine by a score of 21-6. The following week Shrine beat the former league power, St. Ambrose, 19-13.

Captain Tom Martin huddles with Coach Fracassa.

This left the 3-and-1 Shrine Knights with a match-up with the 3-and-1 Detroit Servite High School Panthers. Frank Kolch, who would go on to play for Michigan State University and Eastern Michigan University, and would eventually be drafted by the NFL Pittsburgh Steelers, was in his senior year. The winner of this game would remain at the top of the league with Divine Child High School.

Coach Fracassa designed a defense specifically for Kolch. It was a six-man defensive umbrella behind a five-man defensive front. In the NFL, one extra defensive back makes a "nickel" defense, so coverage with two extra guys is a "dime" defense. Fracassa tried running a dime defense in a high school game, and his strategy worked — Kolch wasn't given open targets. But despite Fracassa's plan, Servite won a low-scoring game, 12-6.

Coach Fracassa realized this game was the key to the season. In the Monday practice afterward, he communicated his frustration to the players. The practice field was surrounded by an 8-foot-high fence, about 70 yards from side to side. Coach told the players to run and touch that side, and then run back and touch this side, "until I blow the whistle." Then he threw the whistle over the fence.

The Knights' next game was against the Harper Woods Bishop Gallagher High School Lancers. The Lancers were 4-1 at the time and their best player was Bill DuLac, a senior offensive guard who would play for Eastern Michigan University after his graduation, then be drafted by the NFL Los Angeles Rams and go on to play for the New England Patriots. Under Coach Fracassa's enthusiastic guidance, the Knights executed the game plan well and beat the Lancers 20-12. The last game of the season was a 35- 9 victory over Detroit Benedictine.

The Detroit Servite Panthers and Dearborn Divine Child Falcons tied for the league title. Because of their victory over the Panthers, the Falcons played the U-D Jesuit Cubs in the first Charity Bowl. The Falcons prevailed over the Cubs by a score of 21-7.

BILL SIMPSON

Bill Simpson was another of the multisport athletes who thrived in the Detroit Catholic High School athletic environment in the 1960s. He was the last NFL player Coach Fracassa had at Shrine High School. Simpson was a junior during Coach's last season, playing in the offensive and defensive backfields. He went on to achieve All-League, All-Catholic, and All-State honorary football team awards in the 1969 season under Coach Dave Woodcock. Simpson was also named to the All-League teams in basketball and baseball in 1970.

After his high school career, Simpson was awarded an athletic scholarship to Michigan State University. Ironically, his freshman football coach was Tony Versaci, who had coached at Dearborn Divine Child High School the previous year. Simpson was an All-Big Ten defensive back for the Spartans in 1972 and was named to the All-America team in 1972 as a defensive back, punter (8th in total yardage in the country), and punt returner (9th in total yardage) in 1972. He also played baseball for the Spartans and was named the All-Big Ten center-fielder in 1974.

BILL SIMPSON

Bill Simpson

Simpson was drafted in the second round by the NFL Los Angeles Rams in 1974. He was the first defensive back selected. In 1977 and 1978, he was given a first-team All-Conference slot.

Simpson played five seasons for the Rams and three seasons with the Buffalo Bills. He holds the NFL playoff record for interceptions, with nine in 11 games. He shares that record with Charlie Waters of the Dallas Cowboys (nine in 25 games) and Ronnie Lott of the San Francisco 49ers and Oakland Raiders (nine in 20 games).

Simpson has kept in touch with Coach Fracassa over the years and, like a lot of others, his calls are greeted by Fracassa with joy. Fracassa said in a recent interview that "We [Bill and I] are still very close friends, we [both] went to Michigan State." Fracassa doesn't forget his players, and they don't forget him.

THE DECISION

One of the biggest decisions of Coach Fracassa's career was made in 1969. In his nine years with the Shrine High School football team, Fracassa had won one Catholic League Championship in a Soup Bowl game (although it was a shared title, without a Goodfellows Game appearance), lost a second Soup Bowl game, and missed three other Soup Bowl games by a single defeat. His teams didn't get to play the final game of any season in his first nine years of coaching. In the 1968-69 season, it was rumored around Shrine High School that Coach Fracassa would be considering other coaching options.

The world that Fracassa had been raised in was changing. In the United States, attitudes had changed and trust in authority was frayed. God and country weren't held in as high regard as they had been when Fracassa was growing up.

The militaristic approach to football coaching was changing, too. Players were less likely to accept imposed values; they were thinking more for themselves, reflecting the changes in the "outside" world. More explaining and teaching were expected of coaches; mindless repetition was less admired as a strategy.

The Detroit Catholic High School Football League was also changing, with parish and school consolidations and closings. Challenges from the ongoing secular social and political clashes were affecting attitudes toward church authority figures. The culture of the Catholic Church was changed after Vatican Council II. The inward-focused, enclosed environment of the parochial school was giving way to a more outward-looking ecumenical approach. More lay teachers joined the faculty at Catholic schools, and tuition rose as costs increased. The enthusiastic support for football seemed to lag. Coach Joe Carruthers, of St. Ambrose, said in 1968: "In my last year there, all discipline seemed to be breaking down. The flower children were coming in and changing the whole neighborhood."

All of these changes likely affected Coach Fracassa's decision to leave Shrine. The instability of the parochial schools in Detroit due to population shifts, economic changes, and attitude changes in communities and churches made the move logical and provided an opportunity for Coach Fracassa to up his game elsewhere. In a recent interview, Fracassa said that he "wanted to go to a Class A, larger school." By choosing to go to Brother Rice, he moved from a selection pool of about 300 boys to one of nearly 600 boys.

Brother Rice was an all-boys school, which meant there was the potential for fewer distractions for the adolescent boys under Fracassa's guidance. Gabriel Moran, an American scholar, and teacher in the fields of Christian theology and religious education, noted that "The Christian Brothers were known for running good schools, well-organized and academically demanding. ... The Catholic schools were known for their discipline, a word whose root meaning is not punishment but teaching." The wealthy suburban location of Brother Rice, which had been founded in 1960, projected a sense of security for the future of the school, its football team, and its coach.

BROTHER RICE

Birmingham Brother Rice — a private, all-boys, college preparatory school northwest of Detroit — was established in 1960, and was a recent newcomer compared to the longstanding central Catholic high schools in Detroit. Significant growth in population had occurred in Oakland County in the 1950s, and a group of parents saw the need for Catholic elementary and high schools in the region.

The Archdiocese of Detroit had 30 acres of land on Lahser Road in Birmingham that would provide the site for a high school. Cardinal Edward Mooney, archbishop of Detroit, approached the Congregation of Christian Brothers in New York, an order with a background in education. Six Christian Brothers, led by Br. Norbert Hueller as principal, were invited to staff and administer the school, which was named for the Congregation's founder, Edmund Ignatius Rice. Starting with 200 students in the first year, enrollment increased to 800 students by 1964.

The high school's 1964 yearbook noted that "For Brother Rice High School, there were no ancestors, there was no past. The quest for tradition was beginning at the zero mark." The school was quick to establish a tradition of academic and athletic excellence.

Brother Rice played in their first Soup Bowl Championship game in 1967 against Divine Child, which at the time was led by Gary Danielson and coached by Tony Versaci. Divine Child prevailed, 21-6, and went on to play in the final Goodfellows Game.

In the changing structure of the Detroit Catholic Football League, Brother Rice was in the Central Division — a Class A school, according to the state of Michigan's criteria — and they competed with other large Central Division Catholic schools. Their major competition included Detroit Catholic Central, De La Salle, Orchard Lake St. Mary's Prep, and U-D Jesuit, as well as Divine Child.

1969

Coach Fracassa arrived at Birmingham Brother Rice High School in the fall of 1969 and was invited to give an introductory talk to the Warrior football team he had inherited. The players became restless, and there may have been some murmuring. Coach was unaccustomed to distractions while speaking. In mild frustration, he brought both of his fists down on the podium. The podium crashed to the ground, in pieces. The room became still and quiet. The Fracassa era at Brother Rice had begun with a bang.

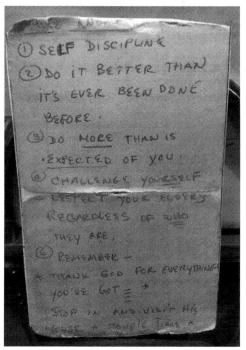

The season turned out to be a good one. Brother Rice finished with eight wins and only one loss. The 14-0 loss was to Detroit Catholic Central, a team that also lost a single game (to Notre Dame, 13-0). Although the teams tied for the league Championship, Detroit Catholic Central went on to the Charity Bowl, having beaten Brother Rice head-to-head. Divine Child beat Detroit Catholic Central 16-0 in Coach Versaci's last high school coaching year.

1969: The actual Fracassa-Mike Knuff index card.

Brother Rice's season included victories over Notre Dame, De La Salle, and U-D Jesuit. In the 13-12 win over Notre Dame, the first game Coach Fracassa had played against Notre Dame since the 0-0 tie in 1963 while coaching Shrine, William Perry kicked the winning field goal. Against Redford St. Mary, Rice running back Steve Jones had a monster game. He rushed for 291 yards, had five touchdowns, and accounted for 30 points — all individual Brother Rice Warrior records. In his first season at Brother Rice, Coach Fracassa repeated the pattern he had experienced at Shrine: It was another great coaching year, with a single regular-season loss that prevented his team from making an appearance in a postseason game. But the biggest impact of Fracassa's first year at Brother Rice wasn't about football at all. It was about the inspirational leadership he provided to the young men. Pat and Mike Knuff were returning senior football players in 1969, having played under several coaches in their previous years at Rice. Coach Fracassa recognized early on that he could build a team around these identical twins, who were talented linemen/linebackers. "We lost our father when we were 10," Pat says, "and Coach was an important male figure in our lives. We had only one year under Coach, and in that time he transformed Mike and me not only into student athletes, but mature young men."

Mike remembers he was having trouble with another coach at Rice and went to talk to Coach Fracassa about it. "Coach listened intently," Mike remembers, "and then he wrote down several bullet points on an index card and told me these are the things he needed from Mike Knuff."

The bullet points were classic Fracassa principles, including discipline and gratitude. "Coach told me to hang onto this and said, 'Every time you need an adjustment, look at it.'" Well, Mike held onto that index card as both he and Pat headed to Cornell University, where they played on a 1971 Ivy League Champion football team and launched successful business careers. Fifty-five years later, at Fracassa's retirement dinner in Dearborn, Mike showed up. When he saw Fracassa during the reception, he pulled that slightly beat-up index card out of his wallet and showed it to his former coach. It was an emotional moment for both men. Fracassa was stunned. Later that night, as he spoke to the hundreds of former players gathered there, he invited the Knuff brothers up on stage and pulled out that index card for all to see. His former players were mesmerized; seeing that little 3x5 index card, they remembered. And through many sets of misty eyes, they embraced and treasured once again the lessons Fracassa had taught them: Not football lessons, but life lessons.

The 1970s

1970

Coach Dick Farley, an NCAA Division III college coach, repeated a well-worn truth in his book, "Why I Never Left Williams College": You learn more about yourself from losing than from winning. Fracassa learned a lot about himself in 1970.

In 1969, the Catholic High School Football League changed the scheduling of games, due to changes in available teams. In 1970, the Central Division high schools played two games against AA Division high schools to start the season. The first game of the season for Brother Rice was against Shrine and resulted in a 14-14 tie. Rice had been favored against Coach Fracassa's former team, which included several players he had coached two years before this game.

This year at Brother Rice, Coach Fracassa had a great team; quarterback Gary Martin, running back and receiver Jim Gerback, captain Tom Hayden, and offensive guard and linebacker Greg Collins led the squad. Collins was the first Rice player coached by Fracassa who would play in the NFL. After the tie game with Shrine, Rice went undefeated in their six regular-season games. The victories included wins over Notre Dame, U-D Jesuit, Detroit Catholic Central, and De La Salle. There was a Central Division semifinal game against Sacred Heart, which Rice won, 40-8. The next game would be the Charity Bowl, for the Detroit Catholic Football League First Division Championship.

Shrine also had a great year. Under Coach Dave Woodcock, the Knights beat Detroit Catholic Central and followed that with an undefeated regular season including a victory over the perennial Division AA champion, Divine Child. Shrine played a semifinal game against East Catholic, which they won 27-0. The next game would be the Charity Bowl — against Fracassa's new team, Brother Rice — for the Detroit Catholic League Football League First Division Championship.

On a wet, snowy, cold evening at the University of Detroit Stadium, underdog Shrine defeated Rice, 18-0. Gary Simpson, Bill's younger brother, kept Brother Rice in the shadow of their own goalpost with his excellent punting. The most valuable player in the game was Tom O'Branovic, who ran for 94 yards on 22 carries. O'Branovic, who would later play at Eastern Michigan University, had earned a varsity letter playing for Coach Fracassa three years earlier.

Ron Ranieri said in a recent interview that this loss was the hardest in Coach Fracassa's long career. Coach never took losing well. He always believed his team was the best prepared, most committed, and most disciplined, so the loss was unexpected. Ranieri remembers a game that Coach Fracassa and his Shrine High School team lost. When Fracassa got back to Shrine after the game, he told his wife to drive home. Coach Fracassa, meanwhile, walked eight miles home from the school, in the dark, to process the defeat. In an interview, Fracassa was asked how he felt after a tough loss. He said, "I can't sleep. I pace the room. I can't eat." When asked what he did to get over it, he said, "Win the next game." And that's what he started to do at Brother Rice.

GREG COLLINS

Greg Collins, an outstanding linebacker and offensive guard for the 1970 Brother Rice squad, was named to the All-State team and was a High School All-American player. He was awarded a scholarship to the University of Notre Dame, and attended what was frequently thought of as "the college of a Catholic mother's dreams." Collins was a member of the 1973 NCAA national champion Notre Dame Fighting Irish football team that beat the Uni-

Greg Collins

versity of Alabama Crimson Tide in the 1973 Sugar Bowl game, 24-23. Behind a strong running attack, Notre Dame finished 11-0-0 under Coach Ara Parseghian. Following his collegiate career, Collins was drafted in 1975 by the San Francisco 49ers and played one year there. He then played for the Seattle Seahawks in 1976 and the Buffalo Bills in 1977, and participated in a total of 38 games over three years.

Eventually, Collins found his way to a career as an actor. In his first television role, he portrayed a football player on "Webster" — a performance that he nailed. Thanks to his handsome and rugged good looks, Collins enjoyed a decade-long acting career in television and the movies. His roles included a host of security guys and police officers, as well as a male stripper. He was in "The Rock" and played the character Halsey in "Armageddon" — two favorite guy classics.

At Shrine, Coach Fracassa didn't have any players who moved on to Hollywood; although Keegan-Michael Key and Kristen Bell attended Shrine and are entertainment stars, neither one played football for Coach Fracassa.

1971

Catholic High School League Champions

In 1971, everything fell into place and Coach Fracassa had his first unbeaten high school football squad as the Warriors won nine games and tied one. The second game of the season was a rematch with Shrine, and memories of the bitter Championship Game defeat the previous November were still fresh. This time, Brother Rice won, 20-7, and Rice statistician Mike Coughlin remembers Fracassa climbing the stairs of the bus, looking at the team with emotion, and saying only "Thank you."

The next game was a tie with Redford St. Mary, 14-14. The rest of the Warriors' games in the Central Division's regular season were victories, including wins over Detroit Catholic Central, Notre Dame, De La Salle, and U-D Jesuit. The semifinal game for the newly named Prep Bowl was played against Redford Covenant, and Brother Rice won the match, 20-0. Bishop Borgess would be Rice's opponent in the first Prep Bowl. The match-up featured the Central vs. A-West Division winners and was played at the Pontiac Silverdome. Coach Fracassa's Warriors prevailed in the Prep Bowl and beat Bishop Borgess, 20-0.

In 1971, Fracassa depended on contributions from several players. The offensive backfield was "quick and athletic," and the squad was "stout defensively," according to the Brother Rice Football alumni community. It was a talent structure that was very much in the Coach Fracassa tradition. Dan Damiani, a multisport athlete, led the team, along with Captain Rick Costantini. Other prominent Rice players on the first undefeated Catholic League Championship team were running backs Gary Lukas and Jim Brunetto, defensive back Tim Zimcosky, and quarterback Mike Ryan.

1972

The 1972 Brother Rice Warriors started the year where they had left off and captured five consecutive victories to start the season. One of them was over

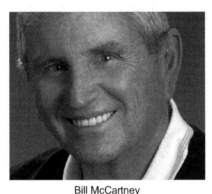
Bill McCartney

Shrine, 28-0. Coach Fracassa didn't enjoy the games against his old school's team because he was concerned that the focus was more on him, his reputation, and his style, rather than the student players. Ron Ranieri, an assistant coach in those early years, said at the time that Coach Fracassa "tries not to be controversial." As it turned out, with repeated schedule rearrangements in the Catholic Football League, the Rice vs. Shrine games became less frequent.

The next two games in 1972 were losses to Notre Dame (7-6) and U-D Jesuit (36-34). The last game of the season was a 7-0 victory over Catholic Central. Brother Rice finished the year with a 6-2 record. The team was led by running backs John Cullen and Steve Lyons, quarterback Mike Ryan, offensive linemen Kevin Stark and Mark Hendricks, and linebacker Mike Stoegbauer. Divine Child beat Catholic Central, 31-7, in the Prep Bowl for the Catholic League A-B Championship. Divine Child was coached by Bill McCartney, who later joined Bo Schembechler at the University of Michigan as an assistant coach. In 1982, McCartney was named head coach at the University of Colorado and led the Buffaloes to Big 8 titles in 1989, 1990, and 1991. His team was the NCAA National Co-Champion in 1990.

1973

A Warrior Creed

I am a Brother Rice Warrior.

I am a man who knows what excellence is and what it takes to reach it.

I know that in order to win, I must dedicate myself through self-discipline and learn, over and over again, the meaning of Pride, Endurance, and Desire.

I truly understand that achieving goals means a constant awareness of my will in paying the price.

I have proven to myself, through training, that battles and victories go to a man who believes in himself.

I realize also that preparing myself with everything I have in me and doing things better than I have ever done them before ... these are the essentials of greatness.

I know what it means and what it is to be a champion.

I understand that achieving greatness is an ever-present challenge and meeting these challenges means sacrifice, perseverance, and complete dedication, again, and again, and again.

Finally, with encouragement, through God, I pledge to live life to its fullest in order that I can live up to the courage and bravery of a true Warrior.

Coach Al Fracassa

Sept. 12, 1973

The 1973 football season got off to a rough start for the Warriors, who recorded three consecutive losses. The first two losses were to Covenant (16-14) and Divine Child (25-13). The first regular-season loss came at the hands of Catholic Central, who posted a 16-0 victory. Catholic Central's best player was Paul Rudzinski, who later played for the MSU Spartans. After his college career, he signed as a free agent with the Green Bay Packers and played for three years, then became an assistant coach for the Edmonton Eskimos in the Canadian Football League for two years.

The rest of the regular-season games in 1973 were victories, and the Warriors posted a 5-3 record. Offensive lineman James Courtney, quarterback Mike Brielmaier, and lineman Jim Fontanesi were outstanding for Rice. The loss to Catholic Central was costly, as Rice failed to make it to the Prep Bowl. In that game, Divine Child beat Catholic Central 7-0, to capture their second Catholic League A-B Championship in a row. They were also the "mythical" (not by the playoff route) Class B State Champions in Michigan.

CATHOLIC CENTRAL

Catholic Central, founded as an all-boys college preparatory school in 1928 by the Archdiocese of Detroit, was operated by the Congregation of St. Basil. It was first located on Harper Avenue in Detroit and has relocated several times; since 2005, it has called a 60-acre campus in Novi home.

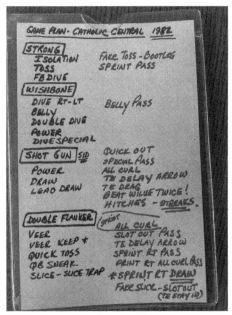

Coach Fracassa's actual game plan card vs. Catholic Central, Oct. 12, 1986.

During Fracassa's career at Brother Rice, Catholic Central was the team that presented the Warriors with the most problems. Fracassa coached 52 games against CC, winning 26 and losing 26. Over the years, both teams won multiple Catholic League and MHSAA State Championships, and both teams included many great high school stars who went on to play college and professional football.

Catholic Central had been a formidable football program for decades stretching back to the 1940s, '50s, and '60s. The Boys' Bowl was a Detroit high school football charity fundraising fixture that began in 1944 with a match-up between Catholic Central and Fr. Edward Flanagan's Boys Town High School from Omaha, Neb., which was considered the best team in the country at that time. Forty-thousand fans attended the first Boys' Bowl game at Briggs Stadium; the contest ended in a 14-14 tie. Over the years, the game grew into a pageant that included a pre-game Mass and breakfast, murals lining the school walls, decorative floats, high school band performances, and even a United States Marine two-jet flyby in 2007. The game was eventually relocated to Pontiac's Wisner Stadium and some other large venues. The opponents were chosen from prominent Catholic League teams, including the Brother Rice Warriors.

Tom Mach speaks at Coach Fracassa's retirement party.

Tom Mach coached the Novi Catholic Central Shamrocks for 41 years, beginning in 1976. At his retirement in 2016, his record was 370-94, third in the state behind Coach Fracassa, with 430 victories, and Coach John Herrington from Farmington Hills Harrison, with 425 victories. Mach led the Shamrocks to 10 Michigan State Championship titles, and coached seven young men who went on to play in the NFL. Mach and Fracassa both built consistently successful programs. Consider that from 1977 to 1996, Catholic Central and Brother Rice won 17 of 20 Detroit Catholic League football Championships. The rivalry was fierce, and the games were legendary — particularly the long stretch that saw them face off annually at Pontiac Wisner Stadium in the Boys' Bowl. Because they also sometimes played against each other in the Catholic League playoffs or the state playoffs, there were seven seasons they battled each other twice. Although Fracassa and Mach were competitors on the field, they maintained a close friendship off of it. Head-to-head, they coached against one another in 45 games; Catholic Central won 24, while Brother Rice won 21.

THE TIMES

The United States was still experiencing crises. The Watergate Scandal, involving a burglary at the Democratic Headquarters in the Watergate Hotel, led to the resignation of President Richard Nixon. Vice President Gerald Ford was appointed the 38th president and pardoned President Nixon, to avoid additional political turmoil. The Vietnam War was winding down; it ended with the fall of Saigon in early 1975. The major issue faced by the country was the boycott of the Arab Oil Producing and Exporting Countries (OPEC) following the United States' support of Israel in the Yom Kippur War. Gasoline prices increased dramatically, which resulted in the speed limit being changed to 55 mph nationwide, and the introduction of daylight saving time.

A combination of civil rights issues, campus activism, the antiwar campaign, women's liberation, and a growing counterculture affected the attitudes of about 30 million young people, leading to a change in values in the 1970s.

With the end of the Vietnam War and the military draft, attention was focused more on personal issues such as relationships, the environment, and lifestyles. The skepticism regarding the institutions of education, the government, the military, and the media, which had reached new heights in the previous decade, persisted. Society changed even more after Bill Gates founded Microsoft in 1975 and Steve Jobs, Steve Wozniak, and Ronald Wayne started Apple Inc. in 1976.

Detroit continued to have problems. By 1975, the majority of the city's population was Black and the number of residents fell to below 1.5 million people. In the case of Milliken v. Bradley, the U.S. Supreme Court reversed a lower court ruling requiring cross-district busing to achieve racial balance in 53 metro Detroit school districts, instead directing a desegregation plan limited to Detroit schools. The decline of the automobile industry, exacerbated by the gasoline shortage, led to 200,000 job layoffs in the city. Coleman

A. Young, a former Tuskegee Airman, was elected the first Black mayor of Detroit in 1974.

The Catholic Church continued to be buffeted by internal and external forces, as well. The changes coming out of Vatican II were associated with more independent thinking and reflected the attitudes of the times. After the Supreme Court overturned state laws against abortion in its Roe v. Wade decision in 1973, Pope Paul VI ratified the Declaration on Procured Abortion in 1974, reiterating the Church's opinion that life begins at conception. Its stance against birth control and other "unnatural" intervention around conception noted in the 1968 encyclical Humanae vitae was reinforced, while the changing roles of women in secular society created additional conflict within the Church.

The Archdiocese of Detroit continued to experience a fall in Catholic elementary and high school enrollment. Nationally, the drop was from a high of 5.5 million students in the 1960s to about 3 million in the mid-'70s. More than 30 high schools that had been members of the Catholic High School

Earl Morrall

League closed their doors in the 1970s, including St. Ambrose High School in 1972. The remaining high school divisions were juggled around and realigned as needed.

Professional football, specifically the NFL, was growing in prosperity and popularity. The Miami Dolphins completed an undefeated season in their 1973 Super Bowl win over the Washington Redskins. Earl Morrall, Coach Fracassa's old teammate at Michigan State, filled in for an injured Bob Griese during the season. Miami repeated as the Super Bowl winners in 1974 — and then the Pittsburgh Steelers and Dallas Cowboys began their rivalry. Terms such as man-in-motion, the shotgun formation, and Hail Mary pass entered the football lexicon. The offensive side of the game was more complex, and rushing and passing were both important components of successful teams.

When the Pontiac Silverdome opened in 1975, the Detroit Lions moved out of the city. The Detroit Pistons followed the Lions to the Silverdome and played their home games there, too. In 1986, the Pistons moved to the Palace of Auburn Hills. The Detroit Tigers remained at Tiger Stadium. In 1974, one of the greatest Tigers, Al Kaline, retired after 22 years. His record included 3,007 career hits, 18 All-Star appearances, and 10 Gold Gloves. The Detroit Red Wings relocated from Olympia Stadium to Joe Louis Arena in 1979, remaining in Detroit.

1974

Catholic High School League Champions
Michigan High School Class A No. 1 Ranking
(Mythical State Champions)

Greatness cannot be achieved without discipline.

This is the year Coach Fracassa began providing his team with a yearly motto. It was also the year that his career took off, and he coached the Birmingham Brother Rice Warriors to their first undefeated, untied championship in the Catholic High School Football League. They were also voted No. 1 in the Michigan Class A High School football rankings, earning a "mythical" State Championship. In a poll taken in 2017 by Jared Purcell, prep sportswriter for *M-Live*, the 1974 team received the highest number of votes, thereby earning accolades as the greatest high school sports team ever in the Detroit metro area. The poll's participants were sports fans from across Michigan, and more than 20,000 votes were cast. The runner-up in that poll was the 1967 Pershing High School State Champion basketball team coached by Will Robinson, featuring Spencer Haywood and Ralph Simpson.

The football season began with victories over Bay City Central and Southfield, followed by games against five teams in the Central Division of the Detroit Catholic High School League. The closest game was against Detroit Catholic Central, in which the final score was 16-6. The team's initial playoff game was against Cabrini High and Rice won it decisively, 50-15. The Catholic League Championship game, the Prep Bowl, was played at Rynearson Stadium in Ypsilanti and saw a match-up between Bishop Foley — quarterbacked by Rick Fracassa, Coach Fracassa's son — and Brother Rice. The powerhouse Warriors won, 35-0.

Altogether, the Warriors scored 270 points in 1974, while allowing only 48 points. Although Coach Fracassa had hundreds of players from his teams go on to play in college, this squad was loaded with outstanding and exceptional players. Thirteen members of the 1974 squad went to NCAA Division I teams, and another four joined Division II or III teams.

One of the 1974 Warriors, Matt Morrall, played on the University of Florida Gators team for three years after graduating from Brother Rice. At a Rice practice one day,

Coach Fracassa and quarterback
Don Hendricks, 1974.

Coach told Morrall to "take a lap" — the routine punishment for a football error. Morrall replied, "Coach, I didn't do anything." Fracassa, whose sense of humor is famous among his ex-players, answered, "It's because of your father that I never got to start a game at Michigan State University." Morrall's father was Earl Morrall, Fracassa's famous college teammate. The rest of the Warriors team loved it.

Other stars of the 1974 team included quarterback Don Hendricks, two-way lineman Kevin Hart, running backs Mike Cullen and Ted Fox, offensive lineman Karl Goebel, end Curt Griffin, and defensive back Pat Callaghan, who tied an all-time Rice record with seven interceptions in just nine games.

RICK FRACASSA

Coach Fracassa's oldest child, Rick, attended Bishop Foley High School, a small, co-ed Catholic school. Founded in 1965, it was named for John Samuel Foley, the first American bishop of Detroit. It took a few years for the school's athletic programs to establish themselves, but by the early 1970s, the football team, led by a young coach named Walt Wyniemko, started to make some noise in the tough AA Division of the Detroit Catholic League.

In 1974, with Rick Fracassa as his senior starting quarterback, Wyniemko scheduled an early season nonconference game against Detroit Cass Tech, one of the top teams in the Detroit Public School League. Cass Tech, with Harlan Huckleby at running back, beat Foley that day, but it was Foley's only loss of the regular season as they dominated their five conference games by a combined score of 138-7 and qualified for the Catholic League playoffs. Waiting for them in the Catholic League First Division semifinals was perennial powerhouse Dearborn Divine Child. Not many folks gave Foley much of a chance, but Rick Fracassa led his team to an upset win, 18-12. He completed passes of 17, 34, 27, and 19 yards as Foley marched down the field in the closing minute of the game. With no time left on the clock, Rick Fracassa lofted a two-yard touchdown pass to tie the game. Foley won the match in overtime and was headed to the Catholic League Championship Game — against, of course, Brother Rice.

"We talk about football all the time at home," Rick Fracassa said in a *Detroit Free Press* article by Hal Schram in the week leading up to the game. "My dad doesn't get much of a chance to see us play, but Coach Wyniemko lets dad take our films home and run them."

According to Schram, Phyllis Fracassa "was treading a neutral path" in this unusual Dad vs. Son showdown. Brother Rice, with a host of stars in 1974 that Mick McCabe of the *Detroit Free Press* called "one of the greatest high school teams in Michigan ever in any sport," won the game 35-0 before 12,000 fans at Rynearson Stadium in Ypsilanti. Rick Fracassa went on to

Michigan State University and later became a key part of the Brother Rice football program, serving as freshman coach for 20 years (1982-2002), where he helped develop the players who would move up to play for his dad.

Jason Fracassa

Rick's son, Jason, also became a great high school quarterback. In 2009, playing for Sterling Heights Stevenson, he set the passing records in the state of Michigan for career yardage (10,615), touchdown passes (97), and pass completions (656). He took Stevenson all the way to the Division 1 State Championship Game in 2009, but his team lost 31-21 — somewhat ironically — to Catholic Central.

KEVIN HART

Brother Rice had three football captains in 1974: Ted Fox, Thomas Gorman, and Kevin Hart. Hart was the star of the team and was named to the All-State and All-American football teams in 1974. He received a scholarship to attend Notre Dame University, where he was a three-year varsity letter award-winner. When he played for the 1977 NCAA College Football Championship Fighting Irish team under Dan Devine, the quarterback was a junior named Joe Montana.

Hart was also a member of the 1974 Brother Rice basketball team, which won the Michigan Class A High School basketball Championship, and was named to the All-League team in that sport. From 2007 to 2015, he was an assistant football coach at Brother Rice, where he worked with the freshman team.

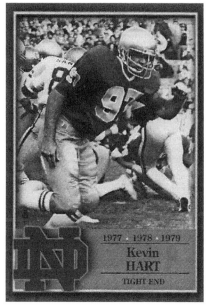

In the book "Thirty Days with America's High School Coaches," Hart was asked to comment on Coach Fracassa. "The players all knew how lucky they were to be guided by this man. These boys never wanted to disappoint him. They never wanted to let him down," he said, adding that Fracassa was about loyalty, humility, and unselfishness. "He would never ask us to do anything that he did not do himself," Hart said. He also pointed out that Coach Fracassa believed "every play-

Kevin Hart

er was vital to the success of the team."

Hart explained that Fracassa wanted each player to be committed to his church, his school, and his teammates. That might include wearing short hair, being self-disciplined, and playing when and where the team needed them. Coach Fracassa once told Hart that the "biggest mission as the freshman coach was to get these young men to be good friends with each other and to trust each other." Hart tried to emulate Fracassa by "Being demanding, but always encouraging. Never let a player leave the practice field feeling dejected or hopeless."

When Hart was occasionally frustrated as a player, he says his father suggested that he should "figure out what [Coach Fracassa] wants, and when you figure it out, give it to him." Hart's father, Leon, had played on three NCAA National Championship teams at the University of Notre Dame in 1946, 1947, and 1949. He won the Heisman Trophy and the Maxwell Trophy in 1949. With the NFL Detroit Lions, he won three NFL Championships in 1952, 1953, and 1957. Leon Hart trusted Coach Fracassa.

1975

Contentment with past accomplishments stifles future achievements.

The year 1975 was the beginning of a state high school football playoff system that ended the reliance on a voting system to determine the "mythical" State Champions. The Michigan High School Athletic Association's plan took the best attributes from 31 state football systems that were in operation at the time. The classifications used were Class A, B, C, and D — from the largest school to the smallest. Each of the roughly 750 high schools was placed in one of the groupings, with about 25 percent of the high schools in each class.

The classes were constructed on a sliding scale to meet that statistical goal. For example, Class A schools might have an enrollment of more than 850 students, Class B schools had 400 to 850 students, Class C schools had 200 to 400 students, and Class D schools enrolled fewer than 200 students. The state was divided into regions or districts. High schools too small for 11-man football teams weren't included.

Each class was comprised of four regions. From each region, one team was selected. That team was determined by wins and a computer point value, calculated for each team based on its record and strength of schedule. These four teams in four classes, 16 teams in all, would play two rounds: a semifinal game and a championship game.

Teams weren't sure under which classification they would compete. This arrangement could result in a team playing for the Class A Championship one year and for the Class B title the following year, depending on computer placement. The computer program was a mystery. The MHSAA playoff system wasn't entirely without problems, but it was an improvement over a vote. The MHSAA Championship playoffs represented a new mountain for Michigan high school teams to climb: It added two games to the end of the season against high-quality competition.

In 1975, Brother Rice started where they'd left off at the end of the previous season: They began with two nonconference wins, followed by five league victories. The first Catholic League playoff game was a successful 36-0 win over Detroit Austin. The team was led on offense by running back Mike Cullen, but he injured his knee late in the season. In the Prep Bowl at Rynearson Stadium, in front of 16,800 fans, the Warriors lost to Divine Child, 7-0. The only score was a seven-yard fumble return. The game wasn't a total loss, however; Terry Simmons set a Rice record for the longest punt (79 yards), and that record still stands.

With that loss, the Warriors' 22-game winning streak, which had begun in 1973, ended. The 1975 team won seven shutout games, scoring 226 points and allowing 15 points. The defense was led by captain K.C. Ryan, who Coach Fracassa called "one of the great defensive players I've ever coached." As of the end of the 2022 season, Ryan is still tied for the Brother Rice record for interceptions in a game (three against Divine Child in 1973) and is the third-rated player in individual tackles (with 21 against Notre Dame in 1974). He attended the University of Notre Dame on a football scholarship. Tom Henry, the Rice tight end in 1975, played for the Western Michigan University Broncos and the Seattle Seahawks. Steve Fuller, Dan MacLean, and Mark Kochanski were also key players. MacLean played for the University of Illinois and years later became the head football coach and athletic director at Detroit Country Day High School.

The upset loss to Divine Child eliminated Brother Rice from the MHSAA high school football playoffs, but their opponent, Divine Child, went on to capture the MHSAA Class B Championship. The MHSAA Class A Championship was won by the Livonia Benjamin Franklin School Patriots. Although news reporters referred to the team as "Franklin Who?" they upset Detroit Southwestern High, 12-9, and then defeated Traverse City High, 21-7, in the Class A Championship Game.

QUARTERBACK CAMP

In the 1973 Super Bowl, future NFL Hall of Fame quarterback Bob Griese threw 11 passes, completing eight for 88 yards and helping the Miami Dolphins cap off a perfect season with a victory over Washington. In 1975, Hall of Fame signal caller Terry Bradshaw completed nine of 14 passes for 96 yards in Pittsburgh's Super Bowl IX victory, also against Minnesota. In

2017, Tom Brady threw an astounding 63 passes, completing 43, for 466 yards in New England's thrilling come-from-behind victory over Atlanta in Super Bowl LI. The next year Brady outdid himself, passing for a Super Bowl record 505 yards in a loss to the Philadelphia Eagles.

Football is an ever-evolving game — move and countermove, action and adjustment. In the Super Bowl era, no position has changed as dramatically as quarterback. Fifty years ago, the quarterback's role was to hand the ball off to powerful fullbacks or shifty tailbacks and throw an occasional pass to keep the defense from crowding the line of scrimmage.

In today's game, the quarterback is the sun around which the football universe revolves. Every NFL team is desperately searching for a franchise quarterback to lead it to Super Bowl glory. In turn, college and high school teams have focused on supplying that demand.

In his early years of coaching at Shrine, Coach Fracassa's teams employed a run first offensive approach. Although Fracassa's dedication to the fundamental principles of blocking and tackling remained firm, he evolved effortlessly and brilliantly into a quarterback guru and passing game innovator at Brother Rice.

Al Fracassa's Quarterback Camp began in 1974 on the weedy playground field at Beer Middle School in Warren because Fracassa needed an income during the summer to supplement his teacher's salary. "I was getting too old to work construction," he said.

Winning a second State Championship in 1977 helped raise Fracassa's profile, as did coaching, in succession, high school All-State quarterbacks Jon English, Brian Brennan, and Dave Yarema. "I was very lucky to have such talented kids playing quarterback for me," he said.

With the increased renown enjoyed by both Coach Fracassa and the Brother Rice football program, attendance at the camp grew steadily. In 1980 the camp was moved to Madison Heights Bishop Foley High. By this time, Fracassa and his assistants were teaching 90-120 aspiring high school quarterbacks each summer.

Brian Paquette was one of the many boys who were four-year camp attendees. "Coach Fracassa is the greatest," Paquette said. "He's an expert on being a great quarterback and he makes me laugh a lot during the drills. Being around him is always a great feeling. He makes the camp fun, and he has a way of making you feel better about yourself. He makes you want to get better."

One day, one of Fracassa's assistants stopped to get his oil changed on his way to work at the camp. He was wearing an Al Fracassa Quarterback Camp T-shirt. When it came time to pay for the service, the owner, Michael Saad, wouldn't accept any payment. "When you see Coach Fracassa, tell him I said hello and let him know I didn't charge you for the service, as a thank-you for all he did for me."

Saad had been a star running back on Dearborn Fordson High School's State Championship team of 1993. Fordson was a culturally diverse high school that included White, Black, Hispanic, Asian, and Arabic students. Fracassa, who wanted his Brother Rice football players to be leaders in acceptance and inclusion, contacted the principal and head coach at Fordson and asked if some of the Fordson football players would speak to the Brother Rice football team. Saad had been one of the students chosen to speak.

"Coach Fracassa came to Fordson to meet with us and discuss what he hoped to accomplish. We all knew who Coach Fracassa was, and I guess I was a little intimidated. When Coach introduced himself, I didn't give him much of a handshake and I was staring down at my shoes most of the time. Coach told me I should have a firm handshake and he told me to always look people in the eye. I'll never forget how he talked to me. He wasn't criticizing me; he was coaching me," Saad recalled.

"The next day we drove to Rice to talk to the football team. Coach Fracassa talked us up to his players. He told them we were great athletes and state champions, and his players should listen to what we had to say. He said we had a great team and a great school because we understood the importance of teamwork and togetherness," Saad added. "He made us feel like kings. When we were done, Coach thanked us and told us we had set a great example for his team. Then he gave us gas money, reminded us to be careful driving back to school, and told us to call him if we ever needed anything."

The incident had a profound effect on Saad. "I was with Coach for two days and those two days stuck with me forever. Something about the way he talked to me gave me confidence. He makes you believe in yourself and makes you feel like you can do anything."

Fracassa was a great quarterback coach, but he was an even better life coach.

1976

You never fail until you stop trying.

The bicentennial Brother Rice Warriors had an up-and-down season. They won every other game through the first six games, then posted two consecutive wins. Led by captains Stephen Arkwright, Kevin Haffey, and Jim Wilberding, they posted victories against Cass Tech, De La Salle, U-D Jesuit, Redford Covenant, and Bishop Gallagher. They lost a 20-17 heartbreaker to Catholic Central, finishing with a 5-3 record. De La Salle that year featured Chris Godfrey, who would go on to play for the University of Michigan

Wolverines and the New York Jets, New York Giants, and Seattle Seahawks. Harper Woods Notre Dame won the Catholic League Championship in the Prep Bowl over Southgate Aquinas High, 22-12. It was one of those rare years without a Catholic League high school playing in the Class A or Class B MHSAA Championship games.

1977

Catholic High School League Champions
MHSAA Class A State Champions
Do it better than it has ever been done before.

Coaches, players, and the public in Michigan agreed that the first attempt to establish a high school football playoff system was too limited and possibly unfair. Many excellent teams were excluded. Scheduling was done to achieve optimal points, and that tactic occasionally disrupted league play.

In 1977, the MHSAA decided to expand the playoffs. Another game was added by using playoff computer points and including the top two teams in each region in each class, allowing 32 teams to participate. There would now be a quarterfinal, semifinal, and championship game in all of the classes.

The 1977 Brother Rice Warriors were a team of overachievers. Fracassa nicknamed his defensive unit the "Termite Defense," as the average weight per player was 163 pounds. This team finished 12-0, with a Catholic League Championship title and an MHSAA Class A State Championship title. Brother Rice was ranked No. 7 in the country at the end of the season.

The season started with two nonconference wins over Andover High and Warren Cousino High. The Catholic Central Division League games were more closely contested, with a 24-14 win over Warren De La Salle and a 17-7 victory over Notre Dame. The closest game was a 9-6 win over the Detroit Catholic Central Shamrocks. The Shamrocks' best player that season was Jeff Wiska, who went on to play for the MSU Spartans, the USFL Detroit Panthers, USFL Oakland Invaders, the Cleveland Browns, and the Miami Dolphins. Rice won the Catholic semifinal game against Notre Dame and then beat Shrine, 30-7, for the Catholic League Championship.

That year, in the expanded MHSAA playoff system, Brother Rice competed in three postseason playoff games. The Warriors beat Clarkston High (10-0) and Lake Shore High (14-7) in the regional and semifinal games, then defeated Portage Central High, 17-7, in front of 25,000 fans in the Pontiac Silverdome to win the MHSAA Class A Championship.

The team was led by underclassmen. Junior Jon English was the quarterback, and junior Marty Martinez and sophomore Brian Brennan were receivers. Martinez had a three-receiving touchdown day against Redford

Bishop Borgess, and still shares the Rice record. One of Fracassa's defensive "Termites" was 150-pound Tony Asher, who later received his M.D. degree from the Wayne State University School of Medicine, which was followed by a training residency in general surgery and neurosurgery at the University of Michigan School of Medicine. He worked as a Howard Hughes Scholar at the National Institutes of Health during his training. Asher is just one of the many young men Coach Fracassa encouraged in the pursuit of academic rather than athletic careers. Defensive standout Mike Haffey, lineman Jim Allor, and placekicker Brian Swanson were also major contributors to the 1977 team. Swanson kicked field goals of 46 and 47 yards — still the second- and third-longest in Brother Rice history.

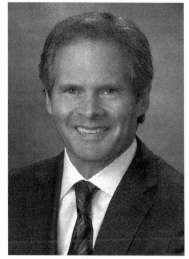

Dr. Tony Asher

JON ENGLISH

Jon English was the quarterback at Birmingham Brother Rice High School from his sophomore year in 1976 through his senior season in 1978. English had games when he completed nine of nine passes (100 percent, against Catholic Central), nine of 10 passes (90 percent, against Bishop Gallagher), and 12 of 14 passes (86 percent, against Warren Cousino). Those were three of the top five best completion percentage games in Brother Rice history.

For his efforts, English was named a three-time Catholic All-League football player. He was named to the Michigan All-State team in his junior and senior seasons, and was a high school All-American football player in his senior year. He participated in track and field as well as football, and scored points at the Michigan State Championship as a junior and senior, finishing third in the high jump in 1979 with a 6'11" leap. This is still a Rice school record.

English, whose father, Wally, was once the offensive backfield coach for the Detroit Lions, began his college career at Michigan State University, then transferred to Iowa

Jon English

State University, eventually ending up as a fifth-year senior at Tulane University. The NCAA believed he violated the spirit of the transfer rule, if not the letter. There was a legal case, English v. NCAA, which was decided in favor of the NCAA.

Although Coach Fracassa would go on to develop other great quarterbacks at Brother Rice and teach hundreds of others through his yearly Al Fracassa Summer Quarterback Camps, English burnished Fracassa's reputation as a "quarterback coach."

1978

Catholic High School League Champions
How good do you want to be?

In 1978, Brother Rice football started strong as the Warriors beat their first two public school opponents, Andover High and Detroit Southwestern. This was the year Coach Fracassa decided to test his team against an out-of-state high school, as the Warriors took on the Barberton Magics from Barberton, Ohio. The Warriors won the game 13-6, and Ed Lynch set a then-school record of 285 yards punting. It turned out to be the only loss for the Magics all season. They finished ranked No. 9 in the state of Ohio and No. 2 in the region. The Magics were led by running back Larry Ricks, who later played for the University of Michigan and the Kansas City Chiefs.

Brother Rice ran the table in the Catholic League Central Division, which included a 21-6 victory over Catholic Central in the Boys' Bowl. The Warriors were ranked No. 1 in the Class A poll, while Catholic Central took the No. 2 spot. The teams met before 13,000 fans at Wisner Stadium in Pontiac, where Brother Rice opened the game in a shotgun formation. Jon English completed all nine of his passes for 75 yards on a windy day and ran six yards for the first touchdown. The key play was a 68-yard punt return by Brian Brennan, who also ran for a two-yard score.

Brother Rice beat Bishop Gallagher, 30-13, in the Prep Bowl game that year, and proceeded to beat Birmingham Groves, 21-7, in their MHSAA regional playoff game. The season came to an abrupt end with a loss to North Farmington High, 26-7, in the semifinal game for the MHSAA Championship. This ended Brother Rice's 24-game winning streak, which had begun in 1976.

English was a senior, and co-captain of the Warriors in 1978. He finished the year completing 62 percent of his passes, accounting for 1,167 yards and 13 touchdowns. Marty Martinez was one of his favorite targets, and in one remarkable game he caught nine passes — the fifth most in Brother Rice history (against Birmingham Groves). In another game he accounted for

149 receiving yards, the fourth most yards in a Brother Rice game (against Redford Bishop Borgess). Martinez attended Stanford University, where he played with John Elway. Ed Lynch, an outstanding punter, made a 69-yard punt that was the fourth longest in Brother Rice history.

BRIAN BRENNAN

Brian Brennan was another player Coach Fracassa admired as one of his "best ever." Brennan was a multisport athlete who played football and basketball at a high level. He was a Swiss army knife for the Brother Rice Warriors, playing running back, wide receiver, kick and punt returner, and defensive back. At the beginning of the 1979 season, he was asked by Coach Fracassa to try another position: quarterback. He injured his shoulder in the Boys' Bowl game, giving Dave Yarema a chance to play quarterback for

a while. Brennan was named to the Michigan All-State football team for the 1979
season, and Fracassa had this to say: "He's
the best; he's going to be a star. He has great
quickness and great awareness of where the
ball is."

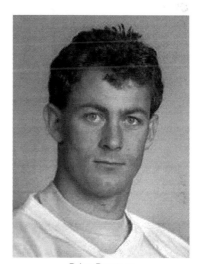

Brian Brennan

Bill Norton also asked a lot of Brennan. Although Brennan was only 5'10", Coach Norton asked him to play guard for the basketball
team. He responded by averaging 14 points
per game and playing the best defense in the
league. Brennan was named to the Michigan
All-State basketball team for the 1979-1980
season, and Coach Norton said: "[Brian's]
major asset is his competitive greatness. He
is a tremendous competitor."

Brennan accepted a football scholarship to Boston College, where he had the pleasure of playing with Doug Flutie, the Heisman trophy-winning quarterback for the team. Brennan caught a school-record 66 passes for 1,149 yards, an average of 17.4 yards per catch, with eight touchdowns his senior year. He was named to the college All-American team for his efforts and was awarded the Thomas F. Scanlan Memorial Trophy for being considered the outstanding senior football player in the areas of scholarship, leadership, and athletic ability.

In 1984, Brennan was the fourth-round draft pick of the Cleveland Browns. He played for the Browns from 1984 to 1991, and for the Cincinnati Bengals and San Diego Chargers in 1992. He finished his career with 334 pass receptions for 4,336 yards and 20 touchdowns, and remains the fourth-leading receiver for the Browns. On Oct. 18, 1987, Brennan had his best career receiving day as far as receptions, with 10 for 139 yards and one touchdown. The passes were thrown by a 36-year-old former Divine Child and Detroit Lions quarterback: Gary Danielson.

1979

Never, never give up.

Coach Fracassa has said, "Ever since I was a young boy, I always enjoyed competing against people who were better than me. Marbles, boxing, horseshoes, follow the leader, basketball, touch football — I loved the challenge of trying to beat the best. I always felt that I was going to be victorious. Most of the time I wasn't, but the competitive spirit was always there. I feel the same way preparing for [a football game]. I hope and pray that my kids do, too."

The 1979 season for Brother Rice began with victories over Lakeshore and Grosse Pointe North. Then, on Sept. 22, 1979, Coach Fracassa and his Brother Rice Warriors traveled 270 miles south to meet Cincinnati Archbishop Moeller High's Crusaders, coached by Gerry Faust. Fracassa wanted to test himself and his team against one of the country's best high school football teams. Moeller, like Brother Rice, was undefeated early in the 1979 football season. Both teams had winning streaks that had ended in 1978, and both teams had been undefeated state champions in 1977. Writing in the *Detroit Free Press* before the game, Hal Schram claimed that "The Brother Rice–Moeller game is the biggest game any Michigan high school football team has ever played."

Gerry Faust

A crowd of 20,792 spectators was at the University of Cincinnati's Nippert Stadium when the two high school teams took the field. Moeller dominated the first half with 282 yards gained, compared to 64 yards for Brother Rice, but led by only 13-7. Brian Brennan was at quarterback for the Warriors, and scored their first-half touchdown on a quarterback bootleg play. As the second half got underway, Moeller halfback Eric Ellington had 178 yards on 10 carries as his team opened a 33-7 lead. The next touchdown for Brother Rice was a Coach Fracassa classic: Brennan dropped back to pass, turned and threw a long lateral on one bounce, and Dave Yarema scooped it up and threw a 68-yard touchdown pass to a wide-open Steve Allen, making the final score 33-14.

Warriors running back Jim Browne remembers that Moeller hadn't given up a first down in their previous games. "We ran a middle screen on the first play for 12 yards and a first down. I went back to the huddle and told the guys we could move the ball against these guys just like we normally do, but it didn't turn out that way. They were a powerful team and they stopped us pretty effectively."

Faust and his Cincinnati Moeller High School Crusaders went on to win the Class AAA Ohio State Championship in 1979 and were believed to be the national high schools' No. 1 team. They won the state and national titles in 1980, and Faust was awarded by being offered the head coaching position at the NCAA's Notre Dame University, becoming the only head coach Notre Dame has ever selected from the high school ranks.

After the Battle of the Titans, the Warriors came out strong in their next game, for an impressive 49-0 victory over Detroit Covenant, which set up a Boys' Bowl match-up with undefeated Catholic Central.

This game between Catholic Central and Brother Rice was played at the Pontiac Silverdome in front of 10,000 fans. The Warriors suffered a severe blow when Brennan injured his shoulder returning the opening kickoff. He was unable to play quarterback and left the game after a few plays on defense. Catholic Central was able to stop Brother Rice's running attack, led by Jim Browne. The only touchdown for

Jim Browne's Raiders brick: All former Raiders players have a brick at the new Las Vegas Stadium.

the team was scored on a pass from Yarema to Allen. Catholic Central won the game, 10-7, thanks to a field goal in overtime.

Brother Rice lost a second Catholic Central Division game to Bishop Gallagher (28-22) that same year, and finished with a 6-3 record. They didn't play in the Catholic League Prep Bowl Championship Game and weren't selected to play in the MHSAA State Championship playoffs.

Brennan was honored as an All-State player despite his injury and enjoyed successful NCAA college football and NFL football careers. His teammate, running back Browne, had an outstanding year. He carried the football 167 times for 1,015 yards — an average of 6.1 yards per carry. Browne attended Northwestern University for two years before transferring to Boston College, where he sat out a year and then played for two years. He was drafted by the Tampa Bay Bandits of the USFL in 1985 and joined the Los Angeles

Raiders in 1987. He returned to Detroit to play for the Detroit Drive of the Arena Football League in 1988.

Jim Ostrowski was an excellent placekicker, and Kevin Kennedy had an outstanding defensive game against Moeller.

Catholic Central went on to celebrate an undefeated 1979 season. The Shamrocks won the Prep Bowl, 16-0, over De La Salle. In the Class A MH-SAA Championship Game at the Pontiac Silverdome, they beat Escanaba High 32-7, to finish as the No. 1 team in Michigan. They held teams scoreless in six games and allowed one score in two games. Catholic Central was led by quarterback Mike Lewis, lineman Dave Yudasz, and running back Aaron Roberts. In 2020, this team was named one of the top five football teams in Michigan in the last 50 years by Mick McCabe of the *Detroit Free Press*.

At this point in his career, Fracassa had dreams of moving on to coach at the college level. In February of 1980, he applied for the head coaching position at his alma mater, Michigan State University. Disappointingly, he wasn't interviewed for the job. Frank "Muddy" Waters, named the head coach, offered Fracassa the position of offensive coordinator for the Spartans, but he declined the offer.

The 1980s

1980

Catholic High School League Champions
MHSAA Class A State Champions

The difference between good and great is a little extra effort.

After the dramatic 1979 season, things settled down in 1980. It was time to return to the business of winning championships. Brother Rice had a maturing quarterback in junior Dave Yarema, a junior safety and receiver in Brad Cochran, and a senior linebacker in Tim MacLean to lead the squad. The season opened with victories over Lake Shore and Grosse Pointe North, both shutouts. Mount Clemens, another public high school, was the next to fall. Yarema threw a 91-yard touchdown pass to Paul Jokisch in that game. The Warriors were undefeated going into Catholic League play.

Coach Fracassa and Brother Rice won their first league game against Bishop Gallagher in another shutout, 29-0. The next game was the Boys' Bowl,

63

played against Catholic Central. Aaron Roberts was back and would be an All-State running back for Catholic Central, but the Warriors won the game, 24-14. Cochran had a 90-yard kickoff return in that game. Brother Rice won the rest of their scheduled Catholic League games against Covenant, U-D Jesuit, and Notre Dame.

This set up a Prep Bowl Catholic Championship Game against De La Salle, led by Steve Phillips, another All-State running back. The Warriors' defense rose to the occasion with a 27-0 shutout, the fourth of the season. The Brother Rice Warriors were undefeated and untied, and were ranked No. 1 in Class A going into the MHSAA playoffs.

The regional playoff game was against Sterling Heights Stevenson. Brother Rice won that game, 25-13, behind 280 passing yards from Yarema and Jokisch's 138 receiving yards. The following week, the team won the semifinal game 49-12 against Detroit Central to move on to the MHSAA Class A Championship Game; Yarema was a key contributor, posting what was then a school-record four touchdown passes.

Steve Allen

The Championship Game against Dearborn Fordson High School, in which defensive play dominated, was held in the Pontiac Silverdome. Brother Rice ran the gadget play and scored a touchdown against Fordson, but the referee blew his whistle thinking the live lateral from Yarema to Jokisch was an incomplete pass and wiped out a Steve Allen touchdown. The Warriors recovered when Yarema completed a 38-yard touchdown pass to Jokisch for the only score in the game. The defense posted another shutout, 6-0, to help lock up the Class A MHSAA title. Mick McCabe of the *Detroit Free Press* reported: "The reason Brother Rice is the Class A state champion is because of its defense. ... Defensive tackle Fred Konkel spent more time in Fordson's backfield than the quarterback, causing a fumble and an interception. ... Linebacker Tim MacLean helped limit Fordson to 156 yards total offense."

The Brother Rice High School Warriors under Coach Fracassa had returned to the mountaintop: they had won three Class A State Championships, two by the MHSAA playoff route, in seven years.

Yarema finished the season with 92 pass completions for 1,489 yards and 23 touchdowns, and was named to the All-Catholic and All-State teams as a junior. Allen, who was a frequent Yarema target, was awarded a spot at the

Air Force Academy and played football for the Falcons during a golden era for Air Force football. Air Force went to bowl games four consecutive years from 1982 through 1985, and won all four against the following opponents: Vanderbilt, Ole Miss, Virginia Tech, and Texas. In 1985, only a regular-season loss to BYU — a game they led 21-7 at halftime — kept them from playing for the National Championship.

BRAD COCHRAN

Brad Cochran was a gifted football player. He was 6'3", weighed 219 pounds, and ran 40 yards in 4.5 seconds. Cochran started his high school football career at Royal Oak Dondero and finished it on an outstanding Brother Rice team. He was a safety for the great 1980 Warrior defensive unit and was named to the defensive All-Metro and All-Catholic teams, along with Tim MacLean. Cochran also returned kicks, played receiver, and filled in at halfback as needed. A track athlete, as well, he was recruited by several colleges and accepted a football scholarship to the University of Michigan.

Brad Cochran

Cochran played well at U of M but opted to transfer to the University of Colorado following an argument with Coach Bo Schembechler. Eventually, tests revealed that Cochran suffered with severe depression due to a treatable hereditary metabolic disorder that was exacerbated by the pressures of big-time college football. After the diagnosis, he left Colorado and returned to his home state of Michigan.

Depression can be mistaken for indifference, and dysphoria associated with anxiety is often misinterpreted as insubordination. Cochran has noted, "By far, that was the worst period of my life."

Despite the challenges he faced, Cochran continued to work out while undergoing successful treatment for his medical issues. "Coach Fracassa and Brother Rice were a sanctuary for me during that time," he remembers. "I would run with those guys three times a week, and Coach gave me a key to the weight room and I would be in there at all hours. I remember a very kind janitor who asked me if I needed a bed in there." Cochran was surprised when Lloyd Carr, U of M's defensive backfield coach, invited him back to the team. Coach Schembechler put him 13th on the defensive back depth chart. The coach said, "Give Cochran credit; he had to earn that starting position."

Cochran was on the starting defensive team for the Wolverines in 1983 and 1984, and was a co-captain of the squad in 1985. That team, quarterbacked by his roommate, Jim Harbaugh, went 10-1-1, beat the University of Nebraska in the Fiesta Bowl, and finished with a No. 2 NCAA college ranking. It allowed only 75 points, an average of 6.8 points per game. Cochran was named a first-team college All-America player that year and was the recipient of the 1985 Toyota Leadership Award for "outstanding performance in the areas of team contributions, academics, and citizenship."

Following that special year, Cochran was drafted by the Los Angeles Raiders. After starting 36 consecutive games with 189 tackles and 12 interceptions in college, he suffered a neck injury in a preseason game, ending thoughts of a professional career. To this day, Cochran's love of and commitment to football continues. He coached his son Tyler's teams as he grew up, and coached the defensive backs for Brother Rice. After high school, Tyler Cochran played for the Wolverines and was the special teams' captain. "I was a blessed guy to have so many great coaches going all the way back to junior high in Royal Oak," Brad Cochran says. "I played for Bo and Lloyd Carr, and Bill McCartney recruited me to Michigan. But Coach Fracassa, he's my favorite — not only as a coach, but as a person."

TIM MACLEAN

"He's the best defensive player I've got. He's our catalyst. He's everywhere. He gets mad at the guys when they don't show any enthusiasm and he hugs them when they do." Coach Fracassa was talking about Tim MacLean, one of the co-captains of the MHSAA Class A Champions. Despite being an undersized linebacker at 5'10" and 185 pounds, MacLean was a three-year starter for the Warriors and was honored as an All-Catholic and All-State team member.

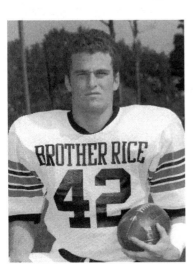
Tim MacLean

MacLean came from a large, sports-playing family that included six boys and a girl. His big brother, Dan, played basketball and football for Brother Rice, and graduated in 1976. Dan went on to play football for the University of Illinois.

Tim had a twin brother, Tom, and the two were inseparable. Both played baseball and basketball, as well as football. Tim and Tom were awarded the Brother Rice Loyalty Award by their senior-class peers. After high school graduation, the pair roomed together at Miami University in Oxford, Ohio, before transferring together to Oakland Community College back home in Michigan. Tim coached a middle school football team at St. Regis, and he and Tom planned to attend Michigan State University together.

According to his brother Dan, Tim was a "very intense, emotional guy, with the unique ability to find out what made you happy. If you were in the dumps, he could get you out of it." Coach Fracassa agreed with Dan. "He gave intensity to our defense. He was probably the most intense player I've ever had the privilege of coaching."

The day started like any other. Tim and Tom took their mother out for lunch, and Tim took flowers to his new sister-in-law. He tossed a football around with his father and some former teammates. In the evening, he made dinner for his brothers. On a whim, Tim, along with his brother Tom, drove to Ann Arbor to surprise their girlfriends. When Tim got out of the car in front of his girlfriend's dormitory, he was struck by a pickup truck. He died two days later.

Athletes are special and the memories they create for others can live forever. Tim's life was lived to the fullest. At his funeral service, Dan noted that "Tim got every hour out of the day." Tim MacLean has a permanent place as a member of the Brother Rice High School Sports Hall of Fame.

1981

Catholic High School League Champion
The harder you work, the harder it is to surrender.

Brother Rice's 1981 season began with optimism. Dave Yarema, the All-State quarterback, and Paul Jokisch, his favorite All-State receiver, were returning for their senior year. The season started with a game against the Cardinal Mooney team from Youngstown, Ohio, at the Pontiac Silverdome. Cardinal Mooney won the Ohio Division II championship in 1980 and would win again in 1982. In this season opener, they beat Brother Rice 16-13.

The Warriors wouldn't lose again. Wins over St. Rita High from Chicago and Toledo, Ohio's, Bowsher High set the table for an undefeated Catholic League Central Division season. The Warriors edged out the Catholic Central Shamrocks, 3-0, in the Boys' Bowl at Pontiac's Wisner Stadium and won the Catholic League Championship Prep Bowl against the Divine Child Falcons, 14-7, in the Pontiac Silverdome. Despite the stellar season, and even though they may have been the best team in Michigan, the Warriors weren't invited to the MHSAA playoffs that year.

In the 1981 season, Yarema passed for 1,115 yards, averaging passing 124 yards per game. He finished his high school career with 3,032 passing yards, 194 completions, 40 touchdowns, and a 53 percent completion rate. Jokisch, a 6'8" receiver, finished his high school career with 72 pass receptions for 1,454 yards and 18 touchdowns. He averaged more than 20 yards per catch. Both Yarema and Jokisch were named to All-State and All-America teams after the season; they were a high school passing tandem for the ages.

Coach Fracassa was disappointed with the failure of his Warriors to make the playoffs. Due to the vagaries of the MHSAA's computer, a co-ed Class B school from Escanaba, a city of about 13,000 people in Michigan's Upper Peninsula, was placed in the Class A division for playoff purposes. In 1979, the Escanaba Eskymos had lost to Catholic Central in the Class A MHSAA Championship Game, but the team returned to the MHSAA Class A Championship Game in 1981 and beat Fraser High in the Pontiac Silverdome. Kevin Tapani, who went on to have a 12-year pitching career in Major League Baseball, led his high school team to victory. The buses coming back across the Mackinac Bridge were greeted with honking horns and flashing headlights from St. Ignace to Gladstone, and from Wells to Escanaba.

DAVE YAREMA

Dave Yarema finished his high school All-America career with a 27-4 won-loss record. Like his coach, Yarema accepted an athletic scholarship to Michigan State University. He was a three-year starter for the Spartans and led the team to two bowl games.

Yarema finished his MSU career with 5,809 passing yards (fifth among Spartan quarterbacks), 464 completions (seventh), 44 touchdowns (fifth), and a 60.5 percent pass completion rate (sixth). On a Spartan Nation/Sports Illustrated website, he was considered the fifth-best quarterback in Spartan history.

"Don't be a big shot" is the mantra Yarema said he took from Coach Fracassa as he began his college career. The coach always stressed that he didn't want the accolades and outward signs of athletic success to define his players. He set an example by practicing humility himself, whether his teams won or lost. Unlike many other coaches, he never tried to embarrass his team's opponent or show them up. Coach Fracassa expected the same of his players, both on and off the field. Fracassa didn't wear his school's colors to a competitor's game and Yarema, likewise, never wore clothing emblazoned with the

DAVID YAREMA

Birmingham Brother Rice
Coach Al Fracassa
6'3" - 187 Quarterback
12 East All-Stars

As quarterback of Brother Rice, David Yarema passed for 40 career touchdowns while running for 15. Along with being named All-League, All-Catholic, All-Metro, and All-State during his junior and senior years, he was also All-American and tri-captain of the Brother Rice football team his senior year.

We congratulate David Yarema

Dave Yarema, Michigan High School All-Star game.

Brother Rice Warrior logo or, later, the Michigan State Spartans logo when attending other sporting events. "I couldn't wear it because I didn't want to let him down," Yarema said.

In 1986, the Michigan State University Spartans were ranked No. 17 in the country and were playing a game against the University of Iowa Hawkeyes. The Spartans were behind by three points, and Yarema was leading his team on a possible game-winning drive. With the ball on the five-yard line, Yarema rolled out and threw an interception, ending any chance for victory. Coach Fracassa wrote a letter to Yarema the next day (as he did with many of his former players), reminding him that guys who are afraid to fail never accomplish anything. It's the courage to try one's best, and the humility to be able to accept the results, that characterized Fracassa's approach to his teams.

PAUL JOKISCH

Coach Fracassa was living at a time when giants walked the halls of Brother Rice. One of those giants was Paul Jokisch, an All-State and All-American in basketball as well as football. He was a Michigan Blue Chip Award-winner in basketball and a Catholic League Athlete of the Year Award-winner.

Jokisch scored more than 1,000 points in his high school basketball career, in addition to his achievements in his stellar football career. After the season, he received letters almost daily from Bill Frieder, U of M's basketball coach, as his first choice was to play college basketball.

Paul Jokisch

The recruiting class that year had a lot of talent; like Jokisch, Roy Tarpley played power forward. Jokisch was on the court as a substitute forward in 39 games for the Wolverines in that first season, and was averaging 3.9 points, 1.7 rebounds, and 0.5 assists, but he was considering a transfer to the University of Tennessee or Notre Dame as a sophomore, in hopes of getting more playing time. When the Wolverines' football coach, Bo Schembechler, politely requested that Jokisch come to spring football practice, his plans to transfer were canceled.

Jokisch played three years for the University of Michigan Wolverines football team and appeared in 37 games. He played receiver at a time when Jim Harbaugh was his quarterback. At the end of his college career, he had

58 pass receptions for 1,088 total yards and six touchdowns. He averaged 18.8 yards per completion; the longest reception was a 67-yard touchdown against the University of Minnesota. Jokisch caught six passes for 130 yards against the University of Illinois, for his best statistical performance.

As a result of his efforts, Jokisch was drafted by the San Francisco 49ers. He had a chronic injury in his last year with the Wolverines, and that slowed him down in his senior year — causing him to drop to the fifth round. The injury, which likely didn't heal completely, also hampered his tryout with the 49ers. Later, Jokisch played four games with the Detroit Drive football team in the Arena Football League.

Jokisch is part of a University of Michigan football family dynasty. His brother, Dan, played football for Bo Schembechler and Gary Moeller at the University of Michigan; his nephew Daniel, Dan's son, played on the 2019 Wolverine football team under Jim Harbaugh; and Jokisch's son, Paul Jokisch III, was a member of Harbaugh's 2022 team.

1982

Life's battles don't always go to the stronger or faster man,
but to the man who thinks he can.

In December of 1982, George Perles, the former St. Ambrose head coach, was given the Michigan State University head coach position, and he offered Coach Fracassa a job with the Spartan defensive staff. Fracassa chose to remain at Brother Rice. He said in a recent interview that he loved coaching high school kids and helping them to become better people.

This was a rebuilding year for Brother Rice, as a lot of the school's football talent had moved on to the next level. A win over Dearborn High to start the season, followed by losses to Muskegon High and Divine Child, left the Warriors with a losing record going into the Catholic Central Division regular season play. A win against Covenant High evened their record at 2-2 heading into the Boys' Bowl game.

George Perles

The game against Catholic Central was held at Ryerson Stadium at Eastern Michigan University. Catholic Central had a great team that year, led by three future NFL players: senior running back Mike Varajon, senior center Brett Petersmark, and junior defensive tackle Mark Messner. The Boys' Bowl game was close, as was usually the case, but the Warriors lost 7-0.

The Warriors won the rest of their regular-season games, including a Catholic League semifinal game over Divine Child, 19-6. The rematch victory made up for the early season loss and set up a rematch with Catholic Central in the Prep Bowl at the Pontiac Silverdome. The Shamrocks prevailed in that game, 10-0 — their second victory over the Warriors for the year. The Catholic League's Central Division-winning Catholic Central and Division AA-winning Divine Child were both placed in the MHSAA Class B grouping and met in the Class B State Championship Game. The Shamrocks won the game to capture that title, while Farmington Hills Harrison won the MHSAA Class A Championship Game over Dearborn Fordson. Catholic Central and Harrison were perennial football powers and competed with Brother Rice for the best team in the Detroit metro area over the next several decades.

1983
Catholic High School League Champions
MHSAA Class A State Champions
Be the best that you can be.

In 1983, Brother Rice found its way back to the football limelight. The squad was led by senior running back Mel Farr Jr.; his brother, Mike Farr, a junior receiver; and Mike Lodish and Bob Kula, both junior linemen. This season it was back to the running game after all those great passing quarterback years.

The season started with a 14-7 win over the Chicago Mount Carmel High Golden Aces, who would wind up winning the 1983 Chicago Catholic League Prep Bowl. The Warriors followed up with victories over Muskegon High School and Aquinas. Although they swept their Catholic League regular season games, they posted a close 7-3 victory over De La Salle.

The Brother Rice Warriors boasted a 13-10 win over always-challenging Catholic Central, whose best player this season was linebacker Mark Messner, who went on to earn All-America honors at the University of Michigan and played for the Los Angeles Rams. Brother Rice met Divine Child in the Catholic League Prep Bowl at the Pontiac Silverdome, where they won the Catholic League Championship over the Division AA winners, 13-10.

When it came to the state playoffs, Brother Rice was placed in the MHSAA Class A bracket. Their regional game was against Birmingham's Seaholm High School, and the Warriors beat the Maples, 21-6. They followed this with a 28-14 win over Detroit Henry Ford II High. Their opponent in the MHSAA State Class A Championship was East Lansing High School. The Warriors won, 15-12. Allen Szydlowski completed 16 of 19 (86 percent) of his passes in that championship game.

This was another undefeated, untied, MHSAA Championship team for

Coach Fracassa and the Brother Rice Warriors. If the 1974 mythical state champions are included, this made four state of Michigan No. 1 teams in 10 years. The star of the team was Mel Farr Jr., a workhorse halfback. Against Chicago Mount Carmel, Farr carried the ball 30 times. Against Detroit Henry Ford, he carried the ball 28 times. He finished the year with 1,216 yards rushing and 15 touchdowns.

MEL FARR JR.

Mel Farr Jr. came from a family of football royalty. He's the son of Mel Farr, the nephew of Miller Farr, and Mike Farr's older brother. Mel Farr Sr. was

Mel Farr Jr.

a running back at the University of California in Los Angeles (UCLA) and was an All-American college player his senior year. He was chosen by the NFL Detroit Lions as the seventh pick in the first round of the draft, and was named the Offensive Rookie of the Year. Mel Farr played for seven years and was chosen to play in the Pro Bowl twice. Mel Farr Jr.'s uncle, Miller Farr, played defensive back for the AFL's Denver Broncos, San Diego Chargers, and Houston Oilers, and was All-AFL for three years. He finished his career with the St. Louis Cardinals after the 1970 AFL-NFL merger.

Mel Jr. decided to follow in his father's footsteps, attending UCLA and wearing his father's number, 22. The Bruins' head coach, Terry Donahue, had been a teammate of Mel Sr. when the Bruins beat Michigan State, 14-12, in the 1966 Rose Bowl.

Mel Jr. played halfback at Brother Rice but switched to fullback when he played for the Bruins. Coach Donahue felt that "The fullbacks are a key ingredient to our offense. The fullbacks are averaging more yards than our tailbacks." Of Mel Jr., Donahue said: "He is very intelligent. He has a real knack for understanding football. What enabled him to play as a freshman was that he adjusted so quickly to the system."

Mel Jr. played for four years for the UCLA Bruins. In his college career, he had 153 carries for 693 yards (4.5 yards per carry) and four touchdowns; he caught 27 passes for 244 yards (nine yards per catch) and two touchdowns; and he returned seven kicks for 56 yards (eight yards per return). He was drafted by the Denver Broncos and played briefly with the NFL Los Angeles Rams.

Mel Farr Jr. is one of a large number of Brother Rice Warriors whose fathers played NCAA college or NFL professional football. Coach Fracassa was able to maximize the performance of these second-generation athletes, allowing them a chance to compete at the next level.

MIKE FARR

When Mel Farr Jr. was a Brother Rice senior, his brother, Mike, was a junior. In spite of the Farr family's penchant for running the ball, freshman team Coach Rick Fracassa thought Mike would make a great wide receiver. Mike thrived in that position, teaming up with quarterback and 1984 team captain Allen Szydlowski. Following his senior year at Rice, Mike was chosen to represent his school in the Michigan All-Star game.

Mike followed his father and brother to UCLA, where he played for four years. He caught 130 passes for 1,514 yards (an average of 11.6 yards per catch) and two touchdowns. He ran the ball five times for 38 yards (7.6 yards per carry) and returned 14 kicks for 28 yards. He graduated with honors and set a record for most catches in a season (66) in 1988.

Mike Farr

When Mike tried out for the Detroit Lions as an undrafted free agent, his hard work and discipline earned him a roster spot. He played for three years with the Lions, including a year when they made the NFL playoffs. In 1991, the Lions were 12-4, won one playoff game, and lost the conference championship. That year, Mike teamed up with quarterback Erik Kramer, a fellow free agent, for 42 receptions. The duo's efforts totaled 431 yards, with an average of 10.3 yards per catch, including 22 first downs and one touchdown. The Lions haven't won a playoff game since 1991.

From Coach Fracassa, Mike says he learned that "nothing was bigger that the team." Mike's belief in discipline and unselfishness has been carried forward from his time with Coach Fracassa; his commitment and philosophy of "never, ever giving up" allowed him to succeed at the college and professional levels.

As an athlete, Mike said he never thought that Coach looked at him any differently. "He didn't feel anything [in regard to color] on the football field," Farr has said. Coach "played the people who performed." Mike said his experience was that any pre-existing attitudes and perceptions at the school "went away" when he and his brother had an opportunity to go to class, talk in the hallway and cafeteria, and interact on the playing field with their White colleagues. The ties still bind: Mike Farr's Brother Rice teammates were at his wedding, and he volunteered to be chairman for a 1983 team reunion.

1984

Commitment to excellence.

It looked like 1984 would be another championship year for Brother Rice High. Mike Farr, Bob Kula, and Mike Lodish, who would all be football stars in college after their senior year, would be returning. The year started with four wins, all without allowing a score by the other teams. In a game against Harper Woods Notre Dame, Allen Szydlowski had a 9-for-10 (90 percent) passing day. But after the team's victories came a shock: Warren De La Salle Collegiate eked out a 23-20 win over Rice, ending the Warriors' 16-game winning streak.

After that disappointing outing, Brother Rice won their last four games, including a 13-10 victory over Catholic Central in the Boys' Bowl. The season closed with a 23-0 shutout against Aquinas High. The one loss to De La Salle kept Rice out of the Catholic League Championship Game and the MHSAA State Playoffs.

De La Salle went on to the Catholic League Prep Bowl at the Pontiac Silverdome, where they lost to Divine Child, 14-10 — their only loss of the season. It was frustrating for Brother Rice because they'd beaten Divine Child 34-0 in the third week of the season. They watched from the outside as the MHSAA Class A Championship was won by Ann Arbor Pioneer. The MHSAA Class B runner-up was Orchard Lake St. Mary, a team that would emerge as another frequent opponent for Brother Rice.

BOB KULA

Bob Kula was a senior lineman who made the Warriors' offense work. He

Bob Kula

protected his quarterback, Allen Szydlowski, during two seasons, with a combined record of 20-1. Prior to Kula's senior year, Coach Fracassa told the *Detroit Free Press*: "A lot depends on what the offensive line does. They've got to be able to hold people out." The paper noted "Kula holds everybody out."

He was so good at holding people out, he was awarded a football scholarship to MSU. There, under Coach George Perles, Kula played offensive tackle for four years. During that span, the Spartans amassed a large number of rushing yards. Running backs Lorenzo White, Blake Ezor, Tico Duckett, and Hyland Hickson followed Kula's blocks.

During Kula's career, the Spartans accumulated 9,965 yards running the ball, 7,437 yards passing the ball, 211 yards rushing per game, and 148 yards passing per game, with 99 team rushing touchdowns and 41 team passing touchdowns. For his contributions, Kula was a consensus college All-American in 1989. He was also the Rimington-Pace Big Ten Offensive Lineman of the year in 1989. Drafted by the NFL Seattle Seahawks in 1990, Kula played two years of professional football with the Montreal Machine of the World Football League.

MIKE LODISH

Mike Lodish was a 6'4", 224-pound lacrosse player. It's terrifying to imagine him coming toward a person with a large stick in his hand. He made the All-State team in lacrosse at Brother Rice, and he also made the All-State football team after the 1984 season.

Lodish accepted a football scholarship to UCLA, where he played for two seasons as the nose tackle. He was small for a defensive lineman but worked his way up from 224 pounds in high school to 270 pounds by his senior year. He won the Bruin Brawn title as the UCLA Weightlifter of the Year when he set new all-time team records for the squat and combined (bench, squat, clean) events. Among his on-the-field accomplishments during his All-Pac10 defensive tackle career were three pass interceptions and a touchdown.

Mike Lodish

A very good player at UCLA, Lodish was drafted in the 10th round by the NFL Buffalo Bills in 1990 and ended up playing professional football for 11 years. He finished his career with 137 tackles, 8.5 sacks, three interceptions, four fumble recoveries, and one touchdown. Lodish ranks second on the list of all-time Super Bowl appearances, with six. He's tied with Don Beebe and Stephen Gostkowski, and is behind Tom Brady, who has 10. Lodish appeared in four Super Bowls with the Buffalo Bills and two with the Denver Broncos.

Lodish is grateful for the time he spent with Coach Fracassa, and appreciates what Coach represented. "He's a man of morals, and God, and discipline, and hard work," he says. "Those are qualities I utilized in my life to persevere to the next level, both academically and athletically. Those are the virtues that were extremely impressionable on me as a youth."

1985

Do things right the first time.

By 1985, the high school football playoffs in Michigan were still believed to be out of the reach of most high school coaches, players, and teams, so a decision was made to add yet another round to the playoffs. Using a computer to calculate playoff points, the top four teams in each of the four regions in four classes would be included, so there would be 64 teams participating. These changes would result in regional games, quarterfinals, semifinals, and championship games in Classes A, B, C, and D.

It was as rare as a solar eclipse or the return of Halley's Comet: a losing season for Brother Rice with Al Fracassa as their coach. In fact, there would only be one in 45 years. The 1985 season opened with a loss to Chicago St. Rita High, 23-21. Although Chris Sullivan completed 22 passes for 256 yards, St. Rita intercepted four. The second game, another loss, came at the hands of Lansing Sexton High, who won 28-13. Sullivan completed 21 of 40 passes for 249 yards; 11 of those passes went to Dave Plunkett. Sexton went on to participate in the MHSAA playoffs and finished 10-1 for the season. The next game was against Canton (Ohio) GlenOak, and Rice lost 29-21. Sullivan completed 21 of 36 of his passes in that game.

The Catholic League Central Division play began with a Rice victory over Notre Dame, followed by losses to De La Salle and Catholic Central. The Boys' Bowl game was close, with a final score of 7-3. Catholic Central started a five-year winning streak over Brother Rice that would last until 1989.

The Warriors took a 1-5 won-loss record into their last three games of the 1985 season. They won their final games by a combined score of 82-13. There was no Prep Bowl or MHSAA state playoff game for Rice that year. Catholic Central won the Prep Bowl over Divine Child, 13-0, and with their future University of Michigan and NFL Kansas City Chief player, Tom Dohring, won the MHSAA Class B Championship Game.

DETROIT (WARREN) DE LA SALLE HIGH SCHOOL

De La Salle was a testy opponent for years in the Catholic League Central Division and they trail only Catholic Central in the number of games played against Rice. Through the 2022 football season, De La Salle had a 26-46 record versus Brother Rice.

Like Brother Rice, De La Salle is an all-boys, private, Catholic secondary school. Founded in 1926, it's run by the De La Salle Christian Brothers. The school was located on the east side of Detroit before moving to its current location in Warren in 1982. From 1982 to 1986, the football team had a record of 38-7, with three 8-1 season records. From 1974 to 1984, the football

76

coach was John Maronto; Ray Barr took over from 1985 to 1988, followed by Coach Ross MacDonald from 1989-99. After several years of rapid turnovers, Paul Verska served as head coach from 2002 to 2014.

De La Salle graduated several football players who would eventually play in the professional ranks. During the Coach Fracassa era at Brother Rice, these greats included John Sokolosky (Wayne State University, Detroit Lions), Chris Godfrey (University of Michigan, New York Jets, New York Giants, Seattle Seahawks), Jerry McCabe (Holy Cross University, New England Patriots, Kansas City Chiefs), Keith Karpinsky (Penn State University, Detroit Lions), and Mike Danna (Central Michigan University and University of Michigan, Kansas City Chiefs).

Following Coach Fracassa's retirement in 2013, Verska took De La Salle to their first MHSAA Division 2 Championship title in 2014.

1986

Catholic High School League Champions

The price of greatness is responsibility.

The 1986 season started with a loss to Flint Powers Catholic High, 17-14; the Chargers finished the season at 9-1. Rice and Powers met on the field seven times over the years, and this was the only Powers victory. The next two games were wins over the Burbank, Ill., St. Laurence High Vikings (23-14) and Traverse City Central (24-7).

The Catholic League Central Division's play began with wins over Notre Dame and De La Salle, followed by another Boys' Bowl game against Catholic Central. The Shamrocks came out ahead, by a close score of 7-3. The Warriors, meanwhile, followed this loss with wins over Harper Woods Bishop Gallagher and Redford Covenant.

Brother Rice's 5-1 record in the Central Division led to an invitation to the Catholic League Championship in the Prep Bowl at the Pontiac Silverdome, where they earned the title of Catholic League Champions with a 12-8 win over Divine Child. That year, none of the Catholic League teams reached the MHSAA Class A or Class B playoff finals.

1987

Believe it.

The only thing worse for Brother Rice than losing once in a season to Catholic Central was losing to them twice. The opening game of the 1987 season was against Flint Powers, which Rice handily won, 28-7. Next came a contest with the Middletown (Ohio) High School Middies. It was a tight game, but the Warriors won 6-0. They finished their public-school matchups with a 13-7 win over Traverse City Central.

Led by quarterback John Gieselman and running back Jason Wolf, Rice won their first two Catholic League Central Division games against Notre Dame and De La Salle. The Warriors dropped the Boys' Bowl game to Catholic Central, 10-7, but won the rest of their Catholic League games. In their last regular season game, the Warriors beat the Orchard Lake St. Mary's Eaglets, 41-13, behind Jason Wolf's four touchdowns. This year, the Eaglets had three players destined for the NFL: Filmel Johnson (University of Illinois, Buffalo Bills), Leonard Renfro (University of Colorado, Philadelphia Eagles), and Sam Rogers (University of Colorado, Buffalo Bills, San Diego Chargers, and Atlanta Falcons).

The Catholic Central loss kept Rice out of the Catholic League Prep Bowl, which the Flint Powers squad won over Southgate Aquinas, 19-0. Rice was invited to the MHSAA Class A playoffs and won their first game by a score of 28-6 over the Ferndale High Eagles. In the regional final, Rice beat Grosse Pointe South, 27-13. Wolf ran the ball 37 times and scored four touchdowns. The semifinal game was against a familiar opponent: Catholic Central. The Warriors lost to the Shamrocks for the second time this season, 14-9, but Catholic Central went on to lose the MHSAA Class A Championship Game to Ann Arbor Pioneer High, 3-0.

After graduating from Brother Rice, Gieselman played at Michigan State. He appeared in two games in 1989 and seven games in 1992, completing 15 of 28 passes for 122 yards. He played professionally with the Massachusetts Marauders (Arena Football League), the Reine Fire (World League of American Football), and the Charlotte Rage (Arena Football League).

1988

Whatever it takes.

By 1988, Brother Rice, under Coach Fracassa, was assembling a new juggernaut that included underclassmen Bob Utter and Pete Mitchell, along with linemen Marc Milia, Dean Moskovic, and Jordan Halter. The season started with victories over three non-league teams: Flint Powers Catholic, Stevenson, and Muskegon. Catholic League Central Division play began on a high note, with victories over Notre Dame and De La Salle.

Rice carried a 5-0 won-loss record into the Boys' Bowl. Their opponent, Catholic Central, enjoyed a four-game winning streak against Coach Fracassa's squad. On a sloppy field at Wisner Stadium, Catholic Central scored two late touchdowns to win 21-7. The Warriors' last two Catholic League games of the season, against Bishop Gallagher and Covenant, were wins. The last game was a 9-7 loss to Orchard Lake St. Mary.

Jason Wolf was awarded a football scholarship to Southern Methodist University, where he was a four-year varsity letterman as both a runner and receiver. He finished his college career for the Mustangs with 235 pass receptions for 2,232 yards and 17 touchdowns; he ran the ball 29 times, for 80 yards and four touchdowns; and had 23 kick returns for 555 yards.

Marc Milia, Michigan High School All-Star game.

Marc Milia, an outstanding lineman on the 1988 Warriors team, went on to become the starting center for the Michigan Wolverines.

In 1988, Rice was excluded from the Prep Bowl and the MHSAA State playoffs. In the Prep Bowl at the Pontiac Silverdome, Catholic Central defeated U-D Jesuit, 28-7, to capture the Detroit Catholic League Championship title. In the MHSAA Class A Championship final at the Pontiac Silverdome, Catholic Central lost to Traverse City Central High, 24-14.

In MHSAA Class C, there was an interesting contender from the Catholic League. St. Martin DePorres won their sixth championship, this time in Class C. In the school's history, they won 12 MHSAA high school state titles in five different classes or divisions — a Catholic League high school record at the time. Two players from the 1988 DePorres team would eventually play in the NFL: Lamar Mills (University of Indiana, Washington Redskins) and Rodney Culver (University of Notre Dame, Indianapolis Colts, and San Diego Chargers). St. Martin DePorres High School, which played its first game in 1967, closed in 2005.

THE TIMES

The year 1988 brought an end to Ronald Reagan's presidency. George H.W. Bush, his vice president, won the election and assumed office in early 1989. In the final years of President Reagan's second term, the Space Shuttle Challenger exploded shortly after its launch in January 1986, Fox Broadcasting Co. made its debut, the Iran-Contra affair made headlines, and President Reagan, visiting Berlin, called for Soviet General Secretary Mikhail Gorbachev to "Tear down this wall."

Under President George H.W. Bush, a renewed "War on Drugs" was declared; the Exon Valdez ran aground in Alaska, spilling more than 10 million gallons of oil into Prince William Sound; and Bush and Premier Gorbachev announced the Cold War could be coming to an end. In 1987, the Dow Jones Industrial Average fell 22.6 percent in a single session on "Black Monday." Prozac hit the market as an approved prescription drug in 1988. James Hansen, a NASA scientist, said in a Congressional meeting that global warming had begun.

In 1988, Detroit was struggling. The population in 1990 was a little over 1 million, and the city was close to 80 percent Black. Although Detroit continued to lose 5 percent of its jobs every year between 1972 and 1992, Mayor Coleman A. Young tried to apply government and private-sector initiatives to develop a service and entertainment center. The decrease in the city's tax revenue led to a challenge in providing education and social services.

Sports in Detroit saw the MLB Detroit Tigers win a World Series in 1984. In 1988, The NBA Los Angeles Lakers, with Earvin "Magic" Johnson of Lansing Everett High and Michigan State, won the championship title over the Detroit Pistons — but the "Bad Boys" of the NBA would win back-to-back NBA titles in 1989 and 1990. In 1988, Kirk Gibson, a football and baseball star at Michigan State University and star of the 1984 Tigers championship team, hit a stunning walk-off home run for the MLB Los Angeles Dodgers, sending them on their way to a World Series triumph.

The National Football League continued to thrive. Although the Chicago Bears had one of the greatest seasons in NFL history in 1985, the San Francisco 49ers dominated the latter '80s, with four Super Bowl wins.

In the Detroit Catholic League, the Central Division winner still played the A-B Division (formerly AA Division) winner in the Prep Bowl at the Pontiac Silverdome. The Michigan High School Athletic Association playoffs came to dominate the high school football scene.

When it came to the Catholic Church, more than 30 parishes in the Detroit Archdiocese were closed between 1975 and 1990, and many high schools closed their doors or underwent consolidation. Hamtramck's St. Ladislaus High, whose Greyhounds were historically one of the best high school baseball teams, closed in 1981. The profile of urban Catholic school students reflected the diverse populations present in the city. As far as sports went, there were fewer school teams in the city, so more high school football games were played against schools outside the Catholic League and, increasingly, against public schools. Detroit De La Salle moved to Warren in 1982, while Detroit Catholic Central moved to Redford in 1978 and then to Novi in 2005.

1989
Catholic High School League Champions
I think I can.

Brother Rice was ready to go in 1989. Bob Utter and Pete Mitchell were the offensive stars, supported by Steve Morrison and Gannon Dudlar on defense. The season started with three consecutive shutout victories over Flint Powers Catholic, Ypsilanti, and Connellsville (Pa.). The Catholic League's Central Division play began with victories over Notre Dame (28-15) and De La Salle (49-6).

Rice's next game loomed large: Their opponent would be the undefeated Catholic Central Shamrocks in the 45th Boys' Bowl game at Wisner Stadium. Catholic Central had a five-game winning streak against Coach Fracassa's squad. "There have been some real tough losses," Fracassa told Mick McCabe, of the *Detroit Free Press*. "They've been very, very close; there haven't been any runaways. And I expect it to be close again." This time, the Warriors could breathe easy, as they won 31-14. Utter completed 11 of 17 passes for 151 yards; six of those passes were to Pete Mitchell, for 107 yards. "Yes, I'm relieved," Coach Fracassa said to McCabe after the game.

The rest of the Catholic League regular season went well, with victories over Bishop Gallagher and Covenant. The Prep Bowl Catholic League Championship Game at the Pontiac Silverdome was a 36-7 victory over Aquinas.

The MHSAA playoffs began with wins over Detroit's Mackenzie High School and Westland's John Glenn High School. The semifinal game against Detroit Martin Luther King was a devastating 6-0 loss for Rice. King went on to lose the MHSAA Class A final to Muskegon, 16-13.

In 1989, Utter completed 92 of 139 passes — a 66 percent completion rate that ranks third for a single season in Brother Rice history. His career 60.5 percent completion rate (193-319) is fourth all-time. Coach Fracassa noted: "Bob has the quickest feet of any quarterback we've had. He can drop back and pass, he can roll out, and he can run the option. Heck, he can even run the quarterback sneak for a lot of yards." Utter was awarded All-Catholic and All-State team honors. Despite being just 5'11" and 173 pounds, he went on to an NCAA Division 1 college career with Iowa State. In his four years there, he played 26 games and completed 165 of 283 passes for 2,302 yards and 10 touchdowns. He ran for 615 yards in 230 attempts and scored nine rushing touchdowns.

Steve Morrison was an elite linebacker/running back, but he also booted a 72-yard punt against Catholic Central, the second-longest in Rice history. His season punting average of 40.8 yards is tied for fourth all time.

STEVE MORRISON AND GANNON DUDLAR

The 1989 season was the last year at Brother Rice for Steve Morrison. He was an All-Catholic and an All-State team performer his senior year, as well

Steve Morrison

as an All-American high school lacrosse player — along with Gannon Dudlar, his defensive football team comrade. When it came to football, Dudlar was an All-Catholic team member along with Morrison, Bob Utter, and Pete Mitchell. Morrison and Dudlar, friends on and off the field, decided to attend the University of Michigan together.

Morrison injured his leg during his freshman year and earned a medical redshirt season from the NCAA, allowing him to become a five-year varsity letter-winner. He played inside linebacker for the Wolverines and was the 1992 winner of the Roger Zatkoff Award as the team's best linebacker. In 1994, he was a team captain and was an All-Big Ten team selection. He finished his college career with

220 tackles (third all-time for the Wolverines at that time) and eight interceptions. He was a semifinalist for the Dick Butkus Award, given to the best linebacker in the country.

During his time with the Wolverines, Morrison met a U of M women's softball player, Mary Campana, the daughter of Falco Campana, one of the

Dr. Gannon Dudlar

"Italian mafia" backfield from Coach Fracassa's Northeastern High School years. After dating for a while, the now-married couple discovered their "small world" connection with Fracassa.

Morrison wasn't chosen in the NFL draft but signed as a free agent with the NFL Indianapolis Colts. In four years, he played in 58 games and started in 29. Like many of Coach Fracassa's players, Morrison eventually went into coaching — first at Brother Rice, followed by Michigan. He also had stints at Western Michigan, Eastern Michigan, and

Syracuse (N.Y.), and is currently associate head coach at Bowling Green State University in Ohio.

Dudlar had an impressive career with the Wolverines. He followed Morrison as the Roger Zatloff Award winner in 1993. In addition to playing football, he managed to continue his impressive lacrosse career, which he enjoyed on the club level at U of M. His father, who played football at Arizona State University, and his brother, Gunner, who played at Richmond University, thought a shot at the NFL might be in Gannon's future, but he took advantage of his educational opportunities and opted for medical school. Dudlar was a three-year varsity letter-winner and was the Wolverines' Athletic Academic Achievement Award recipient in 1993. He graduated from the University of Michigan Medical School and works as an emergency medicine physician in San Francisco.

PETE MITCHELL

Pete Mitchell had a nice career at Brother Rice, with 83 receptions for 1,150 yards and 13 touchdowns. He was on the All-Catholic and All-Metro teams following his senior year. Although he wasn't recruited by some of the well-known NCAA Division 1 football powerhouses, he was heavily recruited by Boston College — not by the coaching staff, necessarily, but by the Brennan brothers.

Pete Mitchell

Brian Brennan was an All-American in 1983 for BC and later played in the NFL. His younger brother, Charlie, was making a name for himself as a defensive back for BC. Both men were former Warrior football players under Coach Fracassa. Matt Metz, of the 1987 Brother Rice team, was another Warrior who made Boston College his NCAA choice.

Mitchell accepted an athletic scholarship at Boston College and played four years as a tight end. He was on one All-America team as a junior and was a consensus NCAA college All-American in his senior year. In his BC career, he caught 190 passes for 2,388 yards and 20 touchdowns. His BC jersey number, 82, was retired, and in 2019 he was nominated for membership in the College Football Hall of Fame, which he entered in 2021.

Post-college, Mitchell was drafted by the NFL Jacksonville Jaguars. His most productive years in professional football were the first four years at Jacksonville, and the following year with the New York Giants. He spent the next two years with the Detroit Lions. His NFL career included 114 games, 279 receptions for 2,885 yards, 160 first downs, and 15 touchdowns.

Mitchell nominated Coach Fracassa for the Don Shula NFL High School Football Coach of the Year Award in 1997. "Coach Fracassa was like a second father to me," Mitchell said. "If you ask any athlete who played for Coach Fracassa, they will probably tell you he was one of the most influential people in their lives. He taught me more than the game of football; he taught me the game of life."

The 1990s

1990

MHSAA Class A State Champions

Count on me.

The enthusiasm for the MHSAA playoffs and the excitement the games generated led to a big change in 1990. The number of teams included in the playoffs doubled when the decision was made to double the number of classes (which were still based on a school's total student enrollment). Instead of four classes (A, B, C, and D), there would now be eight classes: A, AA, B, BB, C, CC, D, and DD. The number of teams participating jumped to 128, and there were regional, quarterfinal, semifinal, and championship games in all eight classes.

What does a football coach do when many of his high-quality players graduate in the same year? Coach Fracassa didn't let himself dwell on the players he had lost, but focused on the players he still had on his team. First, the Warriors had a solid quarterback in Steven Merchant. Second, they had a leader on the defensive side: co-captain Kevin Kalczynski, a second-team All-Catholic League linebacker. The season started with a 35-14 win over Niles High School, in which Merchant had 10 completions on 10 pass attempts. The next game was a 16-7 loss to Ypsilanti. Next up was a 19-6 win over Henry Ford, to finish the games with the public schools. The 1990 Warriors had a strong start to the Catholic League Central Division schedule, beating Divine Child (14-12) and Notre Dame (17-13).

Coach Fracassa and his Warriors had a 4-1 record going into the Boys' Bowl match-up, where their opponent was Catholic Central, which had a 3-2 record. Catholic Central managed to shut down the Rice offense, winning a 32-0 blowout. The previous year, Fracassa had said "This is a big game, but you're not going to die if you lose. But when you lose, you die a little bit. If you don't, why coach?"

A coach can be challenged by an inexperienced team that suffers a big loss. It's important to make needed changes, but not let the team lose confidence. Coach Fracassa, who was remarkable at walking this line, dug down deep and asked his players to do the same. The Warriors won their next game against De La Salle, 21-7, and finished up the Catholic League regular season games with a 17-8 win over U-D Jesuit. Kevin Cook made a critical 45-yard field goal in that game. Brother Rice beat Redford Covenant 17-6 to finish the early season with a 7-2 record, but their loss to Catholic Central kept them out of the Prep Bowl.

The Warriors entered the MHSAA playoffs in the new Class A bracket. The sectional game, a 35-12 win over Royal Oak Dondero, was followed by a regional game victory over Bloomfield Hills Lahser (28-6) and a semifinal win over Northville High (14-7). Jonathan Burtraw ran the ball 40 times — a school record — in the semifinal game.

The first MHSAA Class A Championship Game at the Pontiac Silverdome had Brother Rice facing Midland High School. The game was tied 10-10 at the beginning of the fourth quarter. Michael Moran, who had a previous sack for a safety, blocked a Midland field goal attempt — and momentum shifted to the Warriors' side. Burtraw had touchdown runs of 12 yards and 23 yards in the fourth quarter, sealing the Warriors' 24-10 MHSAA Championship victory. Senior co-captains and defensive standouts Kalczynski, Jason Randall, and Dean Polce were named to the All-Catholic team for their efforts. Kalczynski's 187 tackles rank third all-time at Rice for a single season. His 291 career tackles are fourth all-time.

The Warriors' nemesis, Catholic Central, won the Prep Bowl 31-0 over St. Martin DePorres. The Catholic Central Shamrocks also won the first MHSAA Class AA Championship over Martin Luther King, 21-0. Although the rules had changed, the Warrior-Shamrock rivalry continued.

1991

Pain is temporary, victory is forever.

Quarterback Steve Merchant returned in '91, along with receiver Matt Allen, running back Marcus Harvey on offense, and linebacker co-captain Damon McClendon leading the defense. This season began with a pair of losses. The first, a 32-0 blowout, came at the hands of Farmington Hills Harrison High. Harrison was coached by John Herrington, who would guide his teams to the MHSAA playoffs frequently over the years. The next loss was to Ypsilanti, 7-6. The first win of the season was against Henry Ford, 25-6.

The season's Catholic League play included victories over Divine Child (25-14) and Notre Dame (28-0). Catholic Central handed Rice another loss, with a final score of 35-7. Wins over De La Salle (17-7) and U-D Jesuit (6-0) ended league play. The Warriors failed to qualify for the 1991 Prep Bowl, which saw St. Martin DePorres beat Catholic Central, 16-15, at the Pontiac Silverdome.

To determine eligibility for the Class A, Region 4 MHSAA playoffs, the Warriors faced a key game against Saginaw's Nouvel Catholic. Merchant completed a 66-yard pass to Jason Snooks, while Harvey ran for 196 yards on 25 carries and scored two touchdowns. Harvey broke a halftime tie with a 77-yard touchdown sprint to begin the second half, and Rice prevailed 35-7.

The Warriors beat the Seaholm Maples in the sectional game (14-7) and took out Fraser in the regional match-up (21-0). In the semifinal against Ypsilanti, the Warriors prevailed, 21-14.

The 1991 MHSAA Class A Championship Game was a battle between Brother Rice and East Lansing, and East Lansing pulled out a 14-0 victory. Meanwhile, Catholic Central lost a tight Class AA Championship Game to Saginaw Arthur Hill, 13-12.

1992

Attitude.

The next season was a rebuilding year for the Brother Rice Warriors. Marcus Harvey, now a junior, returned in the running back position, while sophomore Derek Canine was chosen to start at quarterback. Junior David Ewing would be blocking, and senior co-captain Jason Snooks returned as a receiver. In the 1992 season, Snooks averaged 31.7 yards per kickoff return over nine games to rank fifth all-time for Rice.

Brian Kalczynski, a junior, would be leading the defense from his secondary position.

The season's first two games were wins over Detroit's Martin Luther King (14-6) and Ypsilanti (17-7). The victories were followed by a 7-0 loss to Traverse City Central. Catholic League play began with a 28-0 victory over the AA Division's Divine Child.

In the first game of the Catholic League's Central Division, the Warriors posted a 48-20 victory over Notre Dame, but they lost their next two Catholic League games to Catholic Central (14-7) and De La Salle (33-14). They beat U-D Jesuit (34-12) and Fordson (9-3).

The two Catholic League Central Division losses eliminated the Warriors from the Prep Bowl, which Catholic Central won over St. Martin DePorres, 17-6. The team's 6-3 record also eliminated the Warriors from the MHSAA playoffs. Catholic Central avenged the previous year's loss to Saginaw Arthur Hill with a close 21-20 win in the MHSAA Class AA Championship Game. Muskegon Reeths-Puffer High beat Walled Lake Western, 21-18, to claim the 1992 MHSAA Class A title.

1993

Ever to excel.

Coach Fracassa was always quiet, dignified, respectful, and magnanimous in his undefeated championship seasons. In the seasons that fell short of those achievements, he was also quiet, dignified, respectful, and magnanimous. He said nice things about his opponents and nice things about his players every season, regardless of the outcome.

In 1993, the Warriors had several stars returning, including Marcus Harvey, Dan Gibbons, Brian Kalczynski, Marty Weymouth, and David Ewing. Derek Canine returned as a more seasoned junior quarterback. And then there was Willis Marshall, who was a tremendous all-around athlete. An article in the *Detroit Free Press* noted: "In the late '70s and early '80s, Brother Rice was the dominant team in the state. Well, the Warriors are back."

The season started on a high note, with wins over Martin Luther King, 27-0; Sandusky (Ohio) High, 20-14; and Traverse City Central, 14-3. Divine Child was the Catholic League Division AA match-up and the Warriors beat them, 9-7.

The Catholic League Central Division play began with a 27-6 win over Notre Dame. In a Boys' Bowl meeting with Catholic Central, the Warriors experienced their first loss of the season, 17-7. It was the school's fourth loss to Catholic Central in as many years. The following game was another loss, this time to De La Salle, 25-7. In the Warriors' last Catholic League regular season game of 1993, they rolled to a 42-0 win over U-D Jesuit. The Warriors were eliminated from the Prep Bowl, where the Catholic League Championship was won by Catholic Central over Bishop Gallagher, 35-0.

Next up for the Warriors was a meeting with Farmington Harrison High.

In this game, the Warriors bested Harrison by a score of 35-0. The victory earned them a spot in the MHSAA playoffs. The first sectional game was with the Maples of Seaholm High School. In a closely contested game, Seaholm edged the Warriors, 14-13, to extinguish their playoff aspirations. Harrison, whom the Warriors had trounced during the season, won the MHSAA Class A State Championship over Midland's Dow High School, 12-9.

After graduation the following spring, Harvey attended Ball State University, where he was a wide receiver. Gibbons headed to Ohio State University as an offensive tackle. Kalczynski played baseball for the University of Michigan, while Weymouth was drafted by the Seattle Mariners and joined their minor league affiliate in Arizona. Marshall went to Youngstown State University in (Ohio) and played football for 15 more years. Marcus Harvey would finish his career with the most rushing attempts (670) in Rice history and was tied for first in touchdowns with 40. His 3,516 yards rushing are second all-time.

WILLIS MARSHALL

Willis Marshall was another multisport athlete who competed in football, basketball, and track at Brother Rice. He was a freshman on the 1990 MHSAA Class A Championship football team. When he was growing up, his favorite professional players were Walter Payton and Billy Sims. His cousin, Robert Thomas, played football for the Dallas Cowboys and the Arena Football League's Georgia Force.

Marshall attended NCAA Division I-AA Youngstown State University, where his coach was Jim Tressel, who would later coach the Ohio State University Buckeyes. The Youngstown State University Penguins won the NCAA Division I-AA Championship in 1993, 1994, and 1997.

In 1994, as a freshman defensive back, Marshall recorded four tackles and one fumble recovery. In his second year he was converted to a wide receiver and caught 10 passes for 97 yards. As a junior, he caught 24 passes for 305 yards and one touchdown. He led the team in pass receptions, with 40 in his senior year. He accounted for 490 yards and one touchdown for a team that won the NCAA Division I-AA Championship Game.

Marshall wasn't drafted by an NFL team and decided to try the Canadian Football League. He played for two years with the

Willis Marshall

Calgary Stampeders and was on the Grey Cup-winning Canadian League Championship team in 1998. The quarterback of the Stampeders in 1998 was Jeff Garcia, a future NFL player. For the Calgary team, Marshall played in 10 games and had 18 receptions for 161 yards, returned six punts for 112 yards, and had two tackles on defense.

In 2001, he moved on to the Arena Football League, where he had an impressive nine-year career. He started with the Grand Rapids Rampage, where he was named to the Second Team All-Arena Team in 2002. He then moved to the Colorado Crush. In 2005, Marshall was named to the Arena Football League All-Ironman Team for his yeoman work on offense and defense. The Crush won the ArenaBowl XIX, 51-48, over the Georgia Force, and Marshall was named the ArenaBowl's Most Valuable Player, as well as the ArenaBowl Ironman. In 2006, he was named to the Arena Football League All-Ironman Team for his two-way play for the Colorado Crush. In the Arena Football League, Marshall had 646 pass receptions for 7,223 yards and 95 touchdowns, returned 356 kicks for 6,709 yards, and recorded 207 tackles. He was an Arena League Football "Ironman."

On his business website, Marshall has a personal life credo that Coach Fracassa would approve of: "Faith-driven entrepreneur with a firm belief that the difficult things in life only take a day to fix and the impossible within a week."

1994

Character, discipline, team, tradition.

Brother Rice had reason for optimism in 1994. Derek Canine had thrown for more than 1,000 yards in each of the prior two seasons, Sean Regan was a force on the offensive line, and Walter Jenkins was at linebacker. The teammates were tri-captains for the 1994 Warriors team.

Brother Rice's season opener was against MHSAA Class A Champion Farmington Hills Harrison. Rice pulled out a 28-21 victory. They followed with a win over Sandusky (Ohio), 28-6. Providence Catholic (Ill.) was next, and they prevailed over Rice by a score of 59-30.

Catholic Central's division play began with a win over Notre Dame (35-6), followed by a non-league victory over St. Martin DePorres (28-22). Sophomore Ben Rowden had a school record-tying three touchdown receptions in the game. The next league win was over U-D Jesuit, 35-0, which set up the Boys' Bowl game against Catholic Central at Pontiac's Wisner Stadium. The Warriors at long last ended the Shamrocks' four-year stranglehold on the Boys' Bowl title by pulling out a 21-14 victory.

Unfortunately, the Warriors' Catholic League winning streak ended with a 17-14 loss to De La Salle. Although the next game was a 28-0 shutout win over East Catholic High, De La Salle had knocked the Warriors out of the Prep Bowl Catholic League Championship Game. Orchard Lake St. Mary beat De La Salle, 21-7, at the Pontiac Silverdome. Their team was led by Dave Bowens, who would play for Eastern Illinois University followed by 11 years with the NFL.

In 1994, Brother Rice made the MHSAA Class A playoffs. Their first opponent in the sectional game was Berkley High School. In a close contest, Canine completed 24 passes; 14 of those were to Dave Sofran, an emerging star receiver. Berkley squeezed out a 20-19 victory, thereby eliminating the Warriors from further contention. Harrison, a team the Warriors had beaten in the first game of the season, went on to win the MHSAA Class A Championship once again by beating Grand Rapids Forest Hills Central High, 17-13.

Canine finished the season with 130 pass completions on 201 attempts, for 1,506 yards and 17 touchdowns. He would finish his career with a 61.7 percent completion percentage, second all-time for Rice. Sofran caught 59 of those passes (third all-time) for 722 yards and six touchdowns. Jenkins had 64 solo tackles, 20 assists, and four sacks from his linebacker position in his senior year. He went on to play football at Central Michigan University, where he was a three-year letterman. He accounted for 33 tackles from his defensive end position.

1995

Unity is strength.

By 1995, the Detroit Catholic Football League was having difficulty arranging three non-league games prior to league play. The Central Division would no longer exist. The new leagues, Central East and Central West, would consist of two Class A or AA teams, two Class B or BB teams, and one Class C or CC team. This decreased the number of games before league play from three to two.

There would be two "crossover games," allowing the Central East Division's Brother Rice to play the Central West Division's Catholic Central and U-D Jesuit each year, setting up two possible games per year between the Warriors and the Shamrocks. They would meet in the Boys' Bowl, as they had done in the past, and there was a high likelihood that both would also make it to the Prep Bowl.

Catholic Central's head coach, Tom Mach, said: "Not too many people have to play their archrival twice. I think our schedule just got tougher. Getting into the state playoffs after that is going to be a tough act." Coach Fracassa agreed that the teams' schedules had gotten tougher.

The Warriors looked forward to the 1995 season with junior running back Brian Marshall and junior quarterback Eric Marcy. The team captains included Dave Sofran, Joe Kalczynski, Kris Sava, and Tim Craddock.

The season started well, with a 16-14 victory over Farmington Harrison, the previous year's MHSAA Class A Champions. That was followed by a 35-14 win over Terra Haute (Ind.) North Vigo High. The Warriors' first Catholic League game was a meeting with the Central West Division's U-D Jesuit; Brother Rice won the game, 34-0.

The team's first Central East Division opponent was Bishop Gallagher. Brother Rice prevailed, 28-12. This set up a crossover, non-league Boys' Bowl Game with the Catholic Central Shamrocks, which was played at Pontiac's Wisner Stadium. The Shamrocks won the meeting, 26-23, over the Warriors.

The Warriors won their next three Catholic League Central Division East games over Notre Dame (34-21), De La Salle (20-0), and Bishop Foley (28-14), to finish undefeated in the newly created Central East Division and earned a spot in the Catholic League Championship Prep Bowl Game at the Pontiac Silverdome.

Brother Rice's opponent in the Prep Bowl was a well-known foe: Catholic Central. The Warriors fell to the Shamrocks, 17-7. The pair of losses to their archrivals eliminated them from MHSAA Class A State playoffs, bringing to fruition the "tougher schedule" scenario that both Coach Fracassa and Coach Mach had predicted. The Shamrocks went undefeated in 1995 and won the MHSAA Class AA Championship Game over Holt High, 24-0.

Following graduation, Sofran played college football at Northeastern University in Boston. Later, he would coach at Brother Rice following Coach Fracassa's retirement. His teammate, Joe Kalczynski, played baseball in college like his brother, Brian, had done. Joe, a Michigan State University Spartan, was drafted by the Arizona Diamondbacks.

RON KALCZYNSKI AND MIKE POPSON

Two Brother Rice assistant coaches have been honored, along with Coach Fracassa, by being inducted into the Detroit Catholic High School League Hall of Fame. Fracassa was inducted in 1980; Mike Popson, his offensive line coach, entered the Hall of Fame in 1981; and his defensive coordinator, Ron Kalczynski, known as "Coach Kal," was inducted in 1985.

Kalczynski arrived at Brother Rice in 1973 and taught algebra, English, religion, and American and world history. He was an assistant football coach with the Warriors for 18 years. In 1990, he was named an Assistant Football Coach of the Year by the MHSAA. "I know what Ron's doing, but I don't know what he's doing — does that make sense?" Fracassa once said. "We play good defense; we can match up with anybody. That's because of Ron."

In 1982, Coach Kal became head coach of the Warriors baseball team. He guided them to the Michigan State Championships in 1992 and 1994, and they won the Catholic High School League Championship in 1996. Kalczynski coached his sons, Brian and Joe, when they were on the diamond. He stepped down as the head baseball coach after the 1997 season, to

Coaches (from left): Mike Popson, Harold Burkholder, Albert Fracassa, Charles Elmquist.

watch Brian play at the University of Michigan and Joe play at Michigan State. His oldest son, Kevin, had been one of the football stalwarts for the Warriors, while his youngest son, Tim, played baseball for Coach Bob Riker in 2004. His only daughter, Colleen, attended Marian High School and later played softball at Case Western Reserve University. Coach Kal was inducted into the Michigan High School Baseball Coaches Association Hall of Fame in 2000.

"I enjoyed coaching with Al because he reinforced the things I believed in," Coach Kal said. "One of Al's greatest qualities is his ability to be positive around his players. He enjoys what he does, and that rubs off on the players. It's not a job for him, it's a calling."

Mike Popson was a biology teacher at Brother Rice for 29 years. He served as offensive line coach for the football team, and coached track and field. He took over as athletic director at the high school in 1982. The Detroit Catholic High School League named him their Person of the Year in 2001 and Athletic Director of the Year in 2003. His four sons, like Coach Kal's, attended Brother Rice, and like Colleen Kalczynski, Popson's only daughter attended Marian.

How far will an assistant coach go to support a head coach? There's a story that Coach Fracassa and Coach Kal once took a road trip to Barberton, Ohio, to scout an upcoming opponent. They were running late so Coach Fracassa, who was driving, was happy to see a parking spot near a tall fence close to the stadium. As they parked their car, they noticed a large German shepherd with a wrought iron collar chained to the fence. Hesitating to get out of the car, Coach Fracassa decided to delegate: "Hey, Ron, why don't you go and see how long that chain is?" Coach Kal, in no uncertain terms, informed Fracassa, "Heck, no. Are you crazy?" They decided to find another place to park.

1996

Keep fighting.

Brother Rice headed into the 1996 season as one of the favorites to win the MHSAA Class A title. The talent on the offensive side of the ball was impressive, with running backs Brian Marshall and Ben Rowden, quarterback Eric Marcy, and wide receivers Aniema Ubom and David Matthews. The two losses to Catholic Central the year before still hurt.

The season-starting games were both victories. The first was a 35-20 win over Grand Rapids East Kentwood High, and the second was a 10-0 shutout over Toledo (Ohio) St. Francis de Sales. The first Central West crossover game was a 27-8 victory over U-D Jesuit.

The Warriors' first Catholic League Central East game was against Bishop Gallagher, featuring standout brothers Julius and Markus Curry. Both players were defensive backs who went on to play for the University of Michigan and the NFL (Julius for the Detroit Lions, Markus for the San Diego Chargers). The Warriors dug deep and prevailed in the tight game, 6-0.

Although it was a Catholic League crossover game, the Boys' Bowl loomed large on the schedule. In 1996, the Warriors finally emerged from Pontiac Wisner Stadium with a 21-14 win over the Catholic Central Shamrocks.

The Warriors ran the table in the Catholic League Central East Division, with victories over Notre Dame (31-6), De La Salle (24-7), and Bishop Foley (28-7). The team's winning streak reached eight games, and they were ranked No.1 in Class A in the state. Brother Rice represented Central East in the Prep Bowl Catholic High School Championship, where they again faced Catholic Central. This time, the Shamrocks beat the Warriors, 28-0, at the Pontiac Silverdome.

In spite of their Prep Bowl loss, the Warriors made the MHSAA Class A playoffs. In the sectionals, they faced Grosse Pointe North. The game was a high-scoring affair: Marcy completed 26 of 38 passes, including 11 completions for three touchdowns to Matthews. Although the Warriors put their heart into the game, Grosse Pointe North won, 35-31.

One of the stars on the team was Marshall, the Warriors' running back. On the season, he rushed 216 times for 1,243 yards and 14 touchdowns. All totaled, Marshall had 40 career touchdowns for Brother Rice and is tied for first all-time. His 3,808 career rushing yards at Rice are No. 1 all-time. He attended Northwestern University, where he played for three years as a running back and kick-returner. In an interesting 2019 article that appeared in *USA Today*, it was reported that Marshall's seventh-grade, quarterback-playing son, Isaiah, had been offered a (non-binding) scholarship by Coach Jim Harbaugh of the University of Michigan Wolverines. "He's still a kid and we keep him pretty grounded," Marshall said.

1997

National Football League High School Coach of the Year

Carpe diem.

The National Football League High School Coach of the Year Award was created to honor coaches who profoundly impacted the athletic and personal development of NFL players. One coach is nominated by players from each of the NFL teams. In 1997, Coach Fracassa was nominated by Pete Mitchell, a tight end in his third year with the Jacksonville Jaguars who had played college football for Boston College after graduating from Brother Rice. Fracassa was asked to fill out a questionnaire and was vetted by a panel including Paul Tagliabue, the NFL's commissioner.

Fracassa was selected as a finalist, along with four others. He didn't find out he had won the award until the final Monday Night Football telecast of the season. Each of the five finalists had taped a video and had to wait to see whose video would be played on national TV. Sure enough, the Fracassa video aired; the 1997 NFL High School Coach of the Year was Al Fracassa of Birmingham Brother Rice.

Coach Fracassa was invited to attend the Super Bowl as a guest of the NFL. With his wife, Phyllis, he traveled to San Diego for the game between the Green Bay Packers and the Denver Broncos. One of his former Brother Rice Warriors, Mike Lodish, was playing for the Broncos. Fracassa was given a $5,000 cash award, and the Brother Rice football program received a $10,000 grant.

"I believe the greatest task a coach has is striving to bring his team together as a unit," Coach Fracassa said that night to reporters. "Each player, regardless of his ability, is part of the team. Teaching young players to play hard and by the rules is what sportsmanship is all about, because character is what really counts in life."

In 2009, Coach Fracassa was again a finalist for the NFL High School Football Coach of the Year Award. This time he was nominated by T.J. Lang of the Green Bay Packers, a 2005 Brother Rice graduate. Fracassa didn't win that year, but each finalist was given a $2,500 cash award and a $5,000 grant for their high school football program.

When speaking about the 2009 award, the new NFL commissioner, Roger Goodell, said: "The one thing [the NFL players] all have in common is that they received guidance and learned important life lessons from their high school coaches. These five finalists have dedicated their lives to teaching young players how to become leaders both on and off the field, and we congratulate them and all high school coaches for the roles they play."

In 1997, talented players had graduated and left the team, and new talent had to be brought on board. The tri-captains were Jason Barrios, Karl Pawlewicz, and Jamyon Small. The new quarterback was Pat Craddock. The first game was a win over Henry Ford, 24-12; the second was a 15-10 loss to St. Francis de Sales of Toledo, Ohio.

U-D Jesuit fell to the Warriors, 35-0, in the Central East vs. Central West crossover game, which began Catholic League play. The first Catholic League Central East Division game was a 14-0 win over St. Martin DePorres.

The next game of 1997 was another crossover game, the Boys' Bowl, played at Pontiac Wisner Stadium against an old foe: the Catholic Central Shamrocks. It was another close game and the Shamrocks again prevailed over the Warriors, 14-12.

It would be the last Boys' Bowl game for several years. A fight broke out at halftime between the avid supporters of both teams. Coach Fracassa told a reporter from the *Detroit Free Press*: "The hate was not there between the players. We've had clean games."

The next two Catholic League Central East games were victories over Notre Dame (28-0) and De La Salle (27-7). The final Central East league game was played against Bishop Foley; Foley won the tight contest, 7-6. The final game of the regular season for Brother Rice was a 21-19 victory over South Lyon, leaving the Warriors with a 6-3 overall record — which eliminated the squad from the Catholic League Championship Prep Bowl and the MHSAA Class A playoffs.

St. Martin DePorres won the Prep Bowl over Bishop Foley, 20-6, and Catholic Central captured the MHSAA Class AA Championship over Ann Arbor Huron with a final score of 27-7. Harrison beat Midland Dow, 21-6, to take the MHSAA Class A title.

FARMINGTON HILLS HARRISON HIGH SCHOOL

Whenever Brother Rice wasn't winning the MHSAA Class A Championship Game, Harrison was. The public magnet high school opened in 1970 and was named for Gerald V. Harrison, the superintendent of the Farmington Public Schools from 1957 to 1967 — a period of dramatic growth in the school district. The school's first graduating class was in 1972, but the school closed in 2019, less than 50 years later, due to a fall in the student population in the city of Farmington Hills.

Coach John Herrington started the Harrison Hawks football program in 1970. In his 48 years as head coach, his teams captured a record 13 MHSAA state championships in 18 title appearances, including five consecutive championships from 1997 to 2001. The school's enrollment would shift the MHSAA classification to Class A (Class 2) and Class BB (Class 3) from season to season. Coach Herrington's Hawks team faced Coach Fracassa's Warriors squad on eight occasions and won the first match-up in 1991 and the second-to-last meeting in 2010. Harrison had several players who went on to play in the NFL, including Devin Funchess (University of Michigan, Carolina Panthers), Drew Stanton (Michigan State University, Detroit Lions), Aaron Burbridge (Michigan State University, San Francisco 49ers), Chris Roberson (Eastern Michigan University, Jacksonville Jaguars), Nick Luchey (University of Miami, Cincinnati Bengals), John Miller (Michigan State University, Detroit Lions), and Michael Ojemudia (University of Iowa, Denver Broncos). In 2020, Mick McCabe, of the *Detroit Free Press*, ranked the 2000 Hawks among his top five high school football teams in the Detroit metro area in the last 50 years.

Although Coach Fracassa retired as the winningest coach in Michigan high school football, Coach Herrington eventually surpassed him. Herrington's teams posted 443 wins, compared to Fracassa's 430 wins. Herrington also had 34 consecutive winning seasons (No. 4 in the state), compared with Fracassa's 32-year run (No. 8 in the state), and Herrington's teams had a .800 winning percentage (No. 7 in the state).

Coach Fracassa held the record for the highest win total for a high school head coach in Michigan from 2008 to 2017. Marty Budner, of the Hometown Life group of newspapers, reported on a meeting in 2017 between the two coaching giants, when Herrington was about to surpass Fracassa's total. Coach Fracassa, as gracious as ever, said, "It was nice, you know, for a while, but records are made to be broken." He added, "When you have a gentleman like John Herrington breaking your record, you don't mind it. I'm happy that it happened and it's John's turn."

Coach Herrington said, "When I think of Al, I don't think of how many wins he had. I think about how his players reacted to his coaching and how they still react to him all the time. And I hope I'm remembered in the same way once my career is done."

1998

Stay strong.

Coach Fracassa would likely rank 1998 as one of the best years of his career. For starters, he was relieved of his classroom teaching responsibilities at Brother Rice. "Do you believe this?" he said to a *Detroit Free Press* reporter. "It's going to be like college. I'll go and work on my film and coach. It will be all football. I'm going to enjoy this part of my life."

In the fall of 1998, the Warriors had Pat Craddock at quarterback, with Mark Goebel and Mike Scott running the ball. Brooks Hartnett anchored the defense. The season started with two victories over non-league opponents: Grand Rapids East Kentwood fell 26-6, and a tough Toledo (Ohio) St. Francis de Sales team battled all the way before the Warriors won by a point, 14-13.

99

The next game was a Catholic League Central East vs. Central West cross-over game with Catholic Central. It wasn't a Boys' Bowl game, as that series had been canceled, but the Shamrocks' Coach Tom Mach said, "The rivalry hasn't stopped just because it's not being called the Boys' Bowl." The Shamrocks won the game, 35-14, over the Warriors.

The Catholic League Central East Division season started well with wins over De La Salle (14-9), Bishop Foley (28-6), and Notre Dame (35-0). There was also a low-scoring crossover game victory over St. Martin DePorres, 3-0. The DePorres team thrived on taking on traditional powers like Rice and Catholic Central, and when teams played St. Martin DePorres, they knew they were in for a battle against a determined and talented opponent.

As the season was drawing to a close, the 6-1 Warriors met a new Catholic League Central East Division opponent: Orchard Lake St. Mary's Prep. St. Mary's won the match-up, 34-13. Even though the last game of the season was a non-league 41-14 victory over a fine Rockford team, the Warriors' 7-1 record meant they were eliminated from both the Prep Bowl and the MHSAA Class A playoffs.

In the Catholic League Championship Prep Bowl at the Pontiac Silverdome, Catholic Central pulled off a win over Orchard Lake St. Mary's, 22-15. Rockford qualified for the MHSAA Class AA playoffs despite its loss to Brother Rice, as the team had outscored three high-quality playoff opponents (Jenison, Midland, and Lake Orion) by a whopping 114-21. And it was none other than Catholic Central that nipped Rockford, 27-23, in the Class AA Championship Game. It was a classic illustration of the strength of the Detroit Catholic League and its two traditional powers, Catholic Central and Brother Rice. Another traditional powerhouse, Farmington Hills Harrison, won the MHSAA Class A title over Hudsonville, 35-14.

JOHN JAMES

John James was a member of the defensive line for Brother Rice during the 1998 season. After graduation, he was awarded a position at the United States Military Academy at West Point. James graduated from West Point in 2004 with a Bachelor of Science degree in legal studies, and then served eight years in the army. He participated in multiple tours of duty during Operation Iraqi Freedom as an AH-64 Apache helicopter pilot, then attended Ranger School and became a ranger-qualified aviation officer. He reached the rank of captain and returned to civilian life in 2012.

After his military career, James received his master's degree in supply chain management from Pennsylvania State University's Smeal College of Business. He then obtained a master's degree in business administration from the Ross School of Business at the University of Michigan. James joined the James

Group International, a global supply chain management service company. He became its director of operations, and then president. He's also the CEO of Renaissance Global Logistics, a subsidiary based in Detroit.

In 2018, James decided to run for the U.S. Senate. He won the Republican primary election but lost the general election. He ran in 2020, as well, but lost a hotly contested election.

In 2022, James declared his candidacy for the United States House of Representatives in the newly drawn

John James

10th congressional district in Michigan, and he turned to his former coach for assistance. Fracassa was featured in James' first television ad of the political campaign and said: "From the time I coached him in high school, I knew John James had something special, but it wasn't in football." Coach complimented John James on his military service and business acumen and, as the spot came to a neat conclusion, Fracassa noted that James is still "coachable."

Rep. John Edward James assumed office as a member of the U.S. House of Representatives on Jan. 3, 2023.

1999

The power of teamwork.

Looking at Rice's exclusion from the state playoffs in 1998 with an 8-1 record and a 41-14 win over Class AA finalist Rockford, one had to be puzzled by the state playoffs selection methodology. And sure enough, in 1999 the MHSAA expanded the playoffs to 256 teams in eight divisions. All six-win teams would automatically qualify, as would all five-win teams playing an eight-game season. To fill out the brackets, five-win/four-loss teams and four-win/three-loss teams would be added based on playoff points. Class AA teams would be called Division 1, Class A would be Division 2, Class BB would be Division 3, Class B would be Division 4, Class CC would be Division 5, Class C would be Division 6, Class DD would be Division 7, and Class D would be called Division 8.

As a new season began, the Warriors opened with a win over Sterling Heights, 28-7. Tony Gioutsos set a school record with five quarterback sacks for the season, and Gioutsos and Mark Goebel formed a dynamic running back combination. Goebel's 1,585 yards rushing for a season and 2,804 yards rushing for his career are both ranked as third all-time at Brother Rice. The 1999 season would also see an 85-yard touchdown pass reception by Brendan Hart (ninth longest all-time) and outstanding punting from Mark Mueller. Defensive lineman Garret Weston was a powerful presence all season long, and Matt Baker was the squad's junior quarterback. The Warriors' second game was played against the Chicago Brother Rice High School Crusaders. As the *Detroit Free Press* noted, "Brother Rice, you can't lose!" But one of them had to, and the team from Chicago lost this one, 28-7.

The next game was a Catholic League Central East Division vs. Central West Division contest between Brother Rice and Catholic Central. "Catholic Central is big and powerful," Coach Fracassa told the *Detroit Free Press*. "I tell people they must clone their guys. They look the same every year." The Shamrock "clones" beat the Warriors in another close game, 14-10.

The Warriors' Catholic League Central East Division 1999 season was an undefeated one, with victories over De La Salle (21-19), Bishop Foley (38-19), Notre Dame (28-7), and Orchard Lake St. Mary's (63-44), sandwiched around a 28-14 win over St. Martin DePorres in a Central East vs. Central West crossover game. Against the Bishop Foley team, Goebel ran for two touchdowns, Adam Karl scored on a 76-yard end-around play, and Matt Gioutsos had a 55-yard touchdown run. When it came to the Warriors' record-setting 63-point romp over Orchard Lake St. Mary's, Tony Gioutsos scored four touchdowns on 18 carries for 153 yards, and Baker was 8 of 14, passing for two touchdowns. Afterward, Coach Fracassa asked, "Have you ever seen a game like that?"

The Catholic League Central East Division-winning 7-1 Warriors were matched against the Central West Division-winning undefeated Shamrocks in the 1999 Prep Bowl at the Pontiac Silverdome. The Shamrocks won the rematch, 31-12, over the Warriors. Despite the two losses to the previous season's MHSAA Class AA Champions, Brother Rice went on to play in the former MHSAA Class A playoffs, now renamed the Division 2 playoffs.

The Division 2 playoffs added another round to the season-ending championship run, with five wins needed to secure the title. The Warriors' pre-district game was a 20-14 win over De La Salle, followed by a 35-3 victory over Birmingham Groves. The third game's opponent was Pontiac Northern. Brother Rice prevailed, 21-20, in the regional final. Their opponent in the semifinal contest, which Brother Rice won by a score of 24-20, was U-D Jesuit, an old Catholic League Central West foe. The 1999 MHSAA Division 2 finals saw the Warriors facing the Trojans of Saginaw High School.

In what was called by the newspapers "one of the top 30 Michigan high school state finals games in 30 years," the Warriors faced a Saginaw team that would send 24 of its 37 team members on to play college football, 10 of them in Division 1. Six went on to play in the NFL, and one played for the NBA.

The game at the Pontiac Silverdome didn't fall short of expectations. Fracassa had coached against many great teams over the years and pulled off many amazing victories, but the mighty Saginaw team was on a mission, and there would be no upset for the Warriors. Saginaw scored first on a 60-yard touchdown reception by Charles Rogers, a future Michigan State Spartans star, but failed to make the extra point. The Warriors answered with a Tony Gioutsos five-yard touchdown run in the third quarter and took a 7-6 lead. The Trojans then scored on a 17-yard run and a two-point conversion by Terry Jackson, a future University of Minnesota star. Two future Michigan State Spartans sealed the Trojans' 14-7 victory: linebacker Ron Stanley, with 18 tackles, and Jeremiah McLaurin, with a late fourth-quarter pass interception.

MICHIGAN SPORTS HALL OF FAME INDUCTION

In 1999, Coach Fracassa was inducted into the Michigan Sports Hall of Fame. At the 45th annual dinner and ceremony, held at the Cobo Hall Riverview Ballroom, Fracassa and Scotty Bowman (Red Wings coach), Kirk Gibson (Michigan State University wide receiver and Detroit Tigers baseball star), Bill Laimbeer (Detroit Pistons basketball player, Detroit Shock coach), Bob Miller (Detroit Mercy baseball coach), Roger Penske (auto racing owner), and Robin Roberts (Michigan State University basketball and baseball player) joined the greats honored in the past. It was a star-studded induction class, but watching them interact you easily could have come to the conclusion that the major celebrity was Coach Fracassa. All of his fellow inductees wanted to meet him and talk to him. Fracassa accepted the honor with humble gratitude, and then went back to work.

Secret Recipe: The Scout Team

Coach Fracassa's high school coaching career spanned 57 years, and in all but the first three of those years, he served as a head coach. In that time, he won four national Coach of the Year awards, countless state Coach of the Year awards, 10 state championships, and 16 Catholic High School League championships in a league ranked by MaxPreps as the fifth toughest league in the country. On top of all that, four of his teams were ranked nationally. Without question, Coach Fracassa achieved that success, in part, because of his ability to develop exceptionally gifted athletes and to elicit from those players championship-level performances on the football field. Their names and accomplishments are amazing, from Seymour to Simpson, Hart, Goebel, Church, Lodish, Mitchell, Lang, and Alessi.

The "secret recipe" in Coach Fracassa's success can be traced to his experience as a scout-team quarterback on the great Michigan State teams of the early 1950s. Coach Fracassa built football powerhouses at both Shrine and Brother Rice by inspiring his role-players — the back-ups, the scout-team players, the young men who rarely saw game action — to perform at an exceptionally high level in practices, so the first-team players would be as prepared as possible.

"The players I enjoy most are the ones who aren't especially talented. They're not All-Americans, but they're great kids," Coach said. "We constantly remind them that they are a vital part of everything the team accomplishes. We make them understand that they are part of something special, something bigger than themselves, and that without them we cannot be successful.

"Constantly recognizing the contributions of the second-string and scout-team players helps the starters get better, too," Fracassa continued. "The sense of being a part of something bigger than yourself carries over to the team's stars, which keeps them grounded and inspires them to work harder.

"I know what it's like to never get into a game," he added. "I spent my entire college career as a back-up. These kids work so hard for the chance to play just a little. We make sure they know that, through their effort during practices, they share as much in our victories as their teammates who get most of the playing time."

Given that the players who serve as back-ups and scout-team members significantly outnumber the All-Americans, it would be impossible to mention all of them by name. However, thanks to Chuck Tornow, the scout-team strong safety on Brother Rice's 1999 state runner-up team, there's a way to honor all those Shrine and Rice football players who selflessly devoted 100 percent of their efforts to the success of the team.

During the 1999 season, Coach Fracassa received an anonymous letter from a football parent who was dissatisfied with the amount of playing time the team's back-up and scout-team players received. Fracassa shared the letter with the team as a teaching point and Tornow, who embraced his role as a scout-team player, wrote a letter in response. No one asked Tornow to write the letter, but his pride in the role that he played in making the team successful and his realization that he was making a vital contribution to an endeavor that was bigger than himself compelled him to respond.

Dear Parents,

Today Coach Fracassa received a letter about the lack of playing time for the second and third string. It was written by an anonymous parent, who did not discuss it with his or her son, and it berated Coach Fracassa for not letting some of the less-skilled players participate in our very difficult game against Sterling Heights Stevenson last Saturday.

As a senior on the scout team I disagree entirely with said letter. I have been playing football for only three years prior to this season, and despite my lack of playing I have learned a lot about life and what it takes to be a champion. I'm probably not going to play in college; most of us probably won't. But by playing for Coach Fracassa I have learned about leadership, discipline, hard work, fairness, and dedication.

I didn't play on Saturday. In the last two years I've had 17 plays. Not times that I've been put in, but times when the ball has been snapped. But it doesn't matter that I don't play in the games. I contribute to the team during practice. My job is to make Brendan Hart and Mark Goebel and all the other starters better by working as hard as I can during practice.

I sweat and bleed on the practice field so that they are prepared to give all their strength and talent, which are a lot more than I have, during the game so that we can win as a TEAM. The TEAM is the most important part of football. It doesn't matter how many times your son gets to touch a football during a game as long as he practices hard and gives his all.

As a player, ask your son; he will tell you that this is true. Every small part of the whole is important. If it weren't for the efforts of the scout team the starters would not be able to perform at a high level and the team would not be as successful.

I hope that I get some playing time this year. I would like to be a walk-on at Michigan Tech, but if it's a matter of me getting playing time or winning the football game, I would rather sit on the sidelines so that the TEAM can win. During my time at Rice, Coach Fracassa has taught me lessons about life that have affected me positively and made me a better man. That, ultimately, is what playing football is all about.

Chuck Tornow, #46
Scout Team Strong Safety

Coach Fracassa leads his team in prayer.

NFL players from Shrine (from left): Jim Seymour, Bill Simpson, Coach Martin Foley,
Coach Fracassa, Mike Haggerty, Paul Seymour.

Little guys with big hearts were Coach Fracassa's favorites. Two great ones from the early years at Shrine were Tommy Ventitelli (left) and Tommy Toggweiler.

Coach Fracassa gets his team ready to face powerhouse Muskegon in the State Championship game at Ford Field.

Post-game with Devin Church, Ford Field 2011. Coach Fracassa loved his players
and his players loved him.

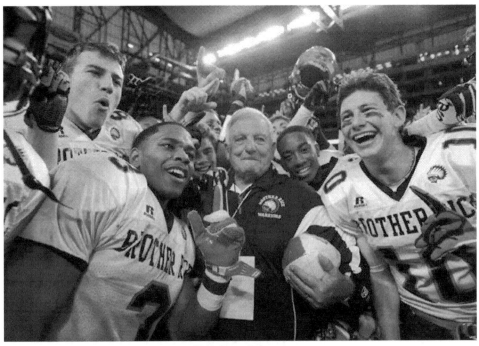

2012 State Champs.

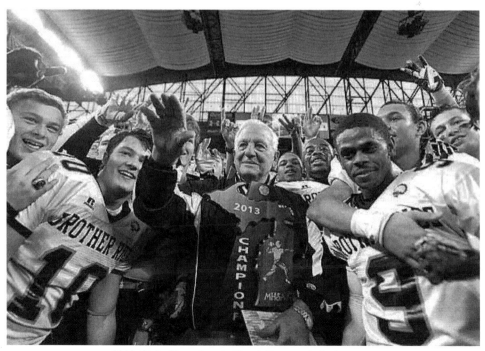

THINKING

If you think you are beaten, you are.
If you think you dare not, you don't.
If you like to win, but think you can't,
It's already a cinch you won't.

If you think You 'll lose, you're lost
For out of the world we find
Success begins with a fellow's will.
It's all in a state of mind.

If you think you are outclassed, you are.
You've got to think high to rise.
You've got to be sure of yourself before
You can ever win a prize.

Life's battles don't always go
To the stronger or faster man.
But sooner or later the man who wins
Is the man who thinks he can.

Life's battles don't always go to the stronger or faster man.

2013: State Champions in Coach Fracassa's final season.

2013: State Champions in Coach Fracassa's final season.

Brother Rice Head Football Coach Adam Korzeniewski (left) and Coach Fracassa.

Phyllis and Albert Fracassa relaxing at home.

Back row, from left: Andiamo owner Joe Vicari, former Brother Rice quarterback Kevin Cassidy, longtime Brother Rice football aide Mike Cassidy, John Vicari. Front row: Albert and Phyllis Fracassa. Joe and John Vicari played high school football for Notre Dame High.

2000-2009

2000
Catholic High School League Champions
MHSAA Division 2 State Champions
Attitude is everything.

By 2000, Coach Fracassa and the Brother Rice Warriors had rediscovered the way to the top. Matt Baker was entering his third year as a starting quarterback, and by this point was both mature and talented. Tony Gioutsos was back to run the ball, and Aaron Jackson and Matt Studenski could catch it.

Once again, the Catholic League shuffled its teams. This time, the Warriors were placed in the new A-B Division with Catholic Central, U-D Jesuit, De La Salle, and St. Mary's.

The season began with a six-win run. The games weren't close, with an average winning margin of 21 points. The losing teams were Walled Lake (28-14), Piqua (Ohio) High (24-14), U-D Jesuit (42-14), De La Salle (30-0), Catholic

Central (24-0), and Detroit Country Day (40-19). The win over the Shamrocks ended Catholic Central's four-game winning streak against the Warriors.

Next was Orchard Lake St. Mary's, and the Warriors suffered their first loss, 23-14. A match-up of A-B Division Brother Rice vs. AA Division Divine Child was next, and at stake was a trip to the Prep Bowl. The Warriors won by a score of 38-7, setting up a rematch with the Shamrocks in the Silverdome with the Catholic League Championship on the line.

The Warriors won the Prep Bowl by a score of 24-7 and beat their rivals, the Shamrocks, for the second time in the season. In the revamped MHSAA Division 2 playoff structure, the Warriors were anticipating five more games.

Brother Rice's balanced offense — with Baker's passing skills, and the running ability of Tony and Matt Gioutsos — and their lock-down defense went to work. Southfield High fell by a score of 35-13, and Southfield Lathrup fell 41-19. The regional title game was a rematch with U-D Jesuit, and the Warriors claimed a 21-0 shutout victory.

The MHSAA Division 2 semifinal game pitted the Warriors against Chippewa Valley High School. The Brother Rice team dominated the game and won 35-14, which meant the Warriors would return to the Pontiac Silverdome to play in the MHSAA Division 2 Championship Game against the Hudsonville High Eagles.

The Championship Game began with a Coach Fracassa special: a double-reverse wide-receiver pass from Lorren James to Studenski for a 50-yard-plus touchdown. In their next possession, the Warriors choreographed a 97-yard, 16-play, eight-minute drive that ended in a Baker-to-Jackson touchdown pass. Later, following a 39-yard Sean Brolley punt return, Baker threw a 35-yard touchdown pass to Studenski. The Eagles scored a late touchdown, but the Warriors claimed a 21-7 victory and the MHSAA Division 2 Championship.

Coach Fracassa had won his fifth state championship. After the previous season's loss in the MHSAA final, he found this victory "very gratifying." In his post-game comments, Fracassa said: "I hoped that we would win it," and added: "I'm happy for the boys."

There were many outstanding athletes on this team, which finished with a 13-1 record. One of those talented players was Gemara Williams, who was given a scholarship to the University of Buffalo in the Mid-American Conference. He played three years for the Bulls as a defensive back, and in 35 games he had four interceptions. Williams drew the attention of NFL teams because of his speed and was signed as an undrafted free agent by the New England Patriots. In 2007, he was part of the Patriots' 18-1 Super Bowl team, contributing as a kick returner and defensive back. Later, he had injury-limited seasons with the Montreal Alouettes and the Edmonton Eskimos of the

Canadian Football League. Defensive lineman Jon Randall had 13 sacks in 2000 (tied for sixth all-time) and also carried on an amazing family tradition of serving as a captain for Coach Fracassa. His brother, Jason Randall, was captain in 1990 (also a State Championship team) and his dad, Mike Randall, was captain for Fracassa at Shrine in 1961.

MATT BAKER

The 2000 season was a great year for Matt Baker. He earned All-State Dream Team honors in the state of Michigan, capping off three years as a starting quarterback. Baker was also a two-time All-State and All-Midwest lacrosse player. In 2001, he was named the Midwest Scholastic Lacrosse Player of the Year and earned All-America team honors. He joined a long list of Brother Rice football players who kept in shape and increased their agility in the spring sport, but Coach Fracassa had other ideas. After the MHSAA Division 2 Championship Game, he joked, "I had hoped he would have another year of eligibility."

Matt Baker

Fracassa believed Baker had a bright future in college football. He received a football scholarship to North Carolina University. He played four years for the Tarheels and made significant contributions in his last two years, playing in 23 games. For his career, he completed 224 passes in 426 attempts (a 53 percent completion rate), with seven yards per attempted pass. These completions accounted for 2,968 yards and 12 touchdowns. Baker was fourth in passing in the Atlantic Coast Conference his senior year.

Although Baker was undrafted by NFL teams, he signed as a free agent with the Houston Texans. He subsequently served on the practice squads for the Dallas Cowboys, the New Orleans Saints, the Arizona Cardinals, the Miami Dolphins, and the Buffalo Bills. Baker had a chance to work with Super Bowl-winning head coaches Bill Parcells and Sean Payton.

Following his stint in the NFL, Baker spent three years coaching NCAA football. He was a graduate assistant coach with the University of Mississippi for two years, then spent a year with Western Michigan University, where he worked with quarterbacks and wide receivers. Baker took a break from coaching, but eventually returned to the Broncos, where he worked with Jon Wassink, the 2019 Wuerffel Award winner (for academic, athletic, and service excellence).

In 2020, Baker joined the staff at John Carroll University. He was promoted and now serves as offensive coordinator and quarterbacks coach for the Blue Streaks. Like many of Coach Fracassa's former players, Baker's love of the game he played so well is being passed to another generation.

2001

Uphold the tradition.

Any time Coach Fracassa had a talent-laden, senior-led championship squad, he had the challenge of re-creating that skill set and chemistry when they graduated. Only three varsity starters returned from the 2000 championship team. Heading into the 2001 football season, Fracassa was five wins away from becoming the Michigan high school coach with the most wins in MHSAA history.

His team's first game was against Cass Tech and Brother Rice won handily, 21-6. The next game was the opening of the Catholic League A-B Central Division schedule, and the opponent was U-D Jesuit. It was a close game, but the Warriors won, 21-20. They followed that with a 37-14 victory over De La Salle.

Next up was a rebirth of the Boys' Bowl game, and Brother Rice would be facing Catholic Central. In the teams' return to Pontiac Wisner Stadium, the Warriors prevailed, 21-14, beating the Shamrocks for the third meeting in a row. At this point in the season, Coach Fracassa was one game away from becoming the winningest coach in Michigan high school history.

The Warriors took their unblemished four-win record into a game against Detroit Country Day. Country Day was coached by Dan MacLean, who had played for Fracassa in the '70s and went on to play for the University of Illi-

Country Day Coach Dan MacLean.

nois. In this match-up, the Warriors were on the losing end of a 16-13 overtime score; the record for most wins would have to wait. According to an article in the *Detroit Free Press*, Coach MacLean — always classy, like his mentor — said: "We didn't gift-wrap it. I was at peace."

The Warriors' next Catholic League A-B Central Division opponent was Orchard Lake St. Mary's. Brother Rice lost, 17-3. The team may have been feeling some pressure about winning that record-setting game for their coach. The *Detroit Free Press* quoted Coach Fracassa as saying: "I think the kids were pressured. I never brought it up, but I know they had it in the back of their minds."

The next game was against St. Martin DePorres, of the Catholic League AA Division. The Warriors won, 23-2, and with the victory, Coach Fracassa achieved 309 wins — a Michigan record for career high school football victories. "It feels good. I'm glad it's over with," he said. "The monkey is off our back." The game against DePorres also earned the Warriors a rematch with Orchard Lake St. Mary's in the Prep Bowl at the Pontiac Silverdome. St. Mary's won their second game of the season against the Warriors, 14-3, to take the Detroit Catholic League Championship title.

The Warriors made the MHSAA Division 2 playoffs and opened with a 17-7 win over Birmingham Groves. In the district final, they beat Southfield High, 24-0. The regional final was a rematch with a Catholic League A-B Central Division foe, U-D Jesuit. The Cubs won the game 28-14, thus ending the Warriors' 7-4 season. One of the Warriors' standouts in 2001 had been Gordon Niebylski, who went on to play offensive guard at Michigan State. Ryan Goethals became the starting center for Georgetown University, and Phillip Jacques played defensive line for the University of Buffalo.

The MHSAA Division 2 Championship was won by Chippewa Valley over Jenison High, 26-13, while Catholic Central won the MHSAA Division 1 Championship over Utica Eisenhower, 24-21.

ORCHARD LAKE ST. MARY'S PREP HIGH SCHOOL

Next to the Shamrocks of Catholic Central, the second-toughest opponent for Brother Rice was Orchard Lake St. Mary's Eaglets. St. Mary's was founded in 1885 on Detroit's east side by Rev. Joseph Dabrowski as a school where Polish-American boys could train for the priesthood. The school moved to the site of the former Michigan Military Academy, on the shores of Oakland County's Orchard Lake, in 1909. The Felician Sisters, based in Livonia, have served the school since 1935. Girls were admitted in 2019.

The Eaglets have been successful in football, reaching the MHSAA state finals 14 times and winning eight times. They competed in Class C in the earlier MHSAA classification and were in Division 4 or Division 5 for the MHSAA playoffs. As the school's enrollment increased in the new millennium, they moved up to Division 3. They joined the Detroit Catholic League Central East Division in 1998 and were considered a Detroit Catholic League A-B Division team in 2000.

The Eaglets also had a great high school football coach. George Porritt came to St. Mary's in 1989 and coached the team for 33 years, retiring in 2021. His teams won 278 games and lost 94 games over that time. He is ranked No. 15 in high school coaching wins in the MHSAA. Porritt also coached basketball and lacrosse at the school.

The Eaglets can boast of a large number of alumni who have made it to the professional football ranks: Dave Bowens (Eastern Michigan University, Denver Broncos, Miami Dolphins, New York Jets, Cleveland Browns); Filmel Johnson (University of Illinois, Buffalo Bills); Scott Kowalkowski (University of Notre Dame, Philadelphia Eagles, Detroit Lions); Grant Mason (University of Michigan, Pittsburgh Steelers); Leonard Renfro (University of Colorado, Philadelphia Eagles); Allen Robinson (Pennsylvania State University, Jacksonville Jaguars, Chicago Bears); Sam Rogers (University of Colorado, Buffalo Bills, Los Angeles Chargers, Atlanta Falcons); Dion Sims (Michigan State University, Miami Dolphins, Chicago Bears); and Morgan Trent (University of Michigan, Cincinnati Bengals, Indianapolis Colts, Jacksonville Jaguars).

Scott Burnstein of *The Oakland Press* described Coach Porritt as "the consummate professional and ultimate molder of men" who "left an indelible mark on the historic St. Mary's athletic program, the Catholic High School League, the Michigan High School Athletic Association ... and on the hundreds of former players ... who benefited from his wisdom." The Detroit Catholic League was, indeed, blessed with the presence of a "Mount Rushmore" of high school football coaches.

2002

Together we stand.

A more experienced Brother Rice was ready for the 2002 season. Doug Pickens was the junior quarterback, paired with running back Anthony Jackson and receiver Jason Horton. The first game was a win over Farmington Hills Harrison, 34-20. Pickens threw for 192 yards and four touchdowns, ending the Hawks' 32-game winning streak. The second game was a high-scoring affair in which Pickens completed a pass at the end of the fourth quarter to repel Oxford High, 35-28. The next encounter was against the Catholic League AA Division's Bishop Foley. The Warriors won this game, too, 35 to 27.

The Catholic High School League A-B Central Division schedule began with the Boys' Bowl game, where Brother Rice again met Catholic Central. The Shamrocks won this meeting, 21-14. Jackson scored a rushing touchdown for the Warriors, but the Shamrocks' Derek Brooks had 194 yards rushing and two touchdowns of his own. The Warriors battled to win the next two league games over De La Salle (28-12) and U-D Jesuit (17-14).

In a match-up with the Detroit Country Day Yellowjackets, Jackson made a school-record, 98-yard kickoff return. The Warriors won, 21-13, setting up the Catholic League A-B Central Division finale with Orchard Lake St. Mary's. Pickens scored on a one-yard run and completed a 25-yard touchdown pass to Brian Mahler, and Jackson ran for another score, ensuring that

Brother Rice beat the Eaglets, 28-21. "They beat us twice last season," Coach Fracassa said to Rod Beard of *The Detroit News*. "It's nice to have beaten three teams (the Cubs, Eaglets, and Yellowjackets) that beat us last year." The final game of the regular season was against a public-school opponent, the perennial powerhouse Muskegon High School, which beat the Warriors, 45-21. The Big Reds would win three MHSAA state championships between 2004 and 2008.

The Warriors were eliminated from the Prep Bowl, which was being played at Detroit's Ford Field, the new home of the Detroit Lions. Catholic Central beat Divine Child, 45-14, to take the Detroit Catholic League Championship.

The MHSAA Division 2 playoff games were up next for the Warriors. The first game was a victory over North Farmington, 42-17. The Warriors then had a rematch with Harrison for the district title, which the Warriors won, 28-7. A Catholic League A-B Central Division foe, De La Salle, was the next team to face Brother Rice. The Warriors shot down the Pilots, taking the regional title with a score of 28-17. The semifinal game, against Allen Park, was a 24-7 Warrior victory.

The Championship Game for the MHSAA Division 2 title paired Brother Rice and Lowell High School. Jason Horton, of Brother Rice, had a school-record 165 receiving yards, including an 86-yard touchdown reception, but Lowell's Mark Catlin had one of the most outstanding performances in MHSAA history: He ran for 259 yards, threw for 152 yards, and had a 28-yard interception return with one minute left in the game. The Lowell High School squad beat the Warriors, 31-14, to capture the MHSAA Division 2 Championship. Other outstanding players for Rice during the 2002 season were linebacker Paddy Lynch, offensive linemen Jerry Aguwa and Phil Schumacher, and defensive linemen Sean Williamson and Roshaun Harris. Meanwhile, Catholic Central beat East Kentwood, 36-26, to win the MHSAA Division 1 Championship.

2003

We can do it.

There was a sense of optimism going into the 2003 football season. Doug Pickens, an excellent quarterback, was returning for his senior year. Running back Mike Radlick and receiver Charley Henneghan would be his primary offensive support. Adam Decker and Cody Nolan anchored the defense. The season opener had the Warriors playing against East Kentwood High, the previous season's MHSAA Division 1 Championship runner-up. The Warriors started the game with confidence but were given a wake-up call in the form of a 44-7 thrashing. They bounced back with definitive wins

Doug Pickens

the next two weeks over Oxford (28-7) and Bishop Foley (42-0).

The Catholic League A-B Central Division play got underway with a 35-7 loss to Catholic Central in the Boys' Bowl. Two league wins for the Warriors followed; they beat De La Salle (9-3) and U-D Jesuit (31-21). Following a narrow 13-12 win over Detroit Country Day, preserved when Jeff Snow blocked two extra points, the final Catholic League A-B Central Division game remained. Orchard Lake St. Mary's handed the Warriors a 20-0 shutout, eliminating them from the Prep Bowl Catholic League Championship Game. Catholic Central, always a dominant team, beat Divine Child, 34-7, to take the title.

The next game for Rice was a 28-0 victory over a public school, Grand Blanc. The win assured the Warriors of a spot in the MHSAA Division 2 Championship playoffs, but their 6-3 record going into the playoffs led some pundits to question their chances. The first pre-district game was a victory over Oak Park, 20-13, followed by a district title win over Birmingham Groves (17-10) and a regional title game win over Sterling Heights (7-3).

The semifinal game for the MHSAA Division 2 Championship was played against the Novi Wildcats, and it turned out to be a game for the ages. The Wildcats took a 21-14 lead into halftime, but in the second half the Warriors came back and took a 28-21 lead thanks to a Pickens-to-Radlick five-yard touchdown pass with 1:33 left in the game. Novi proceeded to tie the game on a 10-yard touchdown pass from Mike Hart to Trevor Hoover with 17 seconds remaining, sending the game into overtime.

In the overtime period, the Warriors went ahead on a 23-yard field goal by John Rea. The Wildcats answered by driving to the Warriors' one-yard line on their possession. The Warriors stopped the Wildcats' Josh Buck short of the goal line, sending them to their second MHSAA Division 2 Championship game in a row. Pickens finished with 19 completions in 29 passing attempts for 191 yards, two touchdown passes, and one rushing touchdown. Henneghan caught nine passes for 112 yards and one touchdown. Keith Dunlap of *The Oakland Press* quoted an emotional Coach Fracassa: "I'm sorry I'm so emotional. I shouldn't be. They counted us out and they're such great kids. They proved their character today and for the last five games, really."

Brother Rice faced Rochester Adams in the MHSAA Division 2 Championship Game, played at the Pontiac Silverdome in front of 13,782 fans. Despite high hopes, the game didn't go well for the Warriors, who made only six first downs and had 18 rushing yards and 81 passing yards. Adams won, 28-7. The Warriors' archrivals, the Catholic Central Shamrocks, won the MHSAA Division 1 Championship with a 24-6 victory over Utica Eisenhower.

Season standouts for Rice were plentiful. Anthony Jackson went on to an outstanding football career as a receiver and kick returner for Cornell University. Wide receiver Brian Mahler continued his athletic career at Harvard University, where he played four years on the Varsity Men's Lacrosse team. Upon graduating in 2007, Mahler joined the U.S. Marine Corps, where he served three years as an intelligence officer, deploying once to the Horn of Africa. He transferred to the Navy in 2010, where he became a Navy SEAL. As the class leader and Honor Man of BUD/S Class 295, Mahler went on to serve as a two-time platoon commander at SEAL Team Five and operations officer at Naval Special Warfare Group Two. Over the course of his career as a SEAL, he deployed twice to Iraq, once to Afghanistan, and led a joint-training exchange in Saudi Arabia. Defensive back Jeff Stachowiak was a leader who had two interceptions and a touchdown reception in the playoff game against Harrison. Marc Roualet was a quarterback who would have played on most teams, but with Pickens throwing 25 touchdown passes (tied for second all-time), Roualet was a backup.

Pickens was named to the All-Catholic and All-State football squads. While that alone is a great achievement, he was also a two-year All-State player in hockey. Being honored in two sports is amazing, but Pickens' best sport was actually baseball, in which he was All-League, All-Catholic, and All-State for three years at Brother Rice. He was honored as "Mr. Baseball" by the Michigan High School Baseball Coaches Association and was named to the All-America baseball team by Rawlings Baseball America. Pickens was also a finalist for the Catholic High School League Athlete of the Year Award. He played college baseball at the University of Michigan and was drafted by the Cleveland Indians as a professional baseball player.

2004

Catholic High School League Champions
Victory begins in the heart.

Every time a great team has a three-year run, there will generally be a recovery period. But some recovery periods turn out better than others. Doug Pickens had led the Brother Rice Warriors to two consecutive MHSAA Division 2 Championship Games, but he had moved on to college. Coach Fracassa found a new quarterback in sophomore Mike Cappetto. Charley Henneghan and Mike Radlick returned as receivers in 2004, Adam Decker returned on defense, and John Goebel was a top-flight running back. Joey

Henry returned two punts for touchdowns during the season, tying a Brother Rice single-season record. Manny Suileman recorded 3.5 sacks, tied for third all-time in a single season.

The new season got underway with a game against Hilliard (Ohio) Davidson which Brother Rice won, 28-12. This victory was followed by two wins over crossover Detroit Catholic League teams. The Warriors beat Notre Dame (33-7) and Flint Powers Catholic (13-7), and took a 3-0 record into Catholic League A-B Central Division League play.

Catholic Central was the first opponent to fall, 14-10, to the Warriors. The Shamrocks' Anthony Szabo ran 87 yards for the first touchdown, but Cappetto — who completed 13 of 18 pass attempts in the game — completed a short pass to Henneghan to even the score. After an interception in the second half, the Shamrocks kicked a field goal to go up by three. Henry made a 20-yard run to the Shamrocks' one-yard line, and Goebel punched it in from there for the margin of victory. Following their defeat of Catholic Central, the Warriors beat Catholic League A-B Central Division rivals De La Salle (17-0) and U-D Jesuit (21-7).

Next up was a non-league game with Country Day, which the Warriors handily won, 30-8. The last game of the Detroit Catholic League A-B Central Division was a 28-7 victory over Orchard Lake St. Mary's, which the Warriors won despite the efforts of the Eaglets' defensive back, Morgan Trent, who would play for the University of Michigan Wolverines, the Cincinnati Bengals, the Indianapolis Colts, and the Jacksonville Jaguars. The Warriors were rewarded with a trip to the Detroit Catholic League's Championship Game, the Prep Bowl, now contested at Ford Field. Rice played St. Martin DePorres and won 24-7, taking the coveted Catholic League Championship title.

The Warriors would take their 9-0 record and No. 1 state ranking into the MHSAA Division 2 State Championship playoffs. They started with a pre-district game against Walled Lake Western and won easily, 55-0. The team now had a 10-game winning streak and had scored 261 points to their opponents' 64 points. The next game was a district final against the St. Mary's Eaglets, a team they had defeated by 21 points just three weeks prior to this game.

The MHSAA district final began with an Eaglets touchdown. Goebel followed up with a 41-yard run but was tackled on the five-yard line. The Warriors forged ahead and took it in for a touchdown. A missed extra point resulted in a 7-6 Eaglets lead. The next score was an 87-yard kick return by St. Mary's Dante Allen, leading to an eight-point Eaglet lead at halftime. In the second half, Goebel added a 45-yard run for a touchdown, but the Warriors failed on an attempted two-point conversion. The Eaglets moved on with an 18-16 victory.

One of the Brother Rice players who concluded his high school career with that game was Decker, who played three years as a linebacker for the Michigan State University Spartans. Another was T.J. Lang, who played football for the Eastern Michigan University Eagles and was drafted by the Green Bay Packers.

T.J. LANG

The stars on a high school football team are most often those who play in the "skill" positions like quarterback, running back, and wide receiver. Of-

T.J. Lang

fensive linemen make it possible for the stars to shine, usually laboring in anonymity. Sometimes they get a chance to play defense and get their name in the paper for tackles and sacks. As a senior, T.J. Lang had 59 tackles, 8.5 sacks, and one fumble recovery. He joined the Eastern Michigan University Eagles and played college football on a scholarship.

In his freshman year, Lang was a defensive lineman for the Eagles. He played 11 games and was credited with four solo tackles and seven assisted tackles. As a result, he heard plenty of cheers. Then he became an offensive lineman and returned to being a cog in the offensive machine — and he was a really good cog. Lang was drafted and signed by the Green Bay Packers as the 109th pick in the fourth round of the 2009 draft. On his Pro Day, Lang stood at 6'4" and 316 pounds, and ran a 5.15-second 40-yard dash.

He played with the Green Bay Packers for eight years and was a member of the team that defeated the Pittsburgh Steelers in Super Bowl XLV in 2011. People noticed him for his play with the Packers, and he was named to the NFL Pro Bowl in 2017. He signed with the Detroit Lions in 2017 and earned a second trip to the Pro Bowl in 2018. Injuries plagued his second season with the Lions, leading to his retirement later that year. Afterward, he did some sideline reporting for the Detroit Lions Radio Network and had a short Hollywood career, appearing in the movie "Pitch Perfect 2."

Through the years, Lang never forgot his high school football coach. He nominated Coach Fracassa for another NFL High School Football Coach of the Year Award. Fracassa was a finalist for the second time in his career, joining four other nominated coaches from across the United States. He didn't win this time, but received a $2,500 cash award and a $5,000 grant for Brother Rice. In his nominating essay, Lang wrote: "Coach Fracassa was an inspiration to me and every player he's ever coached. He taught me humility and the importance of teamwork."

MICHIGAN HIGH SCHOOL FOOTBALL COACHES
ASSOCIATION HALL OF FAME
2004 CROWLEY AWARD-WINNER

The Jim Crowley Award is given in memory of the late former head coach at Jackson Lumen Christi High School — a great coach and a dedicated family man who was tragically killed at the height of his career. The award honors individuals who have made special contributions to the game of football and the Michigan High School Football Coaches Association. Larry Sellers, Crowley Award chair, gave the address at Coach Fracassa's 2004 Crowley Award presentation ceremony. The following is an excerpt from that address:

"Coach Fracassa's won-loss record, numerous Catholic League and State Titles, Regional and State Coach of the Year and Hall of Fame selections (both state and nationally), and his experience as a speaker at numerous Coach of the Year Clinics throughout the country has established a resume of unsurpassed achievement. It is very easy to defend the assertion that he is one of the greatest coaches in the history of Michigan high school football. Simply admiring the achievements mentioned above, however, would do a great disservice to our recipient. The true measure of this man is not a lifetime of gridiron accomplishment, but rather a lifetime of commitment to the virtues of selflessness, sacrifice, dedication and love.

"It is these qualities, particularly his love for his players, that make Al Fracassa a remarkable man and so deserving of the Jim Crowley Award. His devotion to the young men who play for him is absolute and everlasting, and his players respond to that love with the totality of effort that has become the hallmark of Brother Rice football. Coach Fracassa knows the X's and O's of football as well as anyone, but his true genius lies in his unmatched ability to elevate the human spirit. He develops superior football teams because his primary concern is the development of young men of superior character.

"Henry Adams once wrote that 'A teacher affects eternity; he never knows where his influence will end.' Because of him, thousands of young men have learned invaluable lessons on the football field that they later used to establish themselves as honorable, productive adults. Because of him, there are countless former players of his who are now business owners who understand the importance of integrity, doctors who understand the value of compassion, military officers and government officials who understand the necessity of leadership, and husbands and fathers who understand the power of faith and love.

"Coach Al Fracassa's influence has gone far beyond the gridiron and will affect generations of young men and women whom he will never meet. This achievement dwarfs anything his teams have accomplished on the football field; he has brought great credit and distinction to Michigan high school football and to the entire coaching profession.

"It is our honor to present the 2004 Jim Crowley Award to Coach Albert Fracassa of Birmingham Brother Rice High School."

THE TIMES

The social networking website Facebook was launched in 2003, and the first iPhone was sold in the United States in 2007.

In the local sports world, the Detroit Tigers moved from their longtime home at Tiger Stadium to a brand-new facility, Comerica Park, in 2000. In 2002, the Detroit Lions moved from Pontiac and started playing their games at Ford Field in Detroit, adjacent to Comerica Park. At the Palace of Auburn Hills, the Detroit Pistons won their third NBA championship in 2004. In 2006, the Detroit Tigers lost the World Series to the St. Louis Cardinals in five games. The city hosted the MLB All-Star game in 2005 and the NFL Super Bowl in 2006.

The Catholic Church continued to experience less than positive trends in the United States. The number of Catholic elementary school students fell from 1.8 million in 1995 to 1.5 million (-17 percent) in 2010, and the population of students attending Catholic high schools dropped from 638,440 to 611,723 (-4 percent).

The Detroit Catholic High School Football League was under pressure. The drop in the population of Detroit exaggerated the Roman Catholic Church's challenges in the city. Catholic high schools put an unsustainable fiscal burden on the Archdiocese of Detroit and, as a result, more schools were closed, including Harper Woods Bishop Gallagher, Harper Woods Notre Dame, Detroit Holy Redeemer, Detroit St. Martin DePorres, Detroit East Catholic, Detroit Benedictine, Bishop Bor-

Mick McCabe

gess, St. Agatha, and Centerline St. Clement. U-D Jesuit and Detroit Loyola were the only two Catholic high schools left functioning in the city.

Mick McCabe of the *Detroit Free Press* wrote: "It can't be the same without DePorres upsetting Catholic Central or Brother Rice in football. I don't want to turn this into some sappy nostalgic look back at the Catholic League like I'm pining for the good old days when there were more than 70 Catholic high schools. Those days are gone forever, but this was a staggering blow to Catholic education in the Detroit area." He added: "The league will never, ever be the same again. The music has died."

2005

MHSAA Division 2 State Champions
Make a difference.

This season began with a team on a mission. Tailback John Goebel said, "The way the previous year ended was on our minds the whole offseason. We came into the 2005 season and that year's playoffs with revenge on our minds." The season started with a bang, with impressive victories over two out-of-state teams: Evansville (Ind.) Reitz High (48-21) and Toledo (Ohio) St. Francis De Sales High (27-3). The third game, played against Flint Powers Catholic, resulted in another win for the Warriors (30-17).

The Catholic League Central Division schedule began with a match-up against Catholic Central in a Boys' Bowl Game at Ford Field. Brother Rice had an unusually large victory over the Shamrocks, 28-7, behind two interception returns for touchdowns by Matt Pickens. The following league game was a 28-14 win over Divine Child.

The dominance of the Warriors continued with additional Catholic League Central Division victories over U-D Jesuit (21-6) and De La Salle (35-17). Goebel contributed to the win over De La Salle with a 91-yard run from scrimmage.

The Warriors carried a seven-game winning streak, with an average score of 31-12, into their final Catholic League Central Division game against Orchard Lake St. Mary's. Unfortunately, the undefeated Eaglets brought the Warriors' winning streak to a halt with a tight 24-21 victory. The good news was that the Warriors' 4-1 league record had earned the team a trip to the Catholic High School League Championship Game in the Prep Bowl at Ford Field. The bad news was that their opponent would be Orchard Lake St. Mary's. The Eaglets won their second consecutive game against the Warriors, 20-7.

Brother Rice did, however, earn a spot in the MHSAA Division 2 Championship playoffs. Their first pre-district game was against Redford Union

High. Junior quarterback Mike Cappetto completed a touchdown pass to Charlie Gantt and the offensive line, including Gantt, helped Goebel run for two rushing touchdowns, while Matt Shango's three sacks led a stout defense. The Warriors romped over Redford Union, 55-15. The district championship game was against the undefeated and higher-ranked Livonia Franklin High, but the Warriors, having regained their mojo, claimed the victory, 35-21. Although Goebel made an 87-yard run to help secure the victory, Cappetto was injured, and sophomore Andy Lentz took over at quarterback.

The regional championship game placed the Warriors against the undefeated, No.1-ranked Eaglets of Orchard Lake St. Mary's — their third match-up in the same season. "St. Mary's was that big hurdle for us to overcome physically and mentally," Goebel said. With 32 carries for 157 rushing yards and one 11-yard touchdown, he did his part. Teammate Joey Henry had an 18-yard touchdown run with three minutes left in the game, sealing a 17-8 Warrior victory.

The MHSAA Division 2 semifinal game was against the undefeated Rochester Adams Highlanders, who had beaten the Warriors in the 2003 MHSAA Division 2 Championship Game. In this year's game, two Highlander fumbles in the red zone helped the Warriors. Coach Fracassa's squad attempted only three passes in the game but they were carried to a 14-7 victory by Goebel (123 yards), Henry (70 yards), and Chris Colasanti (55 yards) on the ground. Scott Beals punted six times for 300 yards, overcoming the performance of Highlanders quarterback Jacob Ball, who completed 17 of 22 passes for 324 yards. Fracassa was quoted by Jim Spadafore in *The Detroit News* as saying: "It happened to us before and I know how they [The Highlanders] feel. They're a very gallant team."

The MHSAA Division 2 Championship Game, between Brother Rice and the Hudsonville High School Eagles, took place at Ford Field. Young quarterback Lentz completed a 16-yard touchdown pass to Henry and a nine-yard pass to Gantt in the first half. Behind Kaunda Hancock's three interceptions, the defense shut down the Eagles to win the title, 14-7. Pickens had four tackles for a loss. Goebel ran for 84 yards on 18 attempts and had 10 tackles. Any time a running game works, blocking makes it possible. Fullback Mike Radlick and offensive lineman Darris Sawtelle led the way on this Warriors team. Goebel left his mark on the Rice record books; his 1,917 yards rushing in 2005 is second all-time for a single season and his career 2,804 yards rushing are third all-time.

This MHSAA Division 2 State Championship was Coach Fracassa's seventh state championship and his sixth in the MHSAA playoff system. "We played every game thinking it could be Coach Fracassa's last," Goebel said.

"That's how much that man inspired us and meant to us." The championship title could have capped a career of which any high school coach could be proud, but Fracassa, now 72, didn't think he was finished.

JOHN GOEBEL

John Goebel finished his outstanding high school career with an impressive senior year. He accounted for 2,145 all-purpose yards and 21 touchdowns; ran for 1,917 yards — 7.4 yards per carry — for 18 touchdowns; and had 79 pass-receiving yards and one touchdown. As a safety on defense, he had four interceptions and returned one of them 89 yards, for a touchdown. He also had two fumble recoveries, returning one 60 yards for a touchdown, and had 67 tackles and five pass breakups. In his junior year, Goebel ran for 1,173 yards.

John Goebel

For his efforts, Goebel was named to the All-Catholic and All-Area teams. Additionally, he was named to the AP All-State Team and to the All-State Dream Team by *The Detroit News* and was honored as captain of the All-State Dream Team by the *Detroit Free Press*. And that wasn't the end of it. Goebel was selected as the No. 14 Blue Chip Michigan player by the *Detroit Free Press* and was ranked No. 15 by *The Detroit News*. He was also recognized as the Catholic High School League Walt Bazylewicz Athlete of the Year.

Goebel joined the University of Cincinnati Bearcats following his high school graduation. He was hampered by injuries, but managed to carry the ball 178 times for 844 yards and 10 touchdowns in his career. He caught 33 passes for 312 yards and one touchdown, and returned 15 kicks for 301 yards. His best year was 2008, when he finished in the top 10 in every rushing category in the Big East Conference. Goebel played for Coach Mark Dantonio, who would later coach the MSU Spartans.

The closing of Goebel's high school career brought an end to the Goebel family's era at Brother Rice. His father, Karl, had played on the 1974 "mythical" Michigan Class A Championship team. Karl played football for the Ball State University Cardinals and later coached the Brother Rice Warriors for three years. John's brother, Mark, played on the Warriors squad that lost to Saginaw High School in the classic 1999 MHSAA Division 2 Championship finals. Mark played college football for Michigan State.

Mark Snyder, of the *Detroit Free Press*, quoted Coach Fracassa as saying: "With the Goebel family, I coached the father, I coached the two sons, and they all got college scholarships. It's not the championships I stay for. It's the kids."

CHARLIE GANTT

Charlie Gantt was another one of the great players on the 2005 Championship team. He was an exceptional blocking tight end who could also catch the ball. As a senior for the Warriors, he caught 10 passes for 139 yards and four touchdowns, then played linebacker on defense for the last half of the year, recording 37.5 tackles, two sacks, and an interception. He caught the game-winning pass from Andy Lentz in the MHSAA Division 2 Championship Game against Hudsonville High School.

Gantt was easily among the best high school tight ends in the country and was ranked No. 14 in the nation by *rivals.com* and PrepStar. In Michigan, *The Detroit News* placed him No. 9 among all the graduating football players, regardless of position. *Rivals.com*, meanwhile, had him at No. 4. It was no surprise that Gantt earned an athletic scholarship to Michigan State University.

Charlie Gantt

As a redshirt freshman for the Spartans in 2007, Gantt earned a varsity letter. In the next three years, he started 39 consecutive games. In 2008, he was presented with the Tommy Love Award as the team's most-improved player. In his senior year, he was a John Mackey National Tight End of the Week for his four-reception, 38-yard, and one-touchdown performance as the Spartans beat Penn State to clinch a share of the Big Ten title. At the end of the year, Gantt was named to the All-Big Ten second team and received All-America honorable mention honors from *SI.com*. He was also the winner of the Michigan State University Up Front Award, recognizing him as the team's most outstanding offensive lineman.

In his career with the Spartans, Gantt played in 43 games and had 65 pass receptions for 951 yards and nine touchdowns. Among all tight ends in Spartan history, he's tied for third in touchdowns, fifth in receptions, and fifth in receiving yards. Although Gantt was undrafted, he was signed as a free agent by the NFL's Kansas City Chiefs and played in four preseason games; during one of those games, he caught one pass for 16 yards.

Like many Warriors before him, Gantt came from a family of athletic talent. His grandfather, Robert M. Gantt Jr., was a three-sport athlete (football, basketball, track) at Duke University and appeared on the cover of *Look* magazine in 1942, in which he was called "Dixie's finest athlete."

2006

Catholic High School League Champions

Play with passion.

The MHSAA Division 2 State Champions, the Brother Rice Warriors, opened the 2006 season with a five-game winning streak. Mike Cappetto returned at quarterback, having healed from the previous year's injury. Offensive lineman Darris Sawtelle was coming back to protect him. Chris Colasanti and Brian Wing would lead the defense, and Kaunda Hancock would be playing on both sides of the ball. There didn't appear to be any fall-off in talent from the prior season.

The Warriors' first game was a 29-14 win over Detroit Denby. That game was followed by a win over Toledo (Ohio) St. Frances de Sales (35-10) and a cross-state victory over the squad from Traverse City West (28-0). Caulton Ray, a junior Warrior running back, had 161 yards rushing on 23 carries.

There was a break at this point in the season. As reported by Chris Lau of the *Detroit Free Press*, a new $1 million football field on Brother Rice's campus had been completed. The pep rally before the Boy's Bowl game was

Mike Capetto

followed by a ribbon-cutting ceremony at the new "Al Fracassa Field," which was attended by students and alumni. Coach Fracassa was honored for how he "positively influenced and inspired young people."

The Warriors, now carrying an eight-game winning streak over two years, began their Catholic League Central Division play in the Boys' Bowl at Ford Field against Catholic Central. Behind 3.5 sacks by Colasanti, three interceptions, and three fumble recoveries, the Warriors held the Shamrocks to 117 total yards and won 24-0. "We had it tonight," Coach Fracassa said. Lau, of the *Detroit Free Press*, reported that the Shamrocks' coach, Tom Mach, lamented, "There weren't any holes. We have been able to run the ball against most teams, but we couldn't do it against them."

The Warriors ran the table in the Catholic League Central Division in 2006. Their game against Orchard Lake St. Mary's was a 14-7 win, followed by a 16-14 victory over U-D Jesuit. De La Salle was the next team to fall, 10-6. The last league game was a 42-6 romp over Divine Child.

The Warriors once again met De La Salle in the Prep Bowl. It was another close game, but the Warriors prevailed, 24-21, and captured the Catholic High School League Championship. The Warriors were taking a 9-0 record into the MHSAA Division 2 playoffs.

In their first postseason match-up, with Redford Union High, the Warriors won in a 33-0 shutout. The district championship title game was against Dearborn's Henry Ford High School, and the Warriors won impressively (35-6). Joey Henry had a 97-yard kickoff return — the second-longest in Brother Rice history.

The Warriors had won 11 consecutive games in the 2006 season and 16 consecutive games over two seasons, so their chances for the remainder of the season looked bright. Their opponent in the regional championship game would be De La Salle — a team Brother Rice had already beaten twice this season. But a Warriors victory was not to be. De La Salle rose up and beat the high-flying Brother Rice team, 18-7. Muskegon then defeated De La Salle, 32-30, in a closely contested MHSAA Division 2 Championship Game. As Coach George Porritt of Orchard Lake St. Mary's had pointed out the year before, "You try to beat a team three times in a row, it's tough."

In spite of their disappointing loss, the Warriors had a great three-year run with a lot of outstanding performances. Cappetto, the co-captain, had led the team to two Catholic High School Championships and one MHSAA Division 2 Championship. He was a two-time Most Valuable Player for the Warriors and was named to the All-League and All-Area teams his senior year. In his career, he passed for 3,084 yards and 39 touchdowns. One of those was an 85-yard bomb to Hancock in the first game against De La Salle. Cappetto ran for 420 yards and 14 touchdowns, and received a scholarship to play for Duke University.

Kaunda Hancock

Hancock played wide receiver and defensive back for the Warriors. In his senior year, he had 32 pass receptions for 636 yards and six touchdowns. On defense, he had three pass interceptions, 55 tackles, and two forced fumbles; he had two games in which he made 10 tackles. Hancock was an All-State Class A honorable mention player, and Coach Fracassa said: "Great players play well in every game, and Kaunda epitomizes this kind of greatness."

After his high school career ended, Hancock played for Wayne State University and was named to the Great Lakes Intercollegiate Athletic Conference All-Academic Team two years in a row.

CHRIS COLASANTI AND MARC MILIA

Chris Colasanti managed to stand out on a team full of standouts. He was a three-time All-Catholic team honoree, as well as a two-time, first-team Class A All-State selection. In his senior year, he was responsible for 106 tackles and seven sacks. On offense, as a fullback, he ran for 115 yards on 16 carries. He was named to the *Detroit Free Press* Dream Team and earned a scholarship to Penn State University.

Colasanti had dreamt of playing at "Linebacker U" as a Penn State University Nittany Lion. He lettered as a "true" freshman in 2007 and, throughout his career, played in 37 games. In his NCAA career he had 57 solo tackles, 92 assists, and 9.5 tackles for a loss. In 2010, he was third in the Big Ten with 112 total tackles.

Although he was a fine athlete, Colasanti was outstanding in another way.

Chris Colasanti

Despite the rigors of competing on an NCAA Division 1 football team, he was able to graduate from Penn State in four years. He was an Academic All-Big Ten selection three years in a row and was an Academic All-American player his senior year. After receiving his undergraduate degree from Penn State, Colasanti was accepted into Michigan State University's College of Human Medicine and graduated as an M.D. He trained in orthopedic surgery at the New York University School of Medicine and NYU's Langone Orthopedic Hospital.

Colasanti joins Dr. Marc Milia in the small club of former Big Ten football players coached by Al Fracassa who today are working as doctors. Milia was a four-sport athlete at Brother Rice who graduated in 1989. He played college football at the University of Michigan, after being recruited by Bo Schembechler. The Wolverines netted four Big Ten championships during his stay. Milia played a fifth year when Coach Gary Moeller needed him, despite his University of Michigan Medical School acceptance, and he received an All-Big Ten honorable mention.

Milia was more than a football player, having been a three-year Academic All-Big Ten selection. He received his M.D. (cum laude) from the University of Michigan Medical School, then completed his orthopedic training at the University of North Carolina and the University of Pittsburgh. Today, Milia specializes in sports medicine, especially knee and shoulder injuries.

In his election as the Brother Rice Alumni Association Alumnus of the Year in 2021, he credited Coach Fracassa as being the mentor who had the most significant impact on his growth as an individual.

Fracassa coached enough great football players over the years to field an NFL team of his own. He also coached enough great students who became doctors to staff a hospital of his own. Colasanti and Milia would be on both lists.

AGILITY DRILLS

Coach Fracassa instituted his agility drills program at Brother Rice in 1970, after his first season as head coach. The drills were exactly what one would expect them to be: a variety of exercises designed to improve the balance, quickness, and agility of his football players. The rationale behind the drills wasn't solely to improve balance, quickness, and agility; in fact, those physical benefits were only byproducts of the primary purpose of agility drills, which was developing mental toughness.

"Being successful in football is mostly having a want-to attitude," Fracassa often told his players. "If you're mentally tough, if you play with determination, if you never stop fighting no matter how difficult things get, you'll become a champion."

For Coach Fracassa, the word "champion" carried with it two different meanings. The first, and the one the players typically focused on, brought with it the hope that taking part in and completing the drills would put them closer to a league or state title, thus making them champions.

For Fracassa, the second meaning of "champion" was much more important. To him, being a champion meant being a good person, a man of high character who could be counted upon to do the right thing, regardless of the circumstances. Coach Fracassa conducted agility drills because they helped turn his players into better men.

The agility drills consisted of 12 workouts spread out over six weeks, from 6-7 a.m. on Tuesday and Thursday mornings. The Tuesday and Thursday sessions began the same way: The boys would organize themselves into nine even columns, and Fracassa would lead them in 10 minutes of stretching and quick drills to get them warmed up.

On Tuesdays, after the warm-up drills, the players rotated between seven different stations, most of which focused on developing quick feet and balanced lateral movements. At its core, football consists of quick, violent confrontations within confined spaces — and the Tuesday drills prepared the Brother Rice players for those face-to-face, one-on-one battles. The players spent about four minutes at each station and the drills were done with intensity, the pace almost nonstop.

There were no stations during the Thursday drills. After warming up, the boys re-formed into nine columns. Then, one row at a time, the players sprinted, backpedaled, shuffled, and bear-crawled themselves into exhaustion.

For years, there was a debate among agility drill participants as to whether

Tuesday or Thursday was the more physically demanding session. "Definitely Tuesday," said Justin Cherocci, a captain on the '09 team who went from a walk-on to an All-MAC linebacker at Central Michigan. "Each drill was hard and if you really pushed yourself, there was very little time to rest. You could rest a bit between drills on Thursdays."

Most of the players who said Thursday was the most difficult session focused on one event: the ladder drill. Players started at the south end of the

Justin Cherocci

gym. On the whistle, they backpedaled to the first foul line and then sprinted back to the end line. Then they backpedaled to and sprinted back from half court, the far foul line, and finally, the far end line. There was great pride in finishing first in your row, and no one wanted to cross the end line last.

Chris Colasanti, who helped Rice win a state title in 2005 and captained the 2006 squad, remembered the ladder drill well. "The ladder was a beast," Colasanti said. "By the time you crossed the finish line, your legs were screaming and your lungs were burning."

Colasanti had ample reason to vividly recall the ladder challenge. His performance on the ladder during one of the '05 sessions went down in agility drills history. "I knew Chris was going to be a special player," Coach Fracassa said. "He had size, strength, and speed, but I wanted to see what he was made of mentally, how he would respond to a challenge."

Fracassa had Colasanti, a linebacker who weighed 230 pounds, run the ladder drill with the speedy receivers and defensive backs, most of whom weighed at least 50 pounds less. In an impressive performance, Colasanti stayed even with the swift skill players until the final leg of the drill. He started to lose some ground backpedaling to the far end of the gym, and then a little bit more ground on the final sprint home.

Colasanti crossed the end line in third place, which was amazing for a linebacker his size competing against defensive backs and receivers. The same 50-pound weight disadvantage that slowed him down during the final leg of the ladder drill also made it hard for him to stop as he crossed the finish line. "I was running as fast as I could," Colasanti said. "I wanted to finish first."

Normally, players who have yet to run the ladder congregate along the south wall of the gym, waiting for their turn to compete. "It was funny," one player said. "When Chris got close to the finish line, bodies just started running in all directions. No one wanted to get run over!"

For a Warriors football player to take part in all 48 agility drill sessions — that meant perfect attendance in their freshman, sophomore, junior, and senior years — required incredible determination and discipline, and Fracassa took full advantage of the opportunity to stress the importance of two of his favorite virtues.

"It takes a special person to complete all 48 sessions. That's the kind of dedication and mental toughness that you (need) to be successful in life," Coach frequently reminded his players. "You have to pay the price to be great, and the players who make it to all 48 agility drills understand that."

2007

Catholic High School League Champions
As you believe, so you become.

As the 2007 football season dawned, the Warriors of Brother Rice were coming off an 11-1 season. Paul Gyarmati, an All-State Class A second-team honoree was returning as the fullback. Caulton Ray, who had 215 carries for 1,039 yards and 11 touchdowns as a junior, was returning as a senior running back. Andy Lentz was an experienced quarterback, and Nick Thomas was a wide receiver and defensive back. This season, the four players also shared duties as co-captains. The line also featured junior Zach Cherocci.

The Warriors' season got underway with a 10-0 win over Detroit's Denby High School. The opener was followed by another shutout, a 24-0 victory over Pittsburgh's Penn Hills High. The next match-up was against the always-tough Cincinnati (Ohio) Moeller. The Warriors lost the game, 14-6.

The Catholic League Central Division season began with the Boys' Bowl game against Catholic Central. The game was a low-scoring affair, but the Warriors took home a 12-7 victory, helped by Mazen Jaddou's two fumble recoveries. The next game was against Orchard Lake St. Mary's, where Dion Sims was a junior starter for the Eaglets. After high school, he attended Michigan State University and entered the NFL draft after his junior year. His NFL career took him to the Miami Dolphins and the Chicago Bears. Sims' Eaglets enjoyed a big win over the Warriors, 40-21.

The rest of the Catholic League Central Division games went the Warriors' way. Danny Henneghan had an 89-yard punt return, and Ray had a 14-carry, 128-yard, three-touchdown day in a 49-20 win over U-D Jesuit. Kenneth Watkins also played well, and made a 61-yard pass interception return. The next game was a 17-7 victory over De La Salle, and Divine Child also fell to the Warriors, 55-7.

Brother Rice's performance in league play earned the team a spot in the Catholic League Championship Prep Bowl game at Ford Field, where the Warriors got another shot at Orchard Lake St. Mary's. This time, the Warriors romped to a 45-14 win, with Ray running for 156 yards on 23 carries. The Warriors were headed to the MHSAA Division 2 playoffs on a positive note.

In the pre-district game, the Warriors faced Rochester Hills Stoney Creek. Brother Rice pulled out a big 42-8 victory. John Miller had a 64-yard interception return, while Gyarmati made a school-record four tackles for a loss. The district championship game was against Rochester Adams High. The Warriors had beaten the Highlanders two years prior to this game, on their way to the MHSAA Division 2 Championship in 2005, but this time the Highlanders came out on top, taking the game 24-21 on a late fourth-quarter touchdown. The bright spot in the loss was that Ray had a season-high 200 yards rushing on 24 carries and scored two touchdowns. The Warriors finished the year 8-3.

No Catholic High School League teams made the MHSAA Division 1 or 2 Championship finals, but Orchard Lake St. Mary's played East Grand Rapids in what was called "one of the top Michigan high school football state finals in the last 30 years" in the MHSAA Division 3 Championship Game. The contest went to an unbelievable five overtime sessions, and in the end, the Pioneers beat the Eaglets, 46-39. The game was one of the Pioneers' five Division 3 Championships in a row, and one of seven in nine years.

For Brother Rice, Lentz spent most of the year handing the ball off to his impressive backfield tandem. He threw 78 passes and completed 42 of those for 605 yards and seven touchdowns. Thomas was named an All-Catholic and All-Area as a defensive back and wide receiver. He briefly enrolled at Princeton University as a football player but turned his attention to track — a sport in which he was an All-American in the 400- and 800-meter events. He then transferred to the University of Michigan, where his father had run track and cross country from 1978 to 1982.

Ray finished his senior year with 1,150 yards gained on 195 carries, and scored 15 touchdowns. He returned five kickoffs for 112 yards. He was an All-State selection and in the top 20 among Michigan's best senior football players. He began his college career at Michigan State and finished at Western Illinois. Gyarmati was selected for the All-League, All-Area, and All-State teams. In high school, in addition to football, he was a lacrosse player for the Warriors and played on the state championship team his sophomore year. He was awarded a football scholarship to the University of Michigan, where he played as a fullback and on special teams for the Wolverines.

2008

Preparing to be the best.

In 2008, Coach Fracassa was looking for a new quarterback. As the season approached, he also needed a running back. He found the new quarterback in Frankie Popp and the returning running back in Danny Henneghan. Brothers Zach and Justin Cherocci provided some help on the offensive and defensive lines. Fracassa knew the inexperience of this year's team was going to be a challenge.

The season opened with a bang: a 45-7 win over Oak Park. Next up was Muskegon, a tough public-school opponent. The Big Reds handed the Warriors a 42-27 loss. In the next game, a match-up with an out-of-state team, Penn High of Mishawaka, Ind., Henneghan had a game for the ages. He ran for 259 yards on 16 carries — 16.2 yards per carry — with one dash of 90 yards. It wasn't an easy game, but the Warriors prevailed, 30-20.

Brother Rice opened their Catholic League Central Division play with a Boys' Bowl game against the Detroit Catholic Central Shamrocks. The Shamrocks jumped to a 14-3 lead in the first half of the game, but Popp completed a touchdown pass to Nate Saldivar-Garcia to close the lead to three points. The Shamrocks put up 10 more points and led 24-10 with six minutes remaining in the game. Then the Warriors mounted one of the greatest comebacks in Boys' Bowl history. First, Popp completed an eight-yard touchdown pass to Kevonte Martin-Manley with 4:35 remaining. After holding the Shamrocks, Henneghan had a 44-yard punt return to the Shamrocks' 15-yard line, with a penalty moving the ball to the eight-yard line. With 2:45 remaining, Popp hit Mark Makowski with a touchdown pass to even the score. The Shamrocks failed to move the ball on their possession, and the Warriors took over on their 23-yard line with 53 seconds remaining and no timeouts. Popp connected with Makowski for 18 yards and Martin-Manley for 25 yards. The Warriors lined up for a last-second 50-yard field goal. Ryan Kelly made the school-record boot, and the Warriors went home with a 27-24 win — their fifth victory in a row over the Shamrocks!

This exceptional game was followed by two losses to Catholic League Central Division opponents. The first was to Orchard Lake St. Mary's, 31-28; for the Warriors, the highlight was that Saldivar-Garcia had a school-record five kickoff returns for 115 yards. The second loss was to De La Salle, 9-7. The Warriors didn't let those two losses hold them down, however, and they bounced back to beat U-D Jesuit, 49-13. The two losses in Central Division play eliminated the Warriors from Prep Bowl play, but they won games against Powers Catholic High School (33-7) and Orchard Lake St. Mary's (28-21).

The Warriors were 6-3 going into the MHSAA Division 2 playoffs. The pre-district game was against Rochester Adams, the team that had ended their season the year before. The Warriors were up for the challenge and won the rematch, 28-21. The district Championship Game against Lakeland High didn't go as well, as the Eagles beat the Warriors in a close 17-13 game.

Warren De La Salle went on to beat Catholic Central in the Prep Bowl, 28-14, and made it to the MHSAA Division 2 Championship Game, where they lost to Muskegon, 34-14. The 2008 MHSAA Division 1 Championship didn't include any Detroit Catholic League teams.

Although the end of the season was disappointing, the Warriors' stars had consistently played well. Zach Cherocci was named to the All-Catholic, All-Metro, and All-State Division 1-2 teams, and was selected for the All-State Dream Team for his offensive line play. He also was given Brother Rice's Tim MacLean Leadership Award and was cited by the Michigan High School Football Coaches Hall of Fame. In that award ceremony, Zach said: "Coach Fracassa, you are a legend, and I am proud to say I was one of your Warriors. Thank you for being my mentor and my friend." Cherocci played football for Hillsdale College.

Other players who moved on included Shamari Benton, who played linebacker for Central Michigan University, where he had 133 individual tackles and 174 assists. Henneghan followed in his brother's footsteps and played college lacrosse for Penn State. Fullback/linebacker Shaquille Marshall was a devastating blocker and went on to play on the defensive line for Albion College.

LACROSSE AT BIRMINGHAM BROTHER RICE HIGH SCHOOL

Brother Rice had many advantages in building a football juggernaut. As a member of the Detroit Catholic High School Football League, the Warriors faced talented teams almost weekly. The school's location in the economically upscale northern suburbs of Detroit provided safety and continuity, and as the number of Catholic high schools in the Archdiocese of Detroit contracted, additional players became available. Coach Fracassa's reputation and his connections with coaches and players throughout the Midwest were a major bonus.

The school provided the discipline and academic rigor parents sought for their children. In the Catholic tradition, sports were strongly encouraged and supported — a positive when it came to attracting hopeful young athletes and their parents. The Warriors were gifted with wonderful coaches in a variety of athletic pursuits: Coaches Fracassa, Ron Kalczynski, and Bob Riker produced great baseball teams; Coach Bill Norton built State Championship basketball teams; Coaches Fr. Ron Richards and Mike Venos developed the swimming and diving teams; Coaches Lou Schmidt and Kenny Chaput guided the hockey teams; Coach Mike Popson led talented track and field teams; and Coach Jim Rademacher built up the golf teams. But probably the most unique Warrior sport was lacrosse, which was established and coached by Rob Ambrose.

Lacrosse, originally an indigenous tribal sport in the eastern woodlands of North America, was first described by Europeans in the 17th century. The sport had a different set of rules back then; games lasted days, included hundreds of individuals, and fields were up to miles in length. The game served many purposes, including toughening young warriors for combat. In 1763, the Ojibwas used a lacrosse game to get soldiers to drop their guard, allowing the tribe to capture Fort Michilimackinac in northern Michigan.

Lacrosse wasn't a popular high school sport outside of the East Coast in the 1970s. Ambrose coached the first Warrior lacrosse team in 1983, left in 1985, but returned in 1995 and stayed until he retired in 2013. Dave Morrow, who was a captain for the Brother Rice football team, was one of the great Warrior lacrosse players and was recruited by Princeton University, where he was named All-American and led the Tigers to their first NCAA tournament and first NCAA Championship. Since becoming a formal league sport in 1997, the Brother Rice lacrosse teams have won 23 Catholic League Championships. They've also earned 27 State Championships since 1986 and won a National Championship in 2008. Fifty-seven Warriors have been lacrosse All-America players and 40 went on to play for NCAA Division 1 teams.

Many of Coach Fracassa's great football players were also great lacrosse players. The spring sport allowed athletes to work on their speed, balance, and agility. The contributions made by lacrosse players to Fracassa's success were significant, and lacrosse was a boon for attracting athletes and then helping them develop their athletic skills.

2009

Believe.

The Brother Rice Warriors approached the 2009 football season with a championship mindset. Frankie Popp was back at quarterback for his senior year, along with his favorite receivers, Kevonte Martin-Manley and Nate Saldivar-Garcia. Justin Cherocci, who had set a school record for tackles (25) in a single game in 2008, was back to lead the defense. Sean Grisan would anchor the offensive line with running backs Jeff DeClaire and junior Jimmy Pickens.

The Warriors, in their season opener with a Catholic League Central Division game against U-D Jesuit, romped to a 49-0 win. The second game was against an out-of-state opponent, Toledo (Ohio) St. John's Jesuit. Popp had 15 completions in 28 attempts for 177 yards and four touchdowns, Martin-Manley had 110 receiving yards and two touchdowns, and Pickens ran for 123 yards and a touchdown. The Warriors won, 42-21. The next game was a tighter victory (13-6) over Highland Park High School.

The Warriors renewed their Catholic League Central Division play with a game against Catholic Central and, for the first time in six years, they lost to the Shamrocks, 24-7. De La Salle then fell to the Warriors in a close 24-21 game. Popp threw 40 passes, completing 21 of them — eight to Martin-Manley. A crossover game against Divine Child was also a win, 35-22. Then the Warriors hit a rough patch.

A three-game losing streak began with a Catholic League Central Division loss to Orchard Lake St. Mary's, 34-27, despite Popp's 25 pass completions in a school-record 49 attempts (for a school-record 366 yards) and Saldivar-Garcia's nine pass receptions. This loss eliminated the Warriors from Prep Bowl consideration. In the next game, the out-of-state Indianapolis (Ind.) Cathedral High beat the Warriors, 35-7. The third consecutive defeat came at the hands of Detroit Southwestern, which won 19-13.

Brother Rice had a 5-4 record going into the MHSAA Division 2 Championship playoffs and beat Walled Lake Central, 35-7, in the pre-district game. Rochester Adams then fell to the Warriors, 24-7, in the MHSAA Division 2 district final.

Brother Rice met Midland High School in the MHSAA Division 2 regional final and the Warriors had an awesome day, rolling up 35 points and nearly 400 yards of offense in the first half alone. Popp completed 10 of 18 passes for 259 yards and Martin-Manley set a school record of 177 receiving yards, including a school-record 93-yard touchdown pass reception and another touchdown catch for 67 yards. Saldivar-Garcia had four pass receptions for 60 yards and one touchdown. Backup quarterback Tyler Lendzion had a 41-yard touchdown run and DeClaire had 10 carries for 69 yards. Fred Kelly, on the *ourmidland.com* website, reported that Coach Fracassa said: "It's just unbelievable how [the Warriors] came to play. These kids showed me a lot today."

Next up for the Warriors, in the MHSAA Division 2 semifinal game, were the No. 1-ranked Lowell Red Arrows, who brought an 11-1 record into the semifinal. The Warriors jumped to a 6-0 lead early on Popp's 62-yard scoring pass to Nate Slappey in the second play of the game. The second Warriors score came on a Lendzion 19-yard touchdown pass to Saldivar-Garcia at the end of the first half. Although the first half had shown promise, the rest of the game belonged to the Red Arrows. Behind Gabe Dean's 101 passing yards and 110 rushing yards, coupled with Austin Graham's 221 rushing yards, Lowell High School powered their way to a 35-14 win. In the MHSAA Division 2

State Championship Game, the Red Arrows beat Inkster High, 27-6.

The Detroit Catholic League Central Division produced two teams that competed for MHSAA championships in 2009. Catholic Central beat Stevenson, 31-21, for the MHSAA Division 1 Championship. In that game, Coach Fracassa's grandson, All-State quarterback Jason Fracassa, completed 15 of 34 passes for 293 yards for Stevenson, including a 75-yard touchdown pass to his All-State receiver, D.J. Mershman. Meanwhile, St. Mary's lost to East Grand Rapids, 24-2, in the MHSAA Division 3 Championship Game.

Popp finished the season with 131 completions on 277 attempts for 1,930 yards, with 18 touchdowns and 12 interceptions. For his high school career, he threw for 4,001 yards. Co-captain DeClaire was a second-team Academic All-State selection. Co-captain Grisan headed to Northwood University in the fall, along with Jason Fracassa and D.J. Mershman from Sterling Heights' Stevenson High School. Another outstanding player for Brother Rice was linebacker Ed Viverette, who went on to have an outstanding career at Wayne State University. There, he was a four-year football letter-winner (2010-13) who started 37 games, and a three-time All-GLIAC honoree.

Ed Viverette

Viverette concluded his collegiate career first in both forced fumbles (nine) and quarterback hurries (13) in program history, was tied for ninth in tackles (295), and ranked 10th in assisted tackles (147). He was inducted into the Wayne State Athletic Hall of Fame in 2020.

JUSTIN CHEROCCI

There's one player who dominates the Brother Rice individual game records for tackles: middle linebacker Justin Cherocci, who owns five of the top seven games for most tackles. In his junior year he made 193 tackles and followed that with 220 tackles in his senior year. In 2009, he was No. 4 in tackles in the country. Cherocci was on the All-Catholic football team three years in a row, and was on the All-Area team and received an honorable mention for the All-State team as a junior. As a senior, he was on the All-County, All-Metro, and All-State dream teams. Like his brother, Zach, he was honored by the Michigan High School Football Coaches Association Hall of Fame.

Justin Cherocci was awarded a football scholarship to Central Michigan University, where he was a four-year letterman and three-year starter for the Chippewas in the Mid-American Conference. He finished his college career with 161 solo tackles and 239 assisted tackles. He made 20 tackles for a loss and had seven sacks, forced four fumbles, had three recovered fumbles, and made one interception. In 2014, Cherocci led a No. 1 defense in the MAC with 117 tackles and was an All-MAC first-team selection. His 400 career tackles place him at No. 13 since 2005 in the MAC. Cherocci was undrafted by the NFL, but attended the Detroit Lions' rookie mini-camp and was signed to the Lions' 90-man preseason roster in 2015.

Cherocci spoke of Coach Fracassa at the Hall of Fame ceremony when he was a high school senior: "Coach Fracassa, I always wondered what it would be like to be considered a friend and player of yours. I have lived the dream and [I am] very proud to say I was one of your Warriors. Thank you for your friendship, your steadfast belief, and for always looking out for me."

In addition to Zachary, his older brother, Justin was joined by his younger brother, Lucas, as a Brother Rice Warrior. Lucas played on the 2011 and 2012 MHSAA Division 2 Championship Warrior teams. As a linebacker, he had 62 solo tackles, 119 total tackles, and three sacks as a senior. He attended Western Michigan University, of the Mid-American Conference, and saw playing time in eight games over three years for the Broncos.

KEVONTE MARTIN-MANLEY

Kevonte Martin-Manley had a great senior year. In addition to posting a school record for longest pass reception (93 yards), he had 42 receptions for 17.3 yards per catch, scored nine touchdowns, and had the most punt return yards in a game (103). Today, he is fourth in all-time pass receptions (93), third in receiving yards (1,525), and second in touchdowns (20). "Kevonte is one of the best players we've ever had at Brother Rice," Coach Fracassa said. "He's the kind of guy that adds to the traditions we have here." Martin-Manley was named to the All-Catholic and All-County teams as a junior and senior, and to the All-State team as a senior. In addition to his three years of varsity lettering in football, he lettered four years in basketball.

Kevonte Martin-Manley

Martin-Manley was a "two-star" recruit, usually relegated to an NCAA Division 1 mid-major college or FCS (Football Championship School) college rather than an NCAA Division 1 FBS (Football Bowl Championship) college. Initially, he committed to Ohio's Bowling Green State University in the Mid-American Conference, but he wasn't completely convinced he was doing the right thing and set up a final visit to the University of Iowa of the Big Ten Conference. Iowa was interested, but they wanted Martin-Manley to sign a scholarship offer with them that weekend. "During my visit, they said if I didn't commit, they were probably going to offer it to another guy coming in," he recalled. Martin-Manley decided to challenge himself and signed the offer. "I sincerely felt like it was the best option for me," he said. The decision turned out well for both sides.

Martin-Manley had a redshirt year, but then was a four-year player for the Hawkeyes. He was No.1 in the Big Ten in punt return yards and punt return touchdowns (two) in his third year. He played in 50 games and became the all-time leader in receptions (174) at the University of Iowa. He had 1,799 receiving yards, 10.3 yards per catch, and 12 receiving touchdowns. He returned 20 punts for 314 yards and four kickoffs for 82 yards.

After college, Martin-Manley was signed by the Cleveland Browns. An article published on a University of Iowa sorts website called *blackheartgoldpants* described "KMM" as not a player with high-end measurables (size and speed), but one who ran good routes, had good hands, got decent separation, and had a high number of receptions that went for first downs. Martin-Manley didn't play in the NFL, but discipline, hard work, and persistence had made this "two-star" recruit a record-setting college football wide receiver.

After college, Martin-Manley and one of his Hawkeye teammates, Anthony Hinchens, started a sportswear company. The name of the company, "Two Star Clothing," was a nod to his underdog recruiting status.

2010-2013

The Final Years – A Storybook Ending

2010

Catholic High School League Champions
Stay strong – state forte.

A successful group of football players had graduated, but there was talent remaining at Brother Rice High School. Tyler Lendzion was returning and had experience at the quarterback position. Jimmy Pickens would run the ball. Conor Hart at defensive end, Tim "Jumbo" Hamilton at linebacker, and Loran Jaddou at safety would provide talent on the other side of the ball.

The Warriors opened the season with a game against Detroit's Martin Luther King High School. King won, 32-19, behind future University of Michigan player Dennis Norfleet's 254 yards rushing. The next game, against Toledo (Ohio) St. John's Jesuit was another loss, 17-14. The Warriors then regrouped and romped over Highland Park, 35-8. Brother Rice had a rare losing record heading into Catholic League play.

The first game in the Detroit Catholic League Central Division was a 7-0 loss to De La Salle. In the next league game, the Warriors righted the ship, beating U-D Jesuit 21-0. Lendzion looked strong, with a solid 91-yard pass completion to Devin Church. The next game was a 26-3 victory over Orchard Lake St. Mary's.

The Warriors had a 3-3 record going into the next game against the No.1-ranked team in Michigan: Catholic Central. The Shamrocks had a 20-game winning streak coming into the game, which took place on Wayne State University's football field. The Shamrocks scored first, on a field goal. The Warriors responded by kicking one of their own. Lendzion completed a pass to the five-yard line and Church ran the ball in for the game's first touchdown. The score was 10-3 at halftime. The rest of the game was a defensive stand-off. The Warriors had an end-zone pass interception by Travis Ferguson to stop a Shamrock drive. Jaddou and Hamilton rose to the occasion, stuffing several Shamrock plays. Pickens scored a one-yard touchdown in the last minute to make the final score 17-3.

The Warriors' celebration didn't last long, because they were preparing for another game against an out-of-state opponent, Indianapolis (Ind.) Cathedral. Brother Rice won, 14-10, improving their record to 5-3. Their Catholic League Central Division record earned them a spot in the Prep Bowl for the Catholic League Championship against Orchard Lake St. Mary's. The Eaglets' best player was Allen Robinson, who would become an All-American wide receiver for the Penn State Nittany Lions and an All-Pro player during his years with the Jacksonville Jaguars, Chicago Bears, and Los Angeles Rams. But in this game, the Warriors were able to beat the Eaglets for the second time in the 2010 season with a score of 17-14 and captured the Catholic League Championship title.

Next up for the Warriors was a spot in the MHSAA Division 2 State Championship playoffs. The pre-district game was against Farmington Hills' Harrison High School. The Hawks scored first, but a one-yard run by Pickens evened the score. After another Hawks touchdown, Lendzion hit Matt Ogren with a 20-yard touchdown pass and the Warriors briefly took the lead. The Hawks' Tommy Vento threw another touchdown pass, but on the Warriors' side, a Travis Ferguson interception was followed by a Lendzion pass to Nick Dunn for a 21-19 halftime lead. In the second half, after a Hawks field goal, Lendzion scored another touchdown on a six-yard run, to give the Warriors a 27-22 lead. The Warriors were sitting on that five-point lead with 1:48 left in the fourth quarter when they fumbled. The Hawks took advantage of the opportunity and returned the fumble for a touchdown, regaining the lead. They quickly scored again on an interception return for a touchdown, for a final score of 37-27. Harrison went on to win the MHSAA Division 2 Championship with a 38-28 win over Lowell High School.

At the end of the season, Hart, the son of Kevin Hart and grandson of Leon Hart, received a football scholarship to play for Vanderbilt University. Hamilton agreed to play for Central Michigan, Lendzion headed to Michigan Tech, and Jaddou went to Northern Michigan. Pickens decided to play baseball for Michigan State.

Scott Burnstein reported on a local news website, *patch.com*, that Coach Fracassa said: "This group will be remembered. They did some amazing things, especially this last fall with winning the Catholic League [Championship] when everybody considered us dead in the water halfway through the season. I have very fond memories of every one of them."

2011

MHSAA Division 2 State Champions
Anything is possible.

In 2011, Albert Fracassa was 78 years old — an age when most men have finished their careers and moved on to fishing, golfing, or woodworking in their well-earned retirement.

Coach Fracassa told Mick McCabe of the *Detroit Free Press*, "I don't play golf. I don't go on a lot of vacations. I wouldn't know what to do with myself." Despite being the winningest coach in the history of Michigan high school football and having one mythical State Championship and six MHSAA Playoff State Championships, Coach Fracassa wasn't ready to step down.

Although Fracassa was confident, there was some concern among parents and administrators at Brother Rice. The Warriors had won two Detroit Catholic High School League Football Championships in the four years between 2007 and 2010, but they had only one MHSAA Division 2 regional title. The team records going into the playoffs were 7-2, 6-3, 5-4, and 6-3. These weren't bad seasons for a high school football team, but this was Brother Rice.

Coach Fracassa said, "I think coaching football helps me live longer. It doesn't get old. Kids are kids. They never change. They're always the same age. I change, but they stay the same. It seems like 35 years ago they were still the same-looking kids."

Delegating was the key element for Fracassa. "It's still fun for me," he said, and added: "One of the reasons I'm here is that I have great [assistant] coaches. They're good men. I let them coach. It's their baby." Fracassa's health continued to be good following double-bypass surgery in 2007, and Coach Fracassa reported, "I didn't miss a game."

So even though there were doubters among Rice's parents and administrators, Al Fracassa returned for his 52nd year as a high school head football coach, and his 43rd year at Brother Rice High School. He would gloriously prove his doubters wrong.

As he prepared for a new season, Fracassa knew he needed a quarterback. He found one in junior Cheyne Lacanaria. The 2011 team had a senior running back in Devin Church, and senior team captains Cody Ellwanger and Joey Warner led the defense, along with junior Lucas Cherocci.

The season started with two public school games and the Warriors got off to a strong start, beating Detroit's Martin Luther King (28-21) and Ann Arbor's Pioneer High School (27-14). Church emerged as the offense's workhorse, posting 33 carries against the Martin Luther King Crusaders. The first out-of-state game was against Toledo (Ohio) St. Francis de Sales. This game was an easy romp for the Warriors, who won 42-9. Among the game's memorable moments, Church made a 96-yard kickoff return for a touchdown.

Catholic League Central Division League play started with a 21-20 loss to De La Salle, but that disappointment was followed by a 42-7 win over U-D Jesuit. A 10-9 overtime loss to Orchard Lake St. Mary's and a 21-19 loss to Catholic Central left the Warriors with a 1-3 Catholic League Central Division record, eliminating them from Prep Bowl consideration.

After league play, the Warriors had a game with another out-of-state opponent, Cincinnati (Ohio) La Salle, which beat Rice, 21-13. The Warrior offense sputtered with 58 rushing yards and 106 passing yards. The Warriors then pulled themselves together in a game against Harper Woods and won, 38-2, but they watched from the sidelines as Catholic Central beat Orchard Lake St. Mary's, 21-7, in the Catholic League Championship Prep Bowl at Ford Field.

The Warriors had a 5-4 record going to the MHSAA Division 2 playoffs. Had the doubters been correct? That was still to be determined, as it was time for another Brother Rice state tournament run. In the opening pre-district game, against the North Farmington High Raiders, the Warriors took home a 34-8 victory behind a school-record 19.1 yards per carry by Church, who also had a 94-yard kickoff return for a touchdown.

The Warriors' district title match-up was with Farmington Hills Harrison, the No. 1-ranked team in the state, which had eliminated Brother Rice from the MHSAA Division 2 playoffs the year before. The Hawks' roster included Devin Funchess and Mario Ojemudia, who would both play at the University of Michigan, and Aaron Burbridge, who would play for Michigan State. The Warriors' running game was hot that day, with two touchdown runs from Brian Walker and two from Church. Walker finished with 14 carries for 68 yards, while Church had 162 yards rushing on 32 carries. The Warriors were victorious, with a surprising final score of 30-7.

The regional title game was against the Southfield High School Bluejays.

Church had a 54-yard touchdown run on his way to gaining 154 yards for the day, helping the Warriors pull off a 16-6 win. For Brother Rice, it was on to the MHSAA Division 2 Championship semifinal game.

The Warriors' opponent in the semifinal was Martin Luther King — a team they had beaten in the opening game of the season. Walker, Church, and Austin Echols all scored touchdowns. Church finished with 215 yards rushing, and the Warriors had 357 yards rushing for the game as they narrowly edged the Crusaders, 27-26.

The MHSAA Division 2 Championship Game pitted Brother Rice against the Lowell Red Arrows, who were appearing in their third consecutive Division 2 Championship Game and had won it all in 2009. The game was a gem for Church, who ran the ball 33 times for 244 yards. The Warriors' rushing total was sixth-highest in an MHSAA Championship final. Church scored three touchdowns on runs of seven, 15, and 54 yards, and reached 1,919 rushing yards for the season, edging out John Goebel for the school season record. Gabe Dean, a two-year All-State quarterback for the Red Arrows, was held to 190 yards passing and 34 rushing yards. Brother Rice senior linebacker Mark Doman had 13 tackles and junior Jon Reschke had 10 in the Warriors' 24-14 win.

The victory gave Coach Fracassa and his Warriors championships in five different decades and a total of seven MHSAA state titles. Fracassa noted, "When you get older like me, you have to cherish these kinds of days."

The Detroit Catholic League Central Division teams were remarkable in 2011. Catholic Central was in the MHSAA Division 1 Championship Game, but lost to Cass Tech, 36-21. Orchard Lake St. Mary's beat Mount Pleasant High, 45-7, to win the MHSAA Division 3 Championship.

DEVIN CHURCH

Devin Church rewrote the record books at Brother Rice. He was very good throughout the 2011 season, but saved his best for the MHSAA Championship run. In five playoff games, he had 938 yards rushing against some of the best teams in the state. His outstanding effort in the MHSAA Division 2 Championship Game was selected as one of the top 30 Michigan high school state finals performances.

Church was chosen for the *Detroit Free Press* Dream Team and played in the Michigan East/West All-Star Game, and he was also ranked the No. 22 overall college football

Devin Church

prospect in the state of Michigan by *rivals.com*. Church verbally committed to play for Northern Illinois University, but things changed after he visited the University of Illinois and was offered a scholarship to play for the Fighting Illini of the Big Ten Conference. Church was a three-star recruit — he wasn't tall, at 5'9", but he had strength at 190 pounds.

Church was a redshirt in his first year and saw limited action in two years at the University of Illinois. He made the decision to transfer to Eastern Illinois University and played for two years there. In his junior year he ran for 743 yards, caught 36 passes for 254 yards, and was selected for the second-team All-Ohio Valley Conference team. In his senior year he ran for 1,066 yards, caught 41 passes for 386 yards, returned three kicks for 74 yards, scored 13 touchdowns, and was selected for the first-team All-Ohio Valley Conference team.

2012

MHSAA Division 2 State Champions
Never give up.

Sportswriter Mick McCabe made a tongue-in-cheek point in *USA Today High School Sports* that six of seven state football championship teams at Brother Rice had been led by quarterbacks in their junior year. In 2012, Cheyne Lacanaria would be a senior, and McCabe suggested that maybe there was a junior available. "He's the best I've got," Coach Fracassa replied. "I'm not going to jinx Cheyne. I'm not going to say anything."

Sergio Perkovic

Lacanaria wasn't the only player coming back after the Warriors' championship in 2011. Shon Powell, Brian Walker, Greg Marzec, Jason Alessi, Jon Reschke, Lucas Cherocci, and Sergio Perkovic had all been on the 2011 squad. In 2012, Lacanaria's brother, Corey Lacanaria, was also on the team, as a wide receiver.

The opening game was against Cass Tech, the 2011 MHSAA Division 1 Champions, in the Detroit Sports Commission's Prep Kickoff Classic at Wayne State University. Behind a safety, an Alessi field goal, and a 44-yard touchdown pass from Cheyne Lacanaria to Josh Frye, the Warriors were at an even 12-12 with the Technicians at halftime. The sound of suspected gunshots caused both teams to hit the ground in the third quarter, but play eventually resumed. Cass Tech won the outing, 25-18.

The next game was a 28-7 victory over Ann Arbor's Pioneer High School, followed by a match-up with Toledo (Ohio) St. Francis de Sales. In the Warriors' 42-24 win, Cheyne Lacanaria completed nine of nine passes for 181 yards and two touchdowns. His brother, Corey, caught seven of those passes for 165 yards and one touchdown.

The Catholic League Central Division play got underway with a pair of wins. The Warriors dominated De La Salle, 28-0, and the next week they won 21-3 over U-D Jesuit. Cheyne Lacanaria completed a 47-yard pass to his brother in the fourth quarter of that game, setting up a short rushing touchdown to seal the win. The next week, the Warriors fell 21-14 to the 2011 MHSAA Division 3 Champions, Orchard Lake St. Mary's, in their third Catholic League Central Division game.

The last regular-season Catholic League Central Division game was against Catholic Central. The Warriors trailed 14-10 in the fourth quarter before Walker made a four-yard touchdown run. The defense, led by Reschke's 10 tackles, together with a late interception and a pass deflection on the goal line in the closing seconds by Alessi, allowed the Warriors to walk away with a 20-14 victory. Walker finished with 198 yards rushing on 28 carries. The Shamrocks played Orchard Lake St. Mary's in the Prep Bowl at Ford Field, and the Eaglets won with a score of 27-10.

The next part of the Warriors' schedule included two out-of-state opponents. Brother Rice beat both Cincinnati (Ohio) La Salle (30-29) and the Vineland (Ontario) Niagara Academy (38-13).

Heading into the MHSAA Division 2 State Championship playoffs, the Warriors carried a 7-2 record. The team's first playoff game was a 47-26 win over Port Huron, followed by a 38-6 victory over Oxford in the district championship game. The regional championship match-up was with Walled Lake Western. Powell had 144 yards on 11 carries and two touchdowns, Walker had 92 yards and two touchdowns, and Greg Marzec had 132 yards on 10 carries, to lead Brother Rice to a 42-12 win. "Things are going really well for us right now," Coach Fracassa said, in a characteristic understatement.

The Warriors' playoff dominance continued with a 31-3 victory over Wyandotte Roosevelt in the MHSAA Division 2 semifinal game. Both Powell and Walker rushed for touchdowns, and both Cheyne Lacanaria and Alex Malzone threw for touchdowns.

"Whenever you get a chance to play another week of football this time of year, you know it's going to be a great week," Fracassa said. That turned out to be prophetic, as the upcoming Division 2 Championship Game against Muskegon would be one of the greatest games in Michigan high school football history.

At Ford Field, the Warriors began the scoring with a nine-yard touchdown pass from Cheyne Lacanaria to his brother, Corey. Next was another nine-yard touchdown pass, this time made by sophomore Malzone to Frye. Muskegon, a powerhouse team, was undeterred and rallied right back to tie the game. The seesaw battle continued and, with five minutes left in the game, Malzone found Corey Lacanaria on a flea-flicker for a 77-yard touchdown pass. Once again, Muskegon fought right back, scoring on a 51-yard pass to tie the game at 28-28 with 2:30 left. On the subsequent kickoff, Delano Madison fielded the ball on the four-yard line. He took three steps forward, stopped, and hurled a lateral pass all the way across the field to Alessi, who raced 91 yards up the sideline, untouched, to take a 35-28 lead. The Warriors hung on to win, earning back-to-back State Championships for the first time in school history.

Coach Fracassa celebrated his 80th birthday several weeks before his eighth MHSAA State Playoff Championship. Would he be coming back? According to Mick McCabe, after the game, Fracassa said, "I have to go home and talk to my wife about this. I love the game. It's done so much for me. Sports mean a lot to me and I like to give it back."

A number of stars from the 2012 team went on to play college football. Reschke recorded 352 tackles in his high school career, 43 for a loss, with 16.5 sacks. He was named to the All-State and Dream teams and was an All-American honorable mention player. He played at MSU for four years. Anthony Dalimonte spent four years with the University of Michigan, Kyle Marsh played football for Hillsdale (Michigan) College, and Cheyne Lacanaria played for Ohio Wesleyan.

Perkovic made 100 tackles in his career as a Warrior, including 52 solo tackles and 15 sacks, caught 14 passes for 225 yards, and was voted to the All-State football team. He was also a two-time All-American high school lacrosse player, was the Walt Bazylewicz Catholic High School Athlete of the Year, and decided to play lacrosse at Notre Dame, where he was a three-time ACC All-Academic team recipient and second-team college lacrosse All-American his senior year.

2013

Catholic High School League Champions
MHSAA Division 2 State Champions
Honor our tradition.

Coach Fracassa decided to return for one last year of coaching the Brother Rice Warriors. It would be his 54th season as head coach of a high school football team. He had 416 wins under his belt, more than any other football coach in Michigan at the time, and more than all but five coaches in the entire country. He had his returning junior quarter-back, Alex Malzone, who had completed eight of 10 passes for 167 yards in the previous season's Championship Game. He also had running backs Shon Powell and Brian Walker, who together had ac-

Alex Malzone

counted for 2,400 yards on the ground and 35 touchdowns in 2012. Alberto Sandoval, Jack Grisan, Jason Alessi, and Chris Carter were back on defense. The Warriors were riding an eight-game winning streak. Coach Fracassa was honest with his team when he told them: "I'm very eager to return for another year, but after that, I think it's time to step away. One more year is enough."

The season started with two games against out-of-state opponents. The first was Cleveland (Ohio) St. Ignatius, a perennial football power, in the Prep Kickoff Classic. The Warriors began with an 18-yard touchdown pass from Malzone to Damaris Woods. Walker scored on a two-yard touchdown run before a field goal and a 70-yard punt return touchdown from Alessi. A safety on a sack by Sandoval and Jack Dunaway capped the scoring as the Warriors won, 29-20. The next game was a 48-7 win over Toledo (Ohio) St. John's Jesuit. The third game of the 2013 season was against Flint Carman-Ainsworth, and resulted in a 31-6 Warrior victory.

The team's first match-up in the Catholic League Central Division was with De La Salle, which jumped to an early 14-point lead. A field goal by Alessi, from 37 yards out, put points on the board for the Warriors. After a fumble recovery, Powell added another seven on a 21-yard touchdown scamper. The De La Salle Pilots responded by kicking a field goal of their own before halftime. After a defensive start to the second half, Powell scored his second touchdown of the day with 4:15 remaining in the game. The Pilots came back with a touch-down of their own — and with only 24 seconds remaining in the game. Malzone appeared to be sacked on the last play of the game, but the play was ruled an incomplete pass and one second was added to the clock. From 34 yards out, Malzone threw a Hail Mary pass and Alessi came down in the end zone, with the ball, for a last-second 26-24 win. Branden Hunter, of *statechampsnetwork. com*, quoted Coach Fracassa as saying: "This was one of the greatest wins in program history. I don't know how we won the game. This was one of the most fantastic finishes I've ever witnessed as a football coach."

The second Catholic League Central Division opponent of the season was Catholic Central. In front of 7,000 fans in Novi, the Shamrocks took a 14-7 lead in the second quarter before a one-yard touchdown run by Walker evened the score just before halftime. A 32-yard touchdown pass from Malzone to Josh Frye gave the Warriors the lead, but the Shamrocks scored to even things at 21-21. It remained that way until Malzone connected with Patrick Sparks on a 35-yard touchdown pass with 30 seconds left in the game, to clinch a 28-21 win. Fracassa told Scott Burnstein, of State Champs Sports Network: "We're making a bit of a habit of pulling these close ones out with some pretty amazing efforts, and that's all about the kids going out there and making plays."

The next three games weren't as heart-stopping. Brother Rice's last two Catholic League Central Division games were more comfortable wins over Orchard Lake St. Mary's (31-14) and U-D Jesuit (38-0). Interspersed between those two games was a 38-10 win over the Vineland (Ontario) Niagara Academy. The Warriors faced the Shamrocks of Catholic Central in the Prep Bowl at Ford Field, playing for the Detroit Catholic League Championship.

The second match-up of the season between these two football powerhouses wasn't as eventful as the first had been. The Warriors held the Shamrocks to 110 yards on offense while totaling 299 yards of their own. The scoring began with a 32-yard Alessi field goal and a 36-yard touchdown run from Walker. It ended with a passing touchdown from Malzone to Corey Lacanaria and a second field goal from Alessi. The Warriors were the Detroit Catholic League Champions! The 20-7 victory gave Coach Fracassa a career record of an even 26 wins and 26 losses against the Shamrocks.

The Warriors carried a 17-game winning streak into the MHSAA Division 2 Championship playoffs. Birmingham Groves was easily dispatched, 42-0, in the pre-district game. In the district title game against Birmingham Seaholm, Malzone completed 17 of 22 passes for 236 yards and two touchdowns — both to Corey Lacanaria, who caught six passes for 106 yards. Walker was hurt, but Powell carried 18 times for 64 yards as the Warriors romped to a 34-7 win. In the regional title game, the Warriors overpowered U-D Jesuit, 41-14, in a season rematch. Coach Fracassa's squad kept rolling in the semifinal game, winning 43-20 over Detroit's Martin Luther King.

Finally, the MHSAA Division 2 Championship Game at Ford Field pitted Brother Rice against Muskegon in a rematch of the previous year's final. In another Rice vs. Muskegon classic, Malzone led the Warriors to their third straight MHSAA Division 2 Championship, completing an undefeated 14-0 season.

Malzone started with nine consecutive pass completions in the game, hitting Woods for a 16-yard touchdown and Grant Perry for a 34-yard score. The Big Reds tied the game on two rushing touchdowns before Malzone hit Perry for an 18-yard scoring completion prior to halftime. The Warriors' defense stiffened in the second half, allowing the Big Reds minus-nine yards on 13 carries. Malzone connected with Corey Lacanaria for a 21-yard passing touchdown and then scored himself on a 17-yard run off a fake field goal. The Big Reds answered by hitting a long touchdown pass late in the second half, but the Warriors won, 38-21. It was frustrating for Coach Shane Fairfield and his great quarterback, Deshaun Thrower, to lose a second title in a row to the Warriors.

Malzone finished with 20 completions on 24 attempts for 263 yards and four touchdowns, in addition to his rushing score. Corey Lacanaria caught 10 passes for 125 yards and a touchdown, and Perry had five catches for 91 yards and two touchdowns. The game extended the Warriors' unbeaten streak to 22 games. It was a wonderful end to a great season, and a fantastic conclusion to Coach Fracassa's legendary career. The icing on the cake for Fracassa was being named USA Today's 2013 National High School Coach of the Year.

Sage Baltrusaitis

Sage Baltrusaitis, an All-State offensive lineman from the 2013 team, received an appointment to the U.S. Military Academy at West Point and joined the Black Knights football team. Lacanaria finished his high school career with 115 pass receptions for 1,883 yards. He played four years for Ball State University, where he had 161 passes caught for 1,525 yards. Dominic Perkovic finished his high school career with 52 tackles (38 solo) and 13 sacks. He went on to play for the Columbia University Lions, where he was an honorable mention for the All-Ivy League team in his senior year. Walker carried for 879 yards on 144 attempts for the Warriors in 2013 and played college football for NCAA D-II Notre Dame College. Grisan and Woods played football for Saginaw Valley State University.

JASON ALESSI

Jason Alessi was a special athlete, even by Brother Rice standards. A nine-time varsity letter-winner in basketball, football, and lacrosse, he was a jack-of-all-trades on the football field. Initially, the Warriors' football team invited him to play due to his place-kicking skills. At the end of his high school football career, he had made 32 field goals (No. 3 all-time in the state) and was 16 of 18 (No. 2 all-time in one season) in 2013. He was 59 of 59 on extra points in 2013. Alessi played defensive back and had 135 career tackles, 10 interceptions, and three forced fumbles, and scored seven

Jason Alessi

touchdowns as a kick returner. He was first-team All-State his junior year and was on the All-State Dream Team his senior year.

In addition to his football prowess, Alessi was a phenomenal lacrosse player. He was captain of the Warriors squad, which won four State Championships. He was on the All-State Lacrosse team for two years and on the All-America team his senior year. Alessi was voted Michigan High School Lacrosse Player of the Year in 2014, after scoring 85 goals and assisting on 46 as a senior. His lacrosse coach, Ajay Chawla, said, "[Jason] is a guy who comes around every 15 or 20 years. He's been awesome for us. He was a big-time leader for us." Fracassa put it more succinctly when asked about Alessi: "I just love him, that's all."

Alessi was recruited to play lacrosse and football in college, and strongly considered accepting an offer from the University of Michigan to play football. In the end, he decided to attend Yale University, where he would be able to play both football and lacrosse.

At Yale, where he played football for four years, Alessi started as a defensive back, accumulating 208 tackles and four interceptions. He had 17 kickoff returns for 295 yards (a 17.4-yard average) and 45 punt returns for 463 yards (a 10.3-yard average). He was the only player in Bulldog history with two punt returns of 80 yards or more for touchdowns. He was an All-Ivy League Honorable Mention player his senior year, and was the recipient of the Ryan LoProto Award as the Yale player who demonstrated "Ryan's passion and competitive spirit, skill in the defensive secondary, and devotion to teammates."

Alessi also played for four years on the lacrosse team at Yale, and was a New England Intercollegiate Lacrosse Association (NEILA) Second Team Honoree as a junior and a Second Team All-Ivy League Honoree as a senior. He was on the NEILA All-Academic Team as a senior. In the 2018 NCAA National Championship game, played before 29,455 fans at Gillette Stadium in Foxboro, Mass., Alessi scored a goal to help the Bulldogs win their first-ever NCAA title; their last "mythical" lacrosse title had been won in 1883. Alessi was honored to receive the Molly Meyer Humanitarian Award, given to "the senior student-athlete whose character exemplifies selfless devotion along with compassion and concern for their team and the community at Yale and beyond."

Alessi was the kind of player and person that Coach Fracassa hoped to produce during his coaching career at Shrine and Brother Rice. Building young men of character, commitment, and perseverance was his goal. Teaching young men football skills, practicing them, and winning games were the tools.

RETIREMENT

Retirement in 2013.

Al Fracassa finished his coaching career with three consecutive MHSAA Division 2 Championships and a 22-game unbeaten streak. That unbeaten streak would be extended to 33 games under Coach Dave Sofran.

Alex Malzone returned in 2014 to rewrite the Brother Rice High School record book, finishing his high school career with 428 completions in 641 passing attempts for 6,254 yards and 69 touchdowns. Grant Perry, meanwhile, caught 176 passes for 2,771 yards and 27 touchdowns in his career.

Bill Khan reported on Coach Fracassa's comments after his last coaching appearance in his "Special to the Second Half" article (*mhsaa.com*). Fracassa said: "I wish I was young enough to coach some more. When you love something so much, it's very difficult to leave. I'm going to still love football; it's done a lot for me."

Coach Fracassa was a legend even before his retirement. He had a high school head coaching career that spanned 11 U.S. presidents (Dwight D. Eisenhower to Barack H. Obama), eight State of Michigan governors (G. Mennen Williams to Rick Snyder), eight City of Detroit mayors (Louis Miriani to Dave Bing), and six popes (Pope John XXIII to Pope Francis). He coached from the baby boom generation to the millenial generation, and maybe to Gen Z.

At his retirement, he boasted a 430-win, 117-loss, 7-tie record, and was ranked No. 1 for victories in Michigan and No. 7 for wins in the United States. He coached his Warriors to one "mythical" State Championship (voted No.

1 in Michigan), nine MHSAA State Championships, and 16 Catholic League Championships, and had four nationally ranked high school teams (No. 8 in 1977, No. 8 in 1983, No. 23 in 2000, and No.11 in 2013). He coached thousands of young men, negotiated college football scholarships for hundreds, and had more than 20 students go on to play in the NFL.

After his final game, Coach Fracassa said, "It's hit me the whole season when I'd go home every night. I couldn't believe it was going to be my last year. I try not to think about it. Football kept me busy, but it's here." He added, "It's time for someone else to take over. I'd like to mention my coaching staff. They did an outstanding job coaching my boys. I hate to take all the credit. They did most of the coaching. I did most of the yelling."

In an interview with Don Horkey that appeared in the *Detroit Catholic*, Coach Fracassa expressed his joy in working with "the kids." He said, "When you win a lot, people think you're a genius. But the kids on my team, they're the ones that make you look good." Vic Michaels, who in 2013 was the Detroit Catholic League's director of athletics, said of Fracassa: "Everyone talks about how valuable Al Fracassa is to the Brother Rice community. He's just as valuable to the Catholic League. For over 50 years he has mentored players and coaches for roles of leadership, not only at Rice but throughout the league and community. When college coaches call him about prospective players, he tells them about players from other schools, in addition to his own at Rice. He equally promotes talent from the Catholic League. He's a class act. He will be missed."

FRANK ORLANDO

Outside of your family, is there anything better in life than a good buddy? Coach Fracassa and Frank Orlando enjoy being buddies. Many years ago, Al and Phyllis Fracassa ran into Frank and his wife, Yvette, at Mass at St. Cletus in Warren. The two men had met before, when Orlando delivered a film to Shrine High School on an errand for St. Mary's of Redford football coach Walt Bazylewicz. Orlando was Bazy's assistant coach. Coach Fracassa invited the Orlandos over to the Fracassa home, and after a glass of wine and some great conversation, a lasting friendship was born.

"Albert and I don't really talk about high school sports," says Frank, who loves telling the story of the first time he met Coach Fracassa, while delivering that film. "The Shrine players were all on one knee in a tiny basement locker room. Coach Fracassa was giving an intense talk to the boys. He was a commanding speaker and it was totally quiet — not a sound, not a peep. He raised his arms high in the air to emphasize a point and I thought to myself, my goodness, is this man the Pope?"

Orlando spent six years at St. Mary's of Redford and 10 at Warren Tower coaching basketball (head coach), baseball (head coach), and football (assistant coach). He had never coached girls' basketball until he went to Country Day, where he would make history.

Consider the similarities between Albert and Frank:

• Both are Hall of Fame Coaches. Orlando is the winningest Michigan girls' basketball coach in history, with a record of 797-126 from 1981 through 2019.

• Both have won multiple state championships. Orlando won 13 as Country Day's girls' basketball coach.

• Both are among only a handful of coaches who have been honored as national coaches of the year. Orlando was honored in 2003, 2018 (Max Preps), and again in 2019, when he was awarded the prestigious Morgan Wooten Award by the Naismith Basketball Hall of Fame.

• Both were highly successful baseball coaches. Orlando won 780 games at Country Day and was inducted into the Michigan High School Baseball Coaches Hall of Fame in 1991.

• Both are retired. Fracassa recently turned 90, while Orlando recently turned 80.

• Both are from Italian immigrant families who settled on the east side of Detroit.

• Both were undersized but intensely competitive college football players.

• Both have three brothers. Sadly, all are deceased.

• Both are loved and cherished by thousands of former players.

• Both have wonderful, supportive wives.

One story that Orlando and Fracassa remember very well took place after the death of Coach Bazylewicz, Orlando's former boss at St. Mary's of Redford. Bazylewicz passed away in 1999, at the age of 77. He and Fracassa had been fierce rivals for many years, and there was the famous 0-0 tie in the Soup Bowl in 1963 between Shrine and Bazy's Notre Dame team. Shrine scored a touchdown on the very first play of the game on a sideline-and-go pass from Dennis Bienkowski to Jim Seymour, but it was called back because one Shrine player had lined up offsides. A four-yard edge in total yards gained was the tiebreaker that allowed Notre Dame to advance to the Goodfellows Game at Tiger Stadium which was played on Friday, Nov. 22, 1963 — the day President John F. Kennedy was assassinated in Dallas.

Fracassa and Orlando were at the funeral home to pay their respects

From left: Albert Fracassa, Vasco Perkovic, Frank Orlando.

to Coach Bazylewicz. As Fracassa approached the coffin and knelt in prayer, he was startled to see a football in the hands of Coach Bazy. Remarkably, the football was inscribed with the date and score of that Championship Soup Bowl game from 1963. It was the game ball!

The Great Coaches: Who Would Make it on Mount Rushmore?

The list of coaches who Al Fracassa competed against is filled with greatness. Fracassa spent most of his career competing in the toughest league in Michigan, the Detroit Catholic League Central Division, and no Michigan high school team has ever tackled a more challenging out-of-state schedule, annually playing against the finest teams from Indiana, Ohio, Illinois, and Pennsylvania — including famous games against Cincinnati (Ohio) Moeller, coached by Gerry Faust. It all makes Fracassa's career victories record even more impressive, as his teams competed season after season against the toughest of foes.

Fracassa's rivals early in his career at Shrine included the likes of George Perles, Tom Boisture, Dan Boisture, Ed Rutherford, Joe Carruthers, Walt Bazylewicz, Tony Versaci, and Bill McCartney. As the years went on in the Catholic League Central Division, there was Coach Tom Mach, who led Catholic Central into the legendary Boys' Bowl battles against Brother Rice. Michigan high school football didn't get much better than Rice vs. Catholic Central at Wisner Stadium in Pontiac. Today, the folks at Catholic Central hold Coach Mach in the same high regard Brother Rice has for Fracassa, and the two men have a warm friendship.

"One of the keys is that if you can teach a young man the power of positive thinking, you can give him a key to life, that he can wake up every morning and have an attitude that life is going to be what he makes it," Mach once said. "If you can make a young man believe in himself, believe in his team, and believe he's going to win, there's nothing he can't accomplish later in life when he starts putting all those lessons together."

Greg Carter

Mach had 370 wins and 10 State Championships in 17 appearances when he retired in 2016, after 41 years at Catholic Central.

But Mach wasn't the only great coach. Greg Carter, from Detroit DePorres, and Paul Verska, from De La Salle, were outstanding Catholic League coaches who've been inducted into the Michigan High School Football Coaches Hall of Fame. Another frequent Brother Rice foe, non-Catholic League Detroit Country

Day, has been beautifully coached for years by Dan MacLean, a Rice grad. Tony Patrito, at Rochester Adams, was another frequent Brother Rice foe, and played the Warriors five times — all state playoff games (Rice won three, lost two). The 2003 game was for the Division 2 State Championship, and Adams won that one, 28-7.

Tony Patrito

Another outstanding Rice opponent was Coach James Reynolds of Detroit Martin Luther King, who won 253 games between 1974 and 2009, and won a State Championship in 2007. Reynolds retired in 2009, but he helped build a program at King that won back-to-back State Championships in 2015 (Coach Dale Harvel) and 2016 (Coach Tyrone Spencer). Brother Rice and King have played eight times since 1989. King won three of the eight, including two of four that took place in the state playoffs.

George Porritt was a giant presence in the Catholic League Central Division. He coached Orchard Lake St. Mary's to 278 victories and seven State Championships in his 32-year career and, along with Catholic Central and De La Salle, his team loomed large on Fracassa's annual schedule as a talented, tough opponent.

Because there were Catholic League playoffs and due to the ever-changing structure of the state playoffs, it wasn't uncommon to play rivals like Catholic Central, De La Salle, and St. Mary's twice per season — and, on occasion, even three times.

Fracassa's record of 430 victories was earned against top-notch teams and great coaches.

One of those top-notch teams was Farmington Harrison, coached by the legendary John Herrington. Herrington retired as head coach at Harrison after the 2018 season with 443 wins (breaking Fracassa's record) and 13 State Championships in 18 appearances during his 49-year career.

"My philosophy didn't change over the years," Herrington once said, "but you've got to change with the culture. I used to play Big Ten fight songs in the locker room, but eventually it was hip-hop. However, I always ran the same offense and handled the kids the same."

Harrison and Brother Rice went head-to-head frequently, playing eight games in all between 1991 and 2011. Three of those were state playoffs. Brother Rice was 2-1 vs. Harrison in state playoff games, and 4-1 in the regular season.

The Mount Rushmore of Coaches: Al Fracassa, John Herrington, George Porritt, and Tom Mach.

A Final Word from Michael Coughlin

My life changed on so many levels on Sept. 11, 1969. It was a Thursday afternoon and I was sitting on the bleachers in the Brother Rice gym, about halfway up, close to the locker room side, along with the entire student body. We were waiting for the Varsity football team to walk out of the locker room and onto the basketball court for a pep rally. I was told that Brother Rice had a new head football coach, Albert Fracassa. I was 15 years old and a sophomore, it was my first year at Rice, and I had never heard of him. The football team came out onto the basketball floor, all of them sporting brush cuts, and wearing gray shorts and matching T-shirts that said Brother Rice Football. Last to come out of the locker room was the coaching staff, led by a young man with black hair: Coach Fracassa.

What happened over the next 10 minutes changed my life forever. Coach Fracassa walked up to the podium and introduced the captains and the coaching staff, and briefly talked about how the team had practiced very hard all summer long to prepare to be their very best for the season. Then, Coach stopped talking about the team, stopped talking about football, and started talking about what his expectations were about his players. He said: "What's important to me is that my boys will be good sons to their mothers and fathers, that my boys will get good grades in school, that my boys will be good role models to their fellow classmates, that my boys will be good role models outside of school, that my boys will be a good brother to their sisters and brothers." I sat there in the bleachers and said to myself, "This is exactly where I want to be — a student at Brother Rice."

The next day, Friday, Sept. 12, was Coach Fracassa's first game at Rice. I was there, along with my dad, and Rice beat Redford St. Mary's, 48-22. Steve Jones, a running back, had five rushing touchdowns and 291 rushing yards (both stats are still all-time records). After the game, as my dad was driving home, I remember telling him "Dad, we have a really good coach."

I was fortunate to play on Coach Fracassa's first undefeated team. Memories of my time with Coach Fracassa include:

• Coach was always interested in you, the player, and asked questions about your life outside of football.

• Coach was the cheerleader for the players who didn't play much. His goal was to play everyone, every game. Many times, he said, "I play as many boys as I can because they have parents in the stands who want to watch their son play, and that's more important than scoring points."

• Another part of Coach's legacy — and he did this countless times — is that he was famous for motivating his players and inspiring them by walking up and down the rows of players during warm-up stretches, repeating, again and again, quotes that, to this day, I can recite because I heard them repeated a billion times. For example: "Character is who you are when no one is watching" and "Don't do it right just once in a while, do it right every single time."

* Those quotes, and many more, were part of Coach's recipe for success. Positive words of encouragement can help change someone's entire life — it did mine!

* You would have to use a chainsaw to cut through my respect for Coach Fracassa.

* Coach had a voice that echoed respect and demanded attention when you heard it.

* You felt lucky to have Coach put his hand on your shoulder or his arm around your neck and talk to you for a few minutes.

* Coach made you believe the impossible was possible.

* I remember Coach's compassion and empathy when any of his players had a loss in their family.

* I still have the letters Coach wrote to my mom and grandmother when their lives were at a crossroads.

* I was lucky enough to be with Coach when, before games, he and I would sit next to the goalpost watching the team go through their warmups. During that time, we would just talk about the team. It was priceless for me to listen to Coach's mind as he prepared for the game, mentally. When Coach got into "game mode," he was different for the next two hours. After games, and after he talked to the media, Coach and I many times walked off the field, just him and me, talking about the game. We talked all the way to the bus. I had a front-row seat, watching history. Lucky me.

In 2014, before Coach's retirement dinner at The Henry Hotel in Dearborn, I wrote him a letter, telling him what I thought about the honor that was about to be bestowed upon him:

Coach, the tribute banquet that is being held in your honor is a testament to the character and goodwill that you have maintained, and the positive influence that you have had on so many lives. Coach, you have a place in this world that no one else has. The impact that you have made, well, I will sum it up this way: your "presence" has made a world of difference. I believe I speak for many former players, coaches, and friends when I say that we wish everyone could somehow be touched with the direction that you have given us, because then their lives, too, would be as enriched as ours have been. Finally, this is a quote from a book titled "Coach, Lessons of the game of Life," by Michael Lewis: "There are teachers with the rare ability to enter a child's mind. It's as if their ability to get there at all gives them the right to stay forever." Coach, as our teacher, we thank you for entering our minds.

ASSISTANT FOOTBALL COACHES OF AL FRACASSA

No head football coach wins games by himself. He is usually assisted by un-derpaid or unpaid colleagues. This is a list of Coach Fracassa's assistants through the years, in alphabetical order. Thank you to all of them.

Don Bessolo
Jamie Boerkoel
John Bonasso
Harold Burkholder
Charles Elmquist
Karl Goebel
Mark Goebel
Rich Grisan
Steve Haskell Jr.
Ron Kalczynski
Ken Kanadt
Adam Korzeniewski
Norm Krawezak
Pat Lynch
Brian Marshall

Bob McMacken
Charles Padden
Richard Popp
Michael Popson
Ron Ranieri
Juan Roque
Ben Rowden
David Sofran
Justin Turk
Tom Urban
Nick Vettraino
John Walker
Keith Wirth
Dave Yeager
Larry Zimmerman

FOOTBALL TEAM CAPTAINS OF COACH AL FRACASSA

Football senior captains were chosen by Coach Fracassa in consultation with the team. They might or might not have been the best players on the team. They might be extroverts who led with verbal encouragement, or they might be introverts who led by example. They were expected to lead off-season workouts, be at Mass at 6 a.m. on Wednesdays during the season, and be the first to arrive at practice and the last to leave. Here they are, by year.

1960 John Everly & Jerry McCulloch
1961 Mike Randall
1962 Chuck Lowther
1963 Ron Ranieri
1964 Jim Seymour & Dennis Bienkowski
1965 Dick Landry
1966 Dave Yeager
1967 Mick Brzezinski
1968 Tom Martin
1969 Pat Knuff & Mike Knuff
1970 Tom Hayden
1971 Rick Costanini
1972 John Cullen & Mike Stoegbauer
1973 James Courtney

1974	Ted Fox, Thomas Gorman & Kevin Hart
1975	K.C. Ryan
1976	Stephen Arkwright, Kevin Haffey & Jim Wilberding
1977	James Allor, Michael Haffey & William Prieb
1978	James Beauregard & Jon English
1979	Brian Brennan, Thomas Cote & Mark Moore
1980	Steven Allen, Tim MacLean & James Ostrowski
1981	James Cherocci & Dave Yarema
1982	Matthew Chiodo, Dave Dixon & Mark Nichols
1983	Matthew Dingens, Mike Flynn & Dave Cowden
1984	Douglas Kaiser, Paul Konkel, Robert Kula & Allen Szydlowski
1985	Tom Allen, Chris Sullivan & Kevin Wachowiak
1986	Bill Fitzpatrick & Keith Stonestreet
1987	Chris Brennan & Paul Manning
1988	Scott Merchant & Dean Moscovic
1989	Gannon Dudlar, Pete Mitchell, Steven Morrison & Robert Utter
1990	Kevin Kalczynski, Jason Penzak, Dean Polce & Jason Randall
1991	Robert George, Damon McClendon & Aaron Metz
1992	Jason Snooks & Michael Sullivan
1993	David Ewing, Daniel Gibbons & Brian Kalczynski
1994	Derek Canine, Walter Jenkins & Sean Regan
1995	Timothy Craddock, Joseph Kalczynski, Kris Sava & Dave Sofran
1996	Eric Marcy, Brian Marshall, David Matthews, Ben Rowden & Aniema Ubom
1997	Jason Barrios, Karl Pawlewicz & Jamyon Small
1998	Pat Craddock, Brooks Hartnett & Mike Scott
1999	Mark Goebel, Brenden Hart, Adam Karl & Garret Weston
2000	Matthew Baker, Aaron Jackson, James Navarre & Jonathan Randall
2001	Paddy Lynch, Ross Ryan, Kainan Stewart & Sean Williamson
2002	Karl Eschbach, Anthony Jackson, Ryan Brittain, Mike Decker, Jeff Magnatta & Jeff Stachowiak
2003	Doug Pickens & Cody Nolen
2004	Charlie Ryan, Jim Wojciechowski & Adam Decker
2005	Jim Goebel & Mike Radlick
2006	Mike Cappetto, Chris Colasanti & Brian Wing
2007	Andy Lentz, Caulton Ray, Nick Thomas & Paul Gyarmati
2008	Danny Henneghan, Shaquille Marshall, Zack Cherocci & Shamari Benton
2009	Sean Grisan, Justin Cherocci & Jeff DeClaire

2010 Jimmy Pickens, Loran Jaddou, Tyler Lendzion, Tim Hamilton & Conor Hart

2011 Cody Ellwanger, James Hendrix, Brian Roney & Joey Warner

2012 Anthony Dalimonte, Lucas Cherocci, Cheyne Lacanaria, Kyle Marsh & Sergio Perkovic

2013 Sage Baltrusaitis, Chris Carter, Jack Grisan & Dominic Perkovic

Acknowledgments

We are grateful for the wonderful reading available to us:

1. "The Sixties," 5th edition, Terry H. Anderson, Routledge, New York, NY, 2018.
2. "Voices of Protest: Huey Long, Father Coughlin, and the Great Depression," Alan Brinkley, Vintage Books, New York, NY, 1982.
3. "What Happened to the Roman Catholic Church? What Now? An Institutional and Personal Memoir," Gabriel Moran, 2021.
4. "Detroit: Engine of America," R.J. King, Momentum Books, Troy, Mich., 2019.
5. "Once in a Great City: A Detroit Story," David Maraniss, Simon and Schuster, New York, NY, 2015.
6. "The Origins of the Urban Crisis: Race and Inequality in Postwar Detroit," Thomas J. Sugrue, Princeton University Press, NJ, 2005.
7. "The Warmth of Other Suns," Isabel Wilkerson, Vintage Books, New York, NY, 2010.
8. "Goodfellows: The Champions of St. Ambrose," Rick Gosselin, August Publications, Minneapolis, Minn., 2009.
9. "Bowled Over: Big-Time College Football from the Sixties to the BCS Era," Michael Oriard, University of North Carolina Press, NC, 2009.
10. "Pro Football in the 1960s: The NFL, the AFL, and the Sport's Coming of Age," Patrick Gallivan, McFarland and Co. Inc., Jefferson, N.C., 2020.
11. "1963 Goodfellows Game between NDHS and Denby. Annual Goodfellows Game was a Tradition at Tiger Stadium for 30 years," Richard Bak, 2012, *https://www.ndpma.org/1963-goodfellows-game-between-nd-and-denby-posted*, downloaded 03/10/2022.
12. "Thirty Days with America's High School Coaches," Martin Davis and Rick Nease, © 2022 Martin A. Davis Jr.
13. The *Detroit Free Press*. Downloaded from Newspapers by Ancestry at Newspapers.com, (*newspapers.com*).
14. "Detroit's Goodfellows Game Pioneered Playing for a Good Cause," Ron Pesch, Aug. 31, 2021, downloaded 07/14/2022.
15. "Why I Never Left Williams College, A Coach's Legacy Beyond the Wins and the Hardware," Dick Farley with Dick Quinn, The Print Shop, Williamstown, Mass., 2021.

16. "Fracassa Remembers Unusual 1963 Soup Bowl Game," Don Horkey, Nov. 1, 2013, *Detroit Catholic, detroitcatholic.com*, downloaded 08/20/2022.

17. "Divine Steamroller," *Sports Illustrated*, Oct. 16, 1961.

18. NFF Chapter Leadership Award Recipients 2018, Tony Versaci, National Football Foundation, *footballfoundation.org*, downloaded 08/17/2022.

19. "The Super Bowl. The First Fifty Years of America's Greatest Game," David Fischer, Sports Publishing, New York, NY, 2015.

20. "Coach Al Fracassa, Honoring our Legendary Coach," Friends of Fracassa Committee (M. Rottenberk, M. Randall, T. Fox, R. Seymour, R. Ranieri, P. Callaghan, D. Yeager, P. Lynch, L. Dillon, L. Bitonti), May 10, 2014.

21. "Detroit. An American Autopsy," Charlie LeDuff, Penguin Books, New York, NY, 2014.

22. "1974 Brother Rice football and 1967 Pershing basketball are Detroit's greatest prep teams," Jared Purcell, May 23, 2017, downloaded 10/4/2022 from *Japurcell@mlive.com*.

23. "The Mosquito Bowl," H.G. Bissinger, HarperCollins Publisher, New York, NY, 2022.

24. "1979: Rice Meets Moeller in 'Biggest Game Ever,' " Ron Pesch, Aug. 30, 2019, *mhsaa.com/sports/football*, downloaded 10/12/2022.

25. Mick McCabe: My Top Five Football, Boys and Girls Basketball Teams of 50 years, Mick McCabe, *Detroit Free Press*, June 3, 2020, freep.com, downloaded 10/21/2022.

26. "Cochran: A Crack Back. 'M' Defender Leaves Troubles in Dust," Douglas B. Levy, *Michigan Daily*, Nov. 7, 1984, *digital.bentley.umich.edu/midaily*, downloaded 10/24/2022.

27. "Michigan State Football: Top-10 Quarterbacks," McLain Moberg, Spartan Nation/*Sports Illustrated*, July 14, 2020, *si.com*, downloaded 10/27/2022.

28. "Who Wore it Best at Michigan State: No. 63," Cody Tucker, *Lansing State Journal*, June 29, 2018, *lansingstatejournal.com*, downloaded 10/29/2022.

29. "A Conversation with Coach Fracassa: 'I enjoy the kids,' " Don Horkey, *The Michigan Catholic*, Feb. 7, 2014, *detroitcatholic.com*, downloaded 10/27/2022.

30. "Prep Coaching Legends Fracassa, Herrington, Mach Share Wisdom," David Goricki, *The Detroit News*, Jan. 19, 2018, *detroitnews.com*, downloaded 10/27/2022.

31. "Top 10 Seniors," the *Detroit Free Press*, Sept. 6, 1984, *newspapers.com*, downloaded 11/3/2022.

32. "It's No Replay, That is No. 22 for the Bruins: Two Decades Later, UCLA Once Again Has a Mel Farr Playing in the Rose Bowl," Tracy Dodds, *The Los Angeles Times*, Oct. 23, 1985, *latimes.com/archives*, downloaded 10/28/2022.

33. "Brother Rice Lineman Joins 85 Other CHSL Players Who've Made it to the NFL," Don Horkey, *Detroit Catholic*, June 10, 2021, *detroitcatholic.com*, downloaded 9/27/2022.

34. "NFL Veteran Mike Lodish Tackles Food Industry with Peanut Brittle Company," Al Fenwick, *Sports Illustrated*, Aug. 3, 2015, *si.com*, downloaded 11/3/2022.

35. "Harrison's John Herrington is About to Become the State's All-time Winningest Coach," Marty Budner, Hometown Life, Oct. 10, 2017, *hometownlife.com*, downloaded 10/27/2022.

36. "Burnstein: George Porritt's Impact Off the Football Field as Great as it Was On," Scott Burnstein, *The Oakland Press*, Nov. 11, 2021, *theoaklandpress.com*, downloaded 12/16/2022.

37. "Top 30 Michigan High School Football State Finals Performances Over the Last 30 Years," *Mlive.com*, Dec. 2, 2020, *mlive.com*, downloaded 12/8/2022.

38. "MHSFCA Hall of Fame 2004 Crowley Award: Albert Fracassa," Larry Sellers, *mhsfca.com*, downloaded 11/19/2022.

39. "Albert Fracassa, Nominated by Packers' T.J. Lang, is Finalist for NFL High School Football Coach of the Year," Jan. 20, 2010, *packers.com*, downloaded 12/1/2022.

40. "The Nineties, A Book," Chuck Klosterman, Penguin Press, New York, NY, 2022.

41. "Top 30 Michigan High School Football State Finals Games of the Last 30 Years," *Mlive.com*, Nov. 30, 2020, *mlive.com*, downloaded 12/6/2022.

42. "John James Brings Out Famed High School Coach for First TV Ad of Fall Campaign," Todd Spangler, *Detroit Free Press*, Sept. 1, 2022, *freep.com*, downloaded 1/9/2023.

43. "The Warrior Way," Pat Caputo, *The Oakland Press*, Aug. 6, 2006, *theoaklandpress.com*, downloaded 11/19/2022.

44. Individual Game Records, Brother Rice Warriors Football, *yumpu.com*, downloaded 8/27/2022.

45. "Al Fracassa: He's a Winner of a Coach – and More," Johnette Howard, *Detroit Free Press*, Sept. 8, 1983, *newspapers.com*, downloaded 1/17/2023.

46. Royal Oak Shrine Knights Michigan High School Football Scores, *michigan-football.com*, accessed 7/1/2022 to 2/1/2023.
47. Birmingham Brother Rice Warriors Michigan High School Football Scores, *michigan-football.com*, accessed 7/1/2022 to 2/1/2023.
48. "Rice's Fracassa Lives for Football," Mick McCabe, *Detroit Free Press*, Oct. 8, 2008, *newspapers.com*, downloaded 11/19/2022.
49. "Rice Sends Out 'Coach' on Winning Note," Bill Khan, Special to Second Half, Nov. 29, 2013, *mhsaa.com*, downloaded 1/31/2023.
50. "Here are Michigan's Top High School Football Programs of All Time," Phil Friend, *Detroit Free Press*, Sept. 29, 2022, *freep.com*, downloaded 1/26/2023.
51. Frequently requested church statistics. Center for Applied Research in the Apostolate (CARA), Washington, DC, 2023, *cara. georgetown.edu*, downloaded 12/22/2022

Index

About the Team

Bud Krause is a journalist and owner of afaKrause Advertising, with offices in Michigan and Utah. He graduated from Wayne State University in 1973, where he majored in journalism and played college basketball. He was a quarterback at Royal Oak Shrine High, playing for Coach Al Fracassa's last team at Shrine in 1968. He worked as a reporter for the *Daily Tribune* in Royal Oak, Mich., from 1973-77. He lives in Sylvan Lake, Mich., with his wife, Kelli, their son, C.J., and daughter, Daryn.

Tom Martin was the captain of Coach Fracassa's ninth and last Royal Oak Shrine High team. He was named All-State Class B honorable mention and was recruited by Cornell University in Ithaca, N.Y. His football career was brief due to injury, but he went on to graduate with a Bachelor of Arts in biology, with distinction in all subjects. He received his Medical Doctor from the University of Michigan School of Medicine and completed his pediatric internship, residency, and pediatric cardiology fellowship at Washington University in St. Louis, Mo. He has worked as a pediatrician, pediatric cardiologist, pediatric hospitalist, and an addiction medicine specialist in St. Louis, Mo; Bangor, Maine; and St. John's, Antigua. He is credited with more than 50 publications, including research manuscripts, case reports, reviews, and book chapters. In his retirement, he enjoys his volunteer work for the Bangor Area Recovery Network, providing access to resources for persons with substance use disorders. This work led to his serving as medical director for the Discovery House of Central Maine Inc., providing medication-assisted treatment for persons with opioid use disorder. Martin enjoys living in a house on a lake in Maine with his wife, Judith Josiah-Martin, Ph.D., who teaches social work at the University of Maine in Orono, Maine. Reading, travel, and their two daughters (and their husbands) are the focus of the Martins' free time.

Michael Coughlin is a 1972 graduate of Birmingham Brother Rice, played on Coach Fracassa's first undefeated team in 1971, and has been a statistician for Brother Rice football since 2005. He's a 1977 graduate of Eastern Michigan University (business management), where he met his beloved wife, Rebecca. The couple enjoyed 39 years of marriage before Rebecca was welcomed into Heaven in 2020. Coughlin continues today as head statistician for Brother Rice football.

Jerome J. Malczewski is a 1981 graduate of Birmingham Brother Rice and has been a member of the Brother Rice football staff since 2001. He played football under Coach Fracassa and was also a two-year captain of the wrestling team. Malczewski graduated from the United States Military Academy at West Point in 1985 and subsequently served in the 2nd Armored Calvary Regiment in both the United States and Europe. He and his wife, Linda, have a daughter (Katherine), three granddaughters, and one grandson. Malczewski lives in Grand Blanc, Mich., and continues his work on the Brother Rice football staff.

Ken Cendrowski is a metro Detroit graphic designer. He graduated from the College for Creative Studies with a BFA in advertising design, and has worked in various positions, including graphic designer at a small design shop, art director at medium and large advertising agencies, design director at a publishing company, and principal at Ken Cendrowski Design. His work encompasses relevant marketing solutions through advertising campaigns, direct marketing, logos, corporate ID systems, magazine publications, brochures, event materials, and interactive design. His clients range from cottage industries to Fortune 500 companies, include automotive, information technology, travel, health care, financial, government, and nonprofit organizations. His work has received numerous creative awards including Caddy, Target, Ozzie, American Corporate Identity, and others. Cendrowski has enjoyed being an adjunct faculty at College for Creative Studies, where he teaches visual communications, and business and professional practices courses to third-year graphic design students. In his free time, Cendrowski and his wife enjoy walks with their dogs, Luna and Raina. Ken is a 1974 Austin Catholic Preparatory grad.

Anne Berry Daugherty is a graduate of Michigan State University who followed the footsteps of her father, a sportswriter, into the world of journalism. She currently works on *DBusiness*, *Detroit Design*, and *Michigan BLUE* magazines, as well as other Hour Media projects. Other clients include the Community Foundation for Southeast Michigan, Doescher Advisors, and Neithercut Philanthropy Advisors. Daugherty has also edited a number of books, among them "A Tribute to Golf," "Sage Business Advice," and "Detroit: Engine of America." In her free time she enjoys taking ballet classes, reading, exploring photography, visiting new places and old favorites, and spending time with her family, which includes her husband, two daughters, a Labradoodle, and her daughter's rescue horse.

Special thanks to consultant **R.J. King,** Written in Detroit, a Brother Rice grad.

Made in the USA
Columbia, SC
07 November 2024

a5fc45b9-7199-4fb9-9ad4-5ee098a56fc1R02